D1480891

CANNIBALISM
from Sacrifice to Survival

CANNIBALISM
from Sacrifice to Survival

The Aztecs ▪ The Donner Pass, 1846
Leningrad, 1941 ▪ The Andes Plane Crash
The Jeffrey Dahmer Case ▪ and more. . .

HANS ASKENASY, Ph.D.

Prometheus Books

59 John Glenn Drive
Amherst, New York 14228-2197

Published 1994 by Prometheus Books

98 97 96 95   5 4 3 2

Library of Congress Cataloging-in-Publication Data

Askenasy, Hans, 1930–
    Cannibalism : from sacrifice to survival / Hans Askenasy.
        p.   cm.
    Includes bibliographical references and index.
    ISBN 0-87975-906-2 (cloth : acid-free paper)
    1. Cannibalism—History. I. Title.
GN409.A75   1994
394'.9—dc20   94-22772
                                                              CIP

Printed in the United States of America on acid-free paper.

Contents

Preface and Acknowledgments   7

Introduction   9

Part One: A Historical and Geographical Overview

1. By the Dawn's Early Light   17
2. Recorded History   27
3. Caveats   43
4. Summary   51

Part Two: Motivational Factors for Cannibalism

Introduction   57
5. Natural Famines   59
6. Manmade Famines   67
7. Accidents   83
8. Magic   107
9. Ritual, Religion, and Sacrifice   117
10. Punishment, Indifference, and Unification   123
11. The Gourmets   129
12. The Sadists and the Mad   135
Intermission   143

Part Three: Cannibalism in Culture and Society

13. Werewolves, Witches, and Vampires — 149
14. Special Cases: Medical, Legal, and Psychological — 165
15. Our Preoccupation with Cannibalism — 185

Conclusion — 213

Postscript — 235

Further Readings — 239

Endnotes — 247

Bibliography — 255

Index — 259

Preface and Acknowledgments

I was born in Frankfurt am Main, Germany, a "half-Jewish" son of the city attorney. I remember seeing the *Hindenburg* on its ill-fated flight and, a few years later, a thousand B-17s. It was on my fifteenth birthday, two weeks before our liberation by Patton's Third Army, when one of them dropped a bomb on the last house still standing on our street. We were crouching in the dark cellar with my cat, Mau, in a hatbox; the bomb, fortunately, did not explode.

Surviving Hitler (whom I saw twice), I emigrated to the United States in 1949 and enrolled at the University of California at Los Angeles, earning my B.A. in 1953. Following a number of years as a Marine Corps pilot (including a year and a half's tour in Japan, with many visits to Hiroshima), I returned to UCLA and there received my doctorate in clinical psychology. I am the author of *Are We All Nazis?* dealing with the mental diagnosis of concentration camp guards, and *Hitler's Secret*, a psychobiography of that greatest mass murderer of them all.

Given my concern with violence, death, and man's inhumanity to man, as well as taboos, cannibalism struck me as a worthwhile topic for a book. While social customs in most societies clearly impose prohibitions against our eating one another, other societies appear to offer no such prohibition; in fact, they encourage cannibalism. Why should this be so? Within three years the basic research and manuscript were completed. There were some surprises. I hope you will find it as interesting to read as I found it to write.

While intended primarily for the intelligent layperson, I trust this volume will also be of more than passing interest to the scholar, who will find more specific information and documentation in the Further Readings and Endnotes sections.

Special thanks to my brother Eugene Askenasy, Michael Jarvis, and Maureen Clifford.

Finally, a most enjoyable moment has arrived: that of expressing appreciation to that person without whom this endeavor would never have taken place, and who may now enjoy the fruits of his labor of love, luxuriating like a tired man in a warm scented bath: myself.

Introduction

Throughout this book, you will encounter many weird and bloody things—it is not my fault. Our subject after all is by definition not for the faint-hearted, and Stephen King, no novice in such matters, may be proven wrong in his assertion that you can't beat the Bible as horror literature.

The author

I suspect that the first image that comes to the average person's mind when hearing the word "cannibalism" is some ferocious primitive tribe in the jungles of Africa, New Guinea, or Brazil cooking one of their unfortunate enemies, or perhaps some poor shipwrecked sailor doomed to devour his mate. As we shall see, things are not quite that simple.

Let us begin by asking ourselves three primary questions. First, take this scenario.

We are part of a group of people stranded far from anywhere after, say, a plane crash. There are few if any provisions, and reality soon sets in; we all become painfully aware, for example, that man can live a lot longer without food, i.e., flesh, than water, i.e., blood (about a gallon and a half in an average-sized adult). If the only apparent alternative to certain death is the survival of some through cannibalism, the first of our three questions (with many subquestions) is—What would we do? What *should* we do? If anyone is to be killed, who? The youngest or oldest? The healthiest (fattest) or sickest? Women and children first? Or last? Why? Or is it to be a sort of final lottery with everyone drawing straws? Who is to do the killing? How is that to be done? And the cooking?

The subquestions are endless—How would we decide? On what basis would we answer? What are the implications: psychological, moral, legal, medical, religious, whatever? Do we in fact know what we would do? Do we have any idea what real thirst and hunger are, what the pain of starving to death feels like? And if we should be lucky and survive, are we and our fellow cannibals to be tried in a court of law? On what charges? With what "punishment" to fit what "crime"?

Finally, what if the roles were reversed, i.e., what if you were the judge or juror in a case involving cannibalism? Is he who has never nearly starved to death a fair judge? Is he who has never nearly died from lack of water a fair juror? Who at this point would constitute a jury of our peers? With the old issue of "There but for the grace . . ." taking on a new meaning, how would *you* decide?

I think on reflection that we will find it worthwhile to ponder these problems a bit. As we shall see, famines and accidents have occurred often enough and will occur again—and not always to others.

Our second primary question.

Cannibalism (or *anthropophagy*), defined as "the eating of human flesh by human beings," has often been called one of man's last taboos—*taboo* in turn being defined as something "banned on grounds of morality or [would you believe] taste." But is it man's last taboo? Or perhaps the first? Or the original sin of all races? Or is it, after all, logical, normal, even piquant—in short, in the nature of things?

By far the most common reason for human beings eating one another is what we would expect: hunger. Psychologically speaking this is a less compelling aspect of cannibalism. If there is nothing else to eat, why not human flesh? There is a German proverb, *In der Not frisst der Teufel Fliegen* ("In an emergency, the devil devours flies"). Eating corpses under survival conditions may be disagreeable and distressing, but it is difficult to offer significant logical, legal, or moral objections to it.

But what about normal times? What if the question were asked, "Why should we not eat the dead?" The point has been made. As one social scientist in Papua New Guinea concluded: "Anthropologically speaking, the fact that we ourselves should persist in a superstitious, or at least sentimental, prejudice against human flesh is more puzzling than the fact that the Orokaiva, a born hunter, should see fit to enjoy *perfectly good meat* when he gets it." From an economic or materialistic viewpoint this argument is impeccable. It is, therefore, unreasonable, as anthropologists A. P. Rice and G. Hogg maintain, to call this "most natural appetite for good red meat 'unnatural.'" Further, attempts to persuade cannibals otherwise left them, not surprisingly, unconvinced. Thus the natives in New Caledonia, in the southwest Pacific, are said to have been taken aback by the disgust of Europeans, and asked, "Do you want to forbid us the fish of the ocean?" A nineteenth-century Mayoruna cannibal remarked to another European visitor, "When you die wouldn't you rather be eaten by your own kinsmen than by maggots?" And when a chief of the Miranhas was asked why his people practiced cannibalism, he asserted that it was entirely new to him that some people thought it an abominable custom. "You whites," he noted in an astute manner, "will not eat crocodiles or apes, although they taste good. If you did not have so many pigs and crabs you would eat crocodiles and apes, for hunger hurts. It is all a matter of habit. When I have killed an enemy it is better to eat him than let him go to waste. Big game is rare because it does not lay eggs like turtles. The bad thing is not being eaten, but death, if I am slain, whether our tribal enemy eats me or not; I know of no game which tastes better than men. You whites are really too dainty."

Is this, then, a bad idea whose time has come, or one that should be strangled at birth? The 1973 movie *Soylent Green*, which won an award as best science fiction film of the year, comes to mind. It featured Charlton Heston and the literally and figuratively dying Edward G. Robinson. We find this description in Jay Nash and Stanley Ross's *The Motion Picture Guide*:

> It's around 2020 and the Big Apple is rotten to the core. . . . The population explosion has placed more than forty million people in the greater New York area, many of whom live on the streets, in the subways, in abandoned vehicles and burnt-out buildings. . . .*
>
> [Following something called the suicidetorium] the dead are being shipped along a belt and sent to a large manufacturing device at one end, only to emerge at the other end as the ubiquitous wafers *Soylent Green*. . . .
>
> [In a climactic scene Heston, a detective, exclaims in agony, "Soylent Green is *people!*"] *Soylent Green* was a message picture, and they even hired a technical consultant, a professor and futurist. If this is the way he sees it, he has lost his faith in humankind's intelligence. Then again, he may be right. . . . Avoid taking children because it may cause bad dreams.

Now for our third primary question.

Once upon a time, the Caribbean islands were populated by village people, gentle, kind, and inept at war. During the time of the Incas or thereabouts, raids and invasions began by ferociously warlike groups of cannibals from along the South

---

*Actual population estimates for the year 2000: New York, 16.6 million; Tokyo, 28 million.

American coast. When Christopher Columbus first landed in the Bahamas, he was apparently shocked to discover that the native Carib Indians ate all their male prisoners of war. The admiral himself ventured no farther than into one of the Carib houses, where he saw a number of skulls hung from the ceiling and some baskets full of what he presumed to be men's bones. He called them *caribales*, which came to be pronounced *canibales*, thus giving their name both to the Caribbean Sea and to the custom of eating human flesh (see Figure 6).

The raids continued for generations, great sport for the Caribs. According to someone named de Rochefort, they described the French as "delicious," the English as "so-so," the Dutch as "tasteless," and the Spaniards as "so tough as to be virtually inedible." It was the last who were the Caribs' doom, since killing natives in turn constituted great sport for the valiant Christian soldiers of His Most Holy Majesty in Spain. When the Caribs were finally reduced to a few hundred, "and their temperament to a state usually described as mild and melancholy," one sure way to offend them was to call them cannibals.

Today cannibalism is said to exist perhaps in certain isolated parts of the world: remote regions of New Guinea, tiny pockets of East Africa, the jungle between Argentina and Paraguay, and deep in Brazil's amost inaccessible Matto Grosso. In the Amazon basin cannibals, living much like prehistoric man, now and then are presumed also to consume one of the agents of their destruction, government envoys. Alas.

Yet the mere mention of their name and the implication of their dining habits have always evoked a reaction combining unspeakable horror, revulsion, and yet a strange fascination for most of us. Why should this be so?

Arguably there is probably a preoccupation above all with the aspects of violence, death, and taboo. Torture and killing, with flesh-eating thrown in as a bonus, are also spectacles, entertainment that has been time-tested for approval down through the ages. A modern TV audience hardly needs to be reminded of this, least of all Americans: 1993 U.S. gun deaths numbered forty thousand. By contrast, just thirty-three people were killed by guns in Great Britain, and eighty-two in Japan. Every other home on an American street is inhabited by a gun owner. It is apparently part of human nature, then, to pay rapt attention to such unusual sights and sounds as blood spurting from wounds, loud shrieking and howling, or a part of our anatomy being roasted over a fire. Or, for that matter, to read (or write) about such things.

But are there other reasons, and if so, what are they? And why the sudden and pervasive contemporary interest in this subject in fact and fiction—from the chilling (and Academy Award-winning) *Silence of the Lambs* to *Alive* and Francis Ford Coppola's *Bram Stoker's Dracula* (which during its first weekend of release grossed 31 million dollars), to serial killers like Jeffrey Dahmer in Wisconsin; Chikatilo in Rostov-on-Don (who tortured, murdered, and cannibalized at least fifty-two people); and Omeima Nelson in Orange County, California? Much of this shortly, but what is going on?

These, then, are our three basic questions (with their many subquestions): What would *we* do to survive that plane crash; why should we *not* eat flesh; and how do we explain both the historical interest in cannibalism as well as the sudden resurgence in interest today? Is cannibalism one of man's last taboos?

To arrive at the answers we need first to review the evidence on cannibalism, such as it is. Let us do this together, and I strongly encourage you to critically evaluate the data so that you will feel comfortable agreeing or disagreeing with my conclusions. You are the judge.

Part One

A Historical and Geographical Overview

The near-naked warrior with a stone ax over one shoulder and a pig bone through the nose, peering up at the vapor trails of his more advanced colleague's weapon, is a picture in some ways equal to a multi-volumed world history.

William Arens
The Man-Eating Myth

1

By the Dawn's Early Light

In November 1974, near Hadar in north-central Ethiopia, two anthropologists were exploring the parched gullies of the Afar badlands for fossils. With a brutal noontime sun sending waves of scorching heat across the desert, they were about to return to camp when one of them spotted a piece of bone on an eroded slope, long hidden by layers of sediment and volcanic ash and now laid bare by a rare flash flood. It was from a hominid, a bit of an arm.

Three weeks of extensive exploration of the gully uncovered a hundred more pieces of bone, which proved to be from a single individual—an adult female, 1.1 meters (3 feet, 8 inches) tall, and weighing around sixty-five pounds. She quickly became known as Lucy, a name taken from the Beatles song popular in the camp (more formally, *Australopithecus afarensis*).

The oldest hominid then known as dated by the radiometric potassium-argon method, Lucy died three million years ago. She and her kin lived near rivers and lakes, possibly scavenging meat from carnivores, and caught small prey to supplement a diet of fruits, nuts, roots, and other vegetation.[1]

The evidence for our species eating its own suggests that we have been doing so for about the past two million years, for reasons and in ways we will explore in this book. Some of us still do, and many more may. There are certain situations in which cannibalism invariably occurs—call them "survival" scenarios, such as the aftermath of a thermonuclear war.

Cannibalism

As can be seen from the map on the following page, evidence from prehistoric times places cannibalism mainly in southeast Europe and southwest Asia. In historical times it was largely concentrated in a good part of west and central Africa; Australia and New Zealand; New Guinea, Melanesia (especially Fiji), Polynesia, and Sumatra; portions of India and China; the northern and mainly eastern and central parts of the North American continent; and much of Central and South America. Interestingly, cannibalism appears to be largely absent in other locations: in the vast extensions of Eurasia, in northeast and south Africa, and in much of northern America.

Obviously not all cultures and religions have encouraged or condoned cannibalism (though notably the Catholic church practices transubstantiation, i.e., the supposed consumption of Christ's actual flesh and blood in Communion). Eskimos, reduced to eating human flesh because of starvation, are reported to have looked upon the experience with shame, and to have concealed it as a crime. Other tribes, the Tahitians, for example, "stood out like islands in a sea of cannibalism." Neither the Pygmies nor the Bushmen, Semang, Veddas, Andamanese, Zulu, Masai, or Fuegians are said to have known anything resembling it, and apparently were disgusted when malicious neighbors or indiscreet visitors accused them of such practices. For the Hindus it is a sin even to eat an insect, let alone a person.

Key Chong, in his *Cannibalism in China*, gives a history to 1990 of this behavior in that country. The chapter "Methods" alone is twelve pages long. Here are two examples: "The most popular ways of preparing human flesh were boiling, roasting, baking, and steaming. Next was pickling in salt, wine, sauce and the like." He also states: "Learned cannibalism in China has little to do with religion and superstition while in many parts of the world it has much to do with them. In China it was more closely related to such secular ideals as loyalty to superiors and filial piety toward the parent."

We can speculate that it all began when some of our

Distribution of Cannibalism*
\\\\\\ Evidence from prehistoric time
/////// Reports from recorded time

---

*From Ewald Volhard, *Kannibalismus*, a valuable resource in cannibalism research (Stuttgart, 1939). For more on this, see Further Readings.

ancestors, bypassing their closest relatives, the apes, at first simply found it easier to kill and eat one of their own than hunt a larger, faster, and fiercer beast. Perhaps it was also a matter of taste. Later our ancestors would become more consciously aware of the boundaries of life and death and flesh and blood; formulate ritual and magic; avenge murder; and please and pacify good gods and bad. All these developments had their consequences.

Half a century before the discovery of Lucy, a young anatomy professor in South Africa named Raymond Dart unearthed the skull of an infant creature whose physical development placed it in an evolutionary line with man. Subsequent findings by others, including Louis and Mary Leakey in East Africa, enabled this reconstruction:

> The little ape man was four feet tall, possessed an erect carriage and walked on two feet. His teeth were smaller and more modern than those of previous apes; and bones unearthed in his cave dwellings supported Dart's theory that he had been a toolmaker, a hunter, and carnivorous. His favorite prey seems to have been the baboon who, in terms of anatomy and evolution, was something of a distant cousin at the time. A majority of the baboon skulls had been broken open, possibly to remove and eat the brain. There are also several finds that indicate he may have killed and eaten his own kind. Flourishing over much of Africa from 2,000,000 to 700,000 years ago, this tiny australopithecine may be the world's oldest cannibal.[2]

About 500,000 years ago there lived in the caves of the exotically named Dragon Bone Hill, about forty miles southwest of Peking, a predecessor of yours and mine, appropriately called the Peking man, or *Sinanthropus pekinensis*. Among the debris found in the caves were skulls of other Peking men, nearly all of them broken open at the base, as well as charred leg bones, also split open, presumably to extract the brains and marrow respectively. The victims appear to have been roasted, and these parts may have constituted early man's favorite delicacies. For centuries local peasants had mined the hill for "dragon bones." Believing them to have miraculous healing properties, they ground them up and sold them in medicinal preparations. We will never know how many powdered bones of early man, as one author has put it, "have passed harmlessly through the alimentary canals of dyspeptic Chinese."

Peking man seems to have lived in family groups, and, as you might suspect, Sigmund Freud (in his *Totem and Taboo,* 1913) had a theory about all this. He picked up on a suggestion of Charles Darwin that a dominant old male gorilla jealously guarded his harem of females and drove off the younger males, who had to seek mates outside the group. Accepting this idea, Freud next maintained that one day a group of rebellious brothers, no longer able to endure their sexual deprivation, got together, killed their father, and ate him. In accordance with ritual magic they now acquired part of his strength as well as an identification with him. (Maybe they also acquired a load of guilt.) Then again, Peking man was perhaps not at all sexually deprived but simply hungry—perhaps both. The original Peking bones, representing more than forty individuals, mysteriously disappeared during World War II.*

---

*William Arens, of whom more soon: "As if incest and cannibalism were insufficient makers of a pre-cultural stage, a dash of patricide is added, as the offspring kill and eat their father for hoarding the females. In a subsequent state of remorse, they put incest and cannibalism behind them and set out on the road to civilization. Freud refers to the event as 'this memorable and criminal deed, which was the beginning of many things— of social organization, of moral restrictions and of religion.' In effect, morality in the form of human as opposed to animal social organization, as evidenced by the taboos of incest and cannibalism, was invented."[3]

As usual, the father of psychoanalysis had nothing to say about the psychology of the other sex, or he might have observed that a woman must reject the large majority of the roving bands of men in heat, or else find herself impregnated by one who has already moved on to the next cave (or condo).

21

Cannibalism

In 1891 a Dutch doctor, Eugene Dubois, was excavating with fifty convicted laborers along the Solo River in Java, when he uncovered a flat skullcap. He called the creature *Pithecanthropus erectus*, "upright ape-man," better known as Java man. Today we include both Peking man and Java man in the category *Homo erectus*, "upright man." The oldest example of *erectus* in the fossil record is dated at about 1.6 million years ago. While the early ape-man probably did not venture far afield, *erectus*, with a more complicated brain, presumably wanted to see what was on the other side of the mountain. Specimens have been found in Africa and Asia, and many of their unusually thick skulls show signs of multiple healed fractures—evidence of wholesale skull-bashing in warfare or ritual activity? Around a million years ago *erectus* began to change gradually, and by about 300,000 years ago was replaced by *Homo sapiens*, "wise man"—the name modern man has given to himself and, as has been argued, a distinct misnomer. Says Isaac Asimov: "In fact, if we consider that the human species, with the full capacity for forethought and knowing exactly what it is doing and what may happen, nevertheless has a very good chance of destroying itself in a nuclear holocaust—the only logical conclusion we can come to, by my definition, is that *Homo sapiens* thinks more poorly, and is less intelligent, than any species that lives, or has ever lived, on Earth."⁴

In 1856 (while Charles Darwin was working on *The Origin of Species*), in the Neander Valley in western Germany, limestone miners found an unusual human skeleton in a cave. A beetle-browed, low-sloping skullcap, a pelvis, and some limb bones fell into the hands of a local science teacher, who concluded that the remains were those of a refugee from Noah's flood. Others decided the creature was "some poor idiotic hermit," a sufferer from rickets, or a deserter from the Cossack army that had camped nearby during the Napoleonic wars. Neanderthals (i.e., "Neander Valley men," from the German *Tal*, or valley) appear on the scene in Europe around 125,000 years ago, and disappear around 35,000 years ago. They spread all across Europe, the Middle East, and western and central Asia, and may have engaged in brain-eating, possibly part ceremony, part gourmet meal. Among the most famous archeological sites of cannibalism is Krapina, a Neanderthal site in Yugoslavia. Archaeologists have found bones there from as many as seventy individuals. This is in sharp contrast to other sites, where remains of no more than four individuals have been found. Moreover, the Krapina bones, says Mary Russell of Case Western Reserve University, "were all scratched and badly broken. The idea is that they are the remains of a Neanderthal feast."

Cro-Magnon man (named for the Cro-Magnon cave in southwest France), a caucasoid type using stone and bone implements, followed and seems to have continued the practice, as did his successors.

Evidence discovered in 1984 in pits of the Fontbrégoua cave in Provence, between Nice and Marseille, revealed human bones displaying cut markings and deliberate breakage identical to those on animal bones, suggesting once again that some of our ancestors were butchered and eaten. The nutritious marrow of arm and leg bones in particular seems to have been of interest to these neolithic cave dwellers a mere six thousand years ago. An international team of anthropologists considered as a clinching argument for cannibalism a specific electron microscope finding: at the time the marks were made, the bones were fresh. But others remain unconvinced, and stress that the Fontbrégoua find is far from ironclad evidence; even if it does prove cannibalism, there is no sure way of knowing whether it was survival cannibalism or a systematic, cultural practice of eating other human beings.

Stone Age man also drank out of skulls, understandable at a time before pottery had been invented. So did nomadic Scythians, using skullcaps of persons they particularly hated. In the words of the fifth-century B.C.E. Greek historian Herodotus, "They saw off the part below the eyebrows, and after cleaning out what remains stretch a piece of rawhide round it on the outside."

And since man has created his gods in his image, many of these (including giants and heroes and whatnot) had cannibalistic and sacrificial tendencies, too. According to Greek mythology, Kronos (or Saturn), the son of Heaven and Earth and father of the gods, swallowed his own children because it was prophesied that one of them would overthrow him (see Figure 1). The Christian god, too, was said to have predicted that his chosen people would kill and eat one another for food after having disobeyed him: "You shall eat your own sons and daughters" (Lev. 26:29).

There is a modern and, indeed, whimsical sequence to all this. We read in a recent *Skeptical Inquirer* magazine article:

> Project SETI (Search for Extraterrestrial Intelligence) has been chosen to be the point organization that will announce to the world a "discovery"—it will be that they have established communication with an "alien race" (the lower Greys). The Greys will "land" at either White Sands in New Mexico or at area 51 in Nevada.
>
> The very mention of "the Greys" sends a shudder down one's spine in the more paranoid circles of UFOlogy, as this is said to be the alien race that relishes the taste of human flesh.

It also appears that even our closest living relatives are not altogether immune from eating one another. In her longitudinal studies of chimpanzee families in the East African forests, Dr. Jane Goodall encountered an ape version of cannibalism, though the reasons for it were not clear and possibly based on individual abnormalities.

For example, in 1975 one chimpanzee mother named Passion displayed grotesque behavior when she killed an infant chimp and shared the grisly feast with her offspring. Passion and her children, Pom and Prof, "behaved as if the baby were normal prey," Goodall related. "They were quite calm. There was begging and sharing of the meat. They fed until they couldn't eat any more, then abandoned the remains." The author was further horrified when Pom, apparently taught and helped by the mother, later killed two babies. Passion and Pom may also be responsible for the disappearance of other infants. In 1978, when Pom had a baby of her own, she hid from her mother for two weeks. "I think she was afraid her mother would eat her baby," says Goodall.[5]

Cannibalism among our animal relatives is actually widespread, as detailed in the recently published comprehensive research on this subject, *Cannibalism—Ecology and Evolution among Diverse Taxa,* edited by Elgar and Crespi (1992). Examples: a male lion taking over a harem kills nursing cubs fathered by his predecessor; marauding chimpanzees kill the young of their species, as do sparrows and seabirds; newly born snails devour their siblings (though after sixteen days they become vegetarians); and while some spiders consume their age-weakened mothers (an example of gerontophagy), female black widows will eat their mates if these don't flee quickly enough after copulation (a notable exception is the praying mantis. Contrary to popular notions, an analysis of a large number of videopictures shows no indication of similar behavior among them). Perhaps worst of all are sandsharks. The fight for survival begins in their mother's body: between ten and twenty pea-sized eggs are simultaneously expelled from the ovaries and fertilized in the fallopian tubes. The fastest growing shark embryo, as soon as it breaks through its egg cover, eats the remaining embryos one after the other.

2

Recorded History

Most of the remainder of this book will deal with this most recent period of our human continuum, a mere few thousand years between yesterday's Lucy and, if we don't come to our senses, tomorrow's star wars, or whatever that coming attraction might be. We offer now a few examples to give the flavor (excuse the pun!) of what we'll be discussing. In this chapter I'll recount various tales of cannibalism, old and new, from around the world.

There were and are, to begin with and above all, the great famines, natural or manmade. Many other accidents and incidents were on a smaller scale, and more individual in nature. In recent decades, excavations outside the ancient Minoan palace at Knossos, on the island of Crete, uncovered a room in which human bones were being boiled in a souplike mixture at the time of the palace's destruction between 1400 and 1200 B.C.E. Irish history records the rather singular action of a twelfth-century chieftain who, when his soldiers brought him the head of one of his enemies, tore at the nostrils and lips with his teeth and ate them. Another recent study indicates that the Anasazi of the southwest United States practiced cannibalism.[1] Marco Polo's journals refer to cannibalism, and in sixteenth-century China public executioners had the privilege of being rewarded with the blood and certain parts of their victims' bodies, which they could sell or eat as they saw fit. In fact, as late as the nineteenth century it was not unusual for them to eat the hearts and brains of criminals they dispatched.

There is also the celebrated case of Sawney Beane and his offspring, constituting, it seems, a whole family of professional cannibals. The story, which first appeared in a broadsheet around 1700, is variously attributed to the reigns of James I of Scotland (1406-37) or James VI (1567-1625). If it has a basis in fact, it is presumably a story of famine. Reay Tannahill, in her *Flesh and Blood*, relates one version:

> Sallying forth from their vast and well-hidden cavern, they waylaid travellers, slaughtered them, and took them home for dinner. As the family increased—Sawney and his wife raised eight sons and six daughters, and they in turn produced eighteen grandsons and fourteen granddaughters—the whole mob would go hunting together. People began to shun the coast road on which so many travellers mysteriously disappeared and where severed limbs were often cast up by the tide, "to the Astonishment and Terror of all the Beholders." The Beanes, first and last, were estimated to have disposed of more than a thousand victims.
>
> One day, however, some twenty-five years after Sawney and his wife first took up residence in their cave, a party of horsemen rode into sight while the Beanes were still busy dismembering a woman they had killed. The villains fled, but were traced at last with the aid of bloodhounds. When the pursuers found their way into the secret recesses of the cave, they were met with the sight of arms, legs, and haunches hanging from the roof as neatly as in a butcher's shop. That Mrs. Beane was a thrifty housewife was proved by the other choice cuts that had been put up in pickle. But the law wasted no time on compliments and the whole Beane clan was dragged back to Leith, there to be summarily and painfully exterminated in the year 1435.[2]

Another representative event in 1568 gives us a feeling for how things went for cannibals. It was a ruthless business. According to Ernest Dodge in *Islands and Empires*:

> Alvara de Mendaña sailed with two ships from Callao, Peru, on November 19, 1567, to find the islands that, according to the Incas, produced silver and gold and lay in the ocean to the west. . . . Later he was nearly wrecked on a reef near Ontong, Java, and finally, on February 7, he sighted Santa Isabel Island in the central Solomons. . . .
>
> Mendaña moved his ships on May 12 to the good anchorage of Puerto de la Cruz discovered at Guadalcanal. In raising a cross on a high hill two more natives (one a chief) were killed. Coconuts and chickens were obtained and a party sent inland to look for gold, of which not a trace was found. Food was still short, though the land was under cultivation and dotted with villages. The headhunting people of Guadalcanal were understandably unfriendly. They were also interested in the strangers whose deadly weapons and incessant demands for food made them by turns curious, fearful, and hostile. A foraging shore party, led by Sarmiento, stripped a village of its food, but narrowly escaped massacre. A watering party on Ascension Day was not so lucky and nine of its ten men were killed. Mendaña, upon going ashore, was greeted by natives waving his companions' dismembered limbs. Once again Sarmiento was turned loose and burned every village he could reach. A canoe load of natives bringing a pig, probably as a peace offering, were slaughtered by the Spaniards and their quartered bodies laid about at the scene of the massacre of the watering party. So violence begat violence and retribution.[3]

Somewhat later the great Captain James Cook, on his second voyage to the South Pacific in 1772, discovered New Caledonia, "inhabited by good-natured cannibals." As fate would have it, he was to become probably the most famous person in history to be a victim of this custom. On Valentine's

Day 1779, Cook engaged in a skirmish with perhaps less good-natured Hawaiian natives, who in turn clubbed him to death and then ate him.

In some societies eating one another appears to be a comparatively recent phenomenon, as, for example, among the Polynesians, Solomon Islanders, Congolese tribes, and in the Fijis, where it attained huge proportions; in fact, during the first half of the nineteenth century Fiji had the reputation of being apparently as wild, violent, and cannibalistic as any place on earth.

In 1865 a burglar in West Prussia killed a maidservant and cut flesh from her body in order to make a candle for use in later acts of theft. After being caught in another burglary, he confessed that he ate a part of the corpse of his first victim "in order to appease his conscience."

As recounted by Otto Friedrich in *Before the Deluge,* in Germany in 1924 one Karl Denke, a small shopkeeper, had his house searched by the police after neighbors complained about horrible screams. There they discovered several barrels filed with smoked human flesh, a case full of bones, and a number of pots of human lard. During the years of famine, when the villagers had grown accustomed to eating roasted dogs and cats, Denke had done good business in the sale of "smoked pork," and now, with all his "customers" recoiling in horror, Denke, sentenced to die, hanged himself. He left behind a notebook neatly recording thirty murders, with the date of each killing, and the weight of each victim.[4]

The writer Bertolt Brecht commented sardonically that, "He [Denke] canned the meat and made soap from the fat, buttons from the bones, and purses from the skins. He placed his business on a scientific footing and was extremely surprised when, after his apprehension, he was sentenced to be executed. . . . I contend that the best people of Germany, those who condemned Denke, failed to recognize the qualities of true German genius which the fellow displayed, namely: method, consci-

entiousness, cold-bloodedness, and the ability to base one's
every act on a firm philosophical foundation. . . . They should
have made him a Ph.D. with honors."

Friedrich recounts another notorious case at this time, also
in Germany, that of one Carl Wilhelm Grossmann, a former
butcher. You have to brace yourself for this:

> He often went to the railroad station, which brought to Berlin
> a steady stream of peasant girls from the east, coming to
> the city in search of work. They were helpless and penniless,
> for the most part, and Grossmann must have seemed a
> fatherly sort. He had no difficulty in hiring girls as
> housekeepers. . . . Then came the moment when, as Gross-
> mann later said, "I couldn't control myself."
>
> One night, about an hour after Grossmann had brought
> home a new housekeeper, some neighbors named Iglitzki
> heard so much screaming that Frau Iglitzki sent her husband
> directly to the police of the Fiftieth Precinct. With a policeman
> leading the way, the Iglitzkis proceeded directly to Gross-
> mann's apartment, pounded on the door, and then broke it
> open. What they saw was so extraordinary that Herr Iglitzki
> fainted dead away in the doorway. The housekeeper, Marie
> Nitsche, was lying on the bed, her hands tied behind her,
> her legs and thighs enmeshed in rope, her throat cut. Gross-
> mann, his hands covered with blood, was standing over her,
> quite naked. The policeman beat Grossmann into submission
> and then searched the apartment. In the kitchen, he found
> a half-charred thorax and several hands and fingers. Through
> a crowd of shouting neighbors, who remembered that Gross-
> mann used to carry packages into several butcher shops, the
> policeman dragged Grossmann off to precinct headquarters,
> where the authorities subsequently accused him of murdering
> not just Fraulein Nitsche but also twenty-three other women,
> whose remains, in bits and pieces, were found in the nearby
> Luisenstaedter Canal.
>
> Grossmann refused to confess, however. He claimed that
> he had simply been trying to punish Fraulein Nitsche for

stealing money from him. As for the remains of other women found in his kitchen, and in the canal, he showed neither interest nor remorse. The only thing that seemed to affect him was the news that his pet bird, a siskin named Haenseken, was suffering from his absence. Grossmann told the police that he would talk if he could have his bird, and so, the next day, a detective brought in Haenseken in his cage. Grossmann's handcuffs were taken off, and he was given an hour to coo at his bird. The homicide detective then began to chat with Grossmann about the bird. He suggested that it might need some insect powder. Grossmann agreed, and a policeman was sent to fetch the powder. Then, once Haenseken had been treated and cared for and put back in his cage, Grossmann confessed. He completed the confession by hanging himself in his cell, with a twisted sheet tied to a nail.[5]

Now some more modern examples.

In 1928 one Albert Fish cooked and ate parts of a ten-year-old girl in Greenburgh, New York.

In January 1950, Victor Biaka-Boda, a small, thin, worried-looking man who represented the Ivory Coast in the French Senate, set off on a tour of the hinterlands to let the people know where he stood on the issues, and to understand their concerns. One of their concerns apparently was the food supply. Biaka-Boda's constituents promptly ate him.

In the 1950s members of the secret Mau Mau society opposed white rule in Kenya and employed cannibalism in their initiation ceremonies.

Kon Ichikawa's 1959 movie, *Fires on the Plain*, portrays the disintegrating Japanese army on Leyte in the Philippines near the end of World War II. Just to go on living a few more hours, soldiers were committing any crime, including murder and cannibalism.

In the early 1960s, at the zenith of Haight-Ashbury hippiedom in San Francisco, it was reported that a certain

Anton La Vey, a former police photographer and circus performer and later self-styled founder and high priest of the First Church of Satan and author of *The Satanic Bible* and *The Satanic Rituals Book* (more on this topic later), served a meal of human flesh prepared from a female thigh furnished by a medical student from the University of California. In the late 1960s, there was also a "princess" Leda Amun Ra "who became famous for attempting sex with swans." She was a "well-known and lovely devotee of Hollywood's occult set" who reportedly also indulged in cannibalism. Yet another case of North American cannibalism was discovered in the summer of 1970. Two young men were arrested in Salinas, California, and confessed to murdering a man who had stopped for them when they were hitchhiking in Yellowstone Park. They shot him, cut the body into six pieces, and ate the heart. Both had finger bones in their pockets. One man claimed that his lust for human flesh started when he was seventeen, as a result of an electric shock.

In that same year, also in California, a man arrested in connection with a minor traffic accident told a patrolman that he had "a problem"—he was a cannibal. He next confessed to killing a social worker, dismembering the body and eating the heart.

Issed Sagawa, a Japanese student, consumed parts of his girlfriend in 1981. Based on this event Juro Kara wrote *Letters from Master Sagawa*, winning a leading Japanese literary award. We will have a little more to say about him later.

One Ottis Toole, born in 1947, was suspected of as many as a hundred murders committed between 1961 and 1984. Raised by a Bible-quoting mother who dressed him in skirts and frilly undergarments because she had hoped for a daughter, Toole's grandmother called him "the devil's child," a term of endearment for her since she was a satanist. He began killing when he was fourteen. Traveling throughout the country, Toole chose his victims at random, using whatever weapon was at hand to kill them during his satanic rituals. He also admitted to cannibalism.

In 1985 the German newsmagazine *Der Spiegel* related a discovery in a West German botanical garden: plastic refrigerator containers containing chunks of a corpse. A twenty-eight-year-old woman had apparently murdered her thirty-two-year-old boyfriend, cut up the body, and put the pieces in a freezer bought for the purpose. Because of space restrictions she kept it in her bedroom and did not dispose of the evidence until the stench could not be concealed any more, despite roasting and pouring sauces over it. While clinicians testified to her diminished capacity, they concurred with everyone else that she constituted a danger to society.

In the 1986 movie *The Hitcher* we are treated to a finger in the French fries. In the same year witnesses at the trial of former "Emperor" Jean Bokassa testified that in the Central African Republic he was guilty not only of mass murder during his fourteen-year dictatorship, but also of procuring human bodies for purposes of cannibalism. Philippe Linguissa, who claimed to have been the former imperial cook, swore that, "My boss well and truly did eat a meal [of human flesh] in my presence and he truly liked it." Bokassa countered by claiming he had never seen Linguissa before. Linguissa then concluded by adding that the experience had left him paralyzed and impotent.

Still more in 1986: The *Weekly World News*, a popular publication for those of less than brilliant intellect, ran this headline: "Cannibals Shrink Space Alien's Head." According to the story, a "top" Belgian anthropologist described the specimen as having pointed antenna-like ears, scaly skin, oversized eye sockets, and two brains.

This according to the *Los Angeles Times* in 1988:

Libreville, Gabon—A local witch doctor has confessed to having eaten six people, including two of his own children, over the last decade, the Gabonese daily *L'Union* said Tuesday. It quoted police as saying that 35-year-old Ntem Mba, a railway employee, killed humans and ate their flesh as part of ritual ceremonies. Mba was detained when one of his sons said he was responsible for the recent disappearance of a teacher who had sought his help to solve personal problems.

Here is a review by John Michalczyk in Magilli's *Survey of Cinema* (1993) of the French/Dutch film *The Cook, the Thief, His Wife and Her Lover*:

On the surface, this is the story of an eternal triangle, an illicit affair, and a curious vendetta. Beneath this, however, is a black allegorical comedy about the nature of oppression. In essence, the powerful, manipulative, and abusive creatures themselves fall victim to the violence in which they live. . . .

The narrative is straightforward. As the dark tale unfolds, one grotesque scene follows another to draw the viewer into a disturbing, ethereal world of love and horror. The gourmet restaurant Le Hollandais, a type of apocalyptic microcosm of a society breaking at the seams, provides the setting for the tale. It suggests a quasi-universal world, a cross between a futuristic European restaurant of haute cuisine and a decadent, urban American one where dogs grovel for delicacies in the bountiful garbage bins on the streets. . . .

Georgina Spica, the beloved "possession" of the gangster Albert Spica, finds life oppressive in the presence of her boorish husband. For some odd reason, she tolerates his verbal and physical abuse. On one occasion, in the course of their nightly gastronomic adventures at Le Hollandais, however, she finds some respite from the incessant, degrading remarks of the insufferable animal Spica. She spies a quiet, sophisticated man all alone, poring over classic texts at his table. In a passion of pure, almost anonymous sex, a sizzling love affair commences and progresses nocturnally right under the ugly nose of Albert. Between courses, Georgina and

Cannibalism

Michael briefly meet in the bathroom or in the kitchen, protected by the sensitive, all-seeing cook, Richard. When the affair is detected, Albert almost destroys the restaurant in pursuit of the daring adulterers. They manage to escape to the literary oasis of Michael's book depository, only to have Albert discover Michael and choke him to death with his own texts, notably about the French Revolution. In a spirited act of vengeance, Georgina obliges the cook to prepare Michael's corpse as a gastronomic delight. She turns the table on Albert and forces him to eat the garnished cadaver. With no compunction, she guns him down and finally liberates herself from her oppressor.

And this from the *Arizona Daily Star*:

Moscow (AP)—A family preparing a holiday dinner became worried when a bullet was found in what was thought to be beef, a newspaper said yesterday. They were sickened at the news from the police: They had been preparing human flesh. *Moskovskii Komsomolets* reported that the unidentified Moscow family bought the slab of meat at a state store in southwest Moscow and put it in the freezer. They pulled it out on June 12, [1993,] Russian Independence Day, and began cutting, the newspaper said. When the family dog was offered a piece of the strangely colored meat, "The dog sniffed it, whimpered pitifully and left," the account said. Then the family found the bullet and called the police."

We end with three examples, with some details.

The first: Under the headline "Cannibal Relishes Memories: He's Eaten No One Since He Got Religion," the *Baltimore Morning Sun* offered this uplifting tale to its readers in May 1992.

Wamena, Indonesia—Derek swears he gave up eating people in the 1960s. . . .

"The missionaries told us not to," he said, awkwardly stirring his coffee at a small hotel in a hidden valley of Irian

Jaya, the Indonesian half of the huge island of New Guinea and one of the world's most remote regions. But memories of the taste remain.

"Delicious. Better than pig or chicken," he said, with a hint of nostalgia, in the Baliem Valley capital of Wamena.

Derek's eyes sparkle as he warms to his story of the good old days when a well-built neighbor in an enemy village would be earmarked for the pot.

"Old ones are tough. Young men and women taste better. And babies taste like fish. The flesh is very soft."

"I hope you're not going to print that," warned a foreign researcher in Jayapura, the coastal capital of the province. "There has been no documented evidence of babies being eaten."

"It isn't like the popular image of white missionaries ending up in a boiling cauldron with carrots and potatoes. The main impetus was to absorb the spirit from a strong enemy. It would often be the person they most admired," [a reseacher] said.

In fact, people were cooked in the normal outdoor kitchen over hot stones, wrapped in grass and leaves, according to Derek, a name he took when he became a Christian.

Sometimes the weakest in initiation ceremonies would end up on the table, and in some tribes in Irian Jaya, cannibalism was the final pleasure after tricking an outsider into believing he was a friend.

"They'd invite you to a big party. Only you were the main course. Treachery was the main object rather than the eating," the researcher said.

Locals say cannibalism has all but disappeared, though it may still be practiced in the very remote areas where previously unknown tribes continue to be discovered.

Derek, the reformed cannibal, belongs to the warlike Dani tribe, expert farmers whose valley no outsider had seen until a U.S. explorer in 1938 flew over the mountain walls that had hidden them for centuries.

By the 1950s, Christian missionaries were flying in as part of "God's invasion."

"Once 66 little girls came to the mission with their fingers chopped off as a sacrifice to appease the spirits. . . . People lived under constant fear."

The Indonesian government, which took over Irian Jaya in 1963, has banned chopping women's fingers off at the second knuckle—men lose only the tops of their ears as a gesture of grief—but the practice is still common.

Derek's friend, Hulu, suggests the reason many of the 80,000-strong Dani tribe opted for Christianity was the material rather than spiritual benefits it brought to their Stone Age life.

"They gave us shells, salt, steel axes and sharp knives," he said. . . .

The determined forces of missionaries, tourism and a government intent on modernization have had mixed results in the Baliem valley.

The second example: Closer to home, Egyptian-born Omeima Nelson, twenty-four, "a former model," had just met her husband, well over twice her age and a convicted drug smuggler, in a bar. Not a marriage made in heaven, it was also rather short-lived—as was Mr. Nelson. Omeima told jurors that her husband sexually assaulted her in their Costa Mesa, California, home on November 30, 1991. A few weeks later, during another assault, she reached for a pair of scissors, stabbed him, and then "freaked out," beating him with an iron and other objects until he lay dead. She then butchered, cooked, and ate parts of him. She was arrested after she stuffed some portions of her husband's body into garbage bags and offered a friend $75,000 to help her dispose of it. The friend called police, who made the grisly discovery.

Mrs. Nelson told jurors that she killed Mr. Nelson in self-defense, but prosecutors depicted her as a predator who stalked men and traded sex for money and drugs. She had previously been convicted in 1990 of assaulting a former boyfriend by tying him up and demanding money at gunpoint.

Judge Robert R. Fitzgerald cited the bizarre nature of the

crime and the great public interest for the lengthy prison sentence. Nelson was technically eligible for probation.

"If I don't want to be a judge anymore, I guess I could grant probation," Fitzgerald said facetiously. But he added, "The killing and the aftermath are so bizarre that any thinking judge would not grant probation."

Mrs. Nelson informed two examining psychiatrists (Drs. David Sheffner and Park Elliott Dietz, the latter a well-known forensic clinician and expert for the FBI who had also interviewed Jeffrey Dahmer at length) that she had dressed up in a red hat and red high-heel shoes and put on red lipstick to begin the night-long butchering. With gory specifics, she testified that she castrated her victim for revenge, and boiled his hands to eliminate fingerprints. She also said in a packed courtroom that she boiled Mr. Nelson's head and skinned his body. She had previously told the psychiatrists that she ate her husband's ribs after cooking them in barbecue sauce.

"I did his ribs just like in a restaurant," Sheffner quoted Nelson as saying. She then sat at her kitchen table with the food and said out loud, "It's so sweet, it's so tender and delicious . . . I like mine tender." Nelson later denied eating parts of her husband.

During aggressive questioning by prosecutor Randolph Pawles, Nelson also admitted to mixing up body parts with leftover Thanksgiving Day turkey in the garbage dumpster to avoid detection. Pawles sarcastically asked Nelson for help in finding evidence. He said investigators had yet to discover all the "meat" missing from the large man.

"We're missing about 130 pounds of Bill. You know where he might have gone?"

"No, he was all there," Nelson replied.

A court-ordered sentencing report by the Probation Department offered several different views of Nelson. According to the report, Nelson herself had given wildly differing statements to the police about the death, admitting and then denying involvement and apparently concocting stories to explain body parts found in the back seat of her car. She claimed that someone was trying to set her up, then blamed the slaying on a man who caught a ride with her to a nearby laundromat. She then told police that she believed she should contact Mr. Nelson for help in finding his assailant, even though she knew he was dead.

In denying involvement in the slaying shortly after her arrest, Mrs. Nelson told police that "she could not even cut her own hair much less someone who weighed 230 pounds." She also asked police whether she could plead guilty and request the "gas chair."

Costa Mesa Police Officer Robert Phillips had stated: "Omeima Nelson is the most bizarre and sick individual I've had the occasion to meet. No one needs to look to the Dahmers of Milwaukee or the Hannibal Lecters of the screen. A new predator has emerged, named Omeima."

Outside the court, Deputy Public Defender Thomas Mooney said the statement was overblown.

"It's just outrageous to compare her to Jeffrey Dahmer, and Hannibal Lecter is a fictional character," Mooney said. He added that Mrs. Nelson was upset after the sentence.

"She's very upset, understandably so," he said. "She said to me, 'How could this happen? It was self-defense.' "

Therapist Nancy Kaser-Boyd said the butchering also might have some cultural and religious significance if Omeima Nelson believed that dismembering the body would ensure that she would not meet William Nelson in the "nether world."

On her own behalf, however, Mrs. Nelson told the probation officer that she was really a "warm person who wouldn't hurt a mosquito."

The jury was disturbed by evidence during the trial. A Mr. Hooks, who spoke on behalf of the other eleven jurors, concluded, "All I want to do right now is to go home and go to bed. The evidence photos of dismembered body parts will be hard to erase from memory."

Convicted of second-degree murder (and sentenced to twenty-seven years) in one of Orange County's most grisly slayings, Omeima Nelson wept after the verdict was read. Somehow, however, she had also along the line become engaged to a man in his seventies, and hoped "to return to college someday to become a counselor of abused woman."

And this, according to a 1993 newspaper report: Some besieged Muslims in Sarajevo, unable to get food, turned to cannibalism to survive, according to Bosnia's U.N. ambassador, Muhamed Sacirbey. "I received a call from the military commander in Tuzla, who told me that people in these besieged enclaves in eastern Bosnia were now eating the dead in order to survive," he said. He did not elaborate and the claim could not be confirmed.

Finally, there is this 1994 newspaper report concerning the recent civil war and massacre in Rwanda: "Joseph Wanzam, a 28-year-old member of the minority Tutsi tribe, said his ordeal began in April when he saw his family murdered by rival Hutus. Then, he said, he barely evaded death himself in a massacre at a jungle prison camp and fled on foot to neighboring Uganda. Believed to be the first Rwandan refugee to surface in Los Angeles during the current crisis, [he] told a harrowing story . . . of mass murder and cannibalism."

3

Caveats

It was a reaction I learned from my father: have no respect *whatsoever* for authority; forget who said it and instead look at what he starts with, where he ends up, and ask yourself, "Is it reasonable?"

Richard Feynman,
What Do You Care What Other People Think?

The subject of cannibalism is not without controversy, to put it mildly. The primary reason is a lack of solid evidence. The major caveat: beware of hearsay, or, if you will, hearwrite. The readiness with which many tales and concepts were, and are, accepted and perpetuated by nonobservers mandates wariness when dealing with the exotic.

Critical thinking replaced by free association; a hypothesis offered as self-evident truth; values disguised as facts; facts bent to fit a theory; some loopy sailor's florid memoirs taken at face value; findings distorted and then the distortion attacked; sensational interpretations leaving no cutlet uncooked —the litany goes on. In fact there is a great deal we simply do not, and never will, know though at other times we can also make reasonable guesses given evidence that is factually and psychologically compelling.

There isn't much basic disagreement about the Donner

Party, the siege of Leningrad, or the Andes plane crash; but what really happened with, say, the Tubinambas, the Aztecs, or the kuru victims? The following will give an idea—and alert you to the fact that, on the basis of the evidence presented, you will need to decide how much and whom to believe, and to draw your own conclusions.

Consider the Tupinambas. A rather classic story in cannibal history is that of one Hans Staden, an ordinary seaman on a Portuguese trading ship with an extraordinary tale of human nastiness and degeneration. In the middle of the sixteenth century Staden was captured by the thereafter never-to-be-forgotten Tupinamba Indians in South America, whose special talents were said to include "elaborate rules of etiquette in distributing human cutlets."

There is first the bad news: the recital of horrors with one hideous nerve-wracking scene followed by another. One of Staden's eyewitness accounts offers this pathetic tableau: an unfortunate victim's months-long preparation for his inevitable culinary demise. While as a thoughtful aside he had been provided with a female companion for the days and nights along the way, on the occasion of the big event it was women who were his nemesis. They boasted that they would light the fire, devour him, and "shout and whistle." "Mothers would smear their nipples with blood so that even babies could have a taste of it." The body was finally cut into quarters and barbecued while "the old women who were the most eager for human flesh" licked the grease dripping from the sticks that formed the grill. Females, here as elsewhere in history, were presumed inherently inferior, and therefore often represented as ferocious savages.

But then there is also the good news: miraculously Staden himself does not end up in the casserole, and lives to tell his melancholy and heart-rending tale. Returning to his native Germany, and after recuperating from the ordeal for a few years, he pens his memoirs. Others seem to have become involved in this effort, causing a reference to·"a committee only one of whom was on the scene." At any rate Staden's mind is fresh as to details and verbatim reconstructions. The title alone seems worth the price of the book: *Hans Staden: The True History and Description of a Country of Savages, A Naked and Terrible People, Eaters of Men's Flesh, Who Dwell in the New World Called America. Being Wholly Unknown in Hesse Both before and after Christ's Birth until Two Years Ago, When Hans Staden of Hamberg in Hesse Took Personal Knowledge of Them and Now Presents His Story in Print.* The work also contains woodcuts, with the author readily identified as the one with hands folded in prayer and dressed only in a figleaf (see Figure 4).

There are, unfortunately, some technical problems with all this, and Staden's story deserves careful scrutiny. For example, Staden, who may or may not have been able to read or write, seemed to possess an uncanny ability to understand Tubinamba dialect from the moment of encounter,* an ability equaled only by that of his captors, who, according to him, could not count beyond five, but whose extraordinary linguistic talent was evidenced by their fluency in German (or was it Portuguese?). Thus in one scene, a touching testimony to his piety and memory, Staden repeats the psalm, "Out of the depths have I cried unto Thee." The Indians respond with, "See how he cries; now he is sorrowful indeed."

There is another problem: how anyone could ever have taken Herr Staden seriously. But he has been frequently referred to by other writers in the genre, and even in more abstract discussions on the nature of cannibalism.

One scientist of the American Museum of Natural History joins W. Crocker, a Smithsonian anthropologist, in finding

---

*Aryon Rodriguez, Brazil's leading specialist on native languages, estimates that twelve hundred languages were spoken by tribes of Brazil in the early 1500s, when the Portuguese conquerors came.

Staden's account persuasive: "The information about their entire institution of cannibalism, which covers at least a complete annual cycle, is so detailed and complex that it is unlikely that the whole picture was invented."

William Arens, however, disagrees, concluding laconically: "Finally, it must be added that these famous cannibals, who were supposed to make others disappear into their cooking pots, have instead themselves vanished. As a result of their contact with and treatment by Europeans who were so quick to label them man-eaters, the Tubinamba failed to survive the sixteenth century. As a result, there is no modern information on the traditional culture of this group. Although there may be some legitimate reservations about who ate whom, there can be none on the question of who exterminated whom."[1]

Consider the Aztecs, one of the ancient sun kingdoms of America, those strange civilizations with their strange gods, all of whom the Spaniards would annihilate at a genocidal rate in the name of the true Lord and His Most Catholic Majesty.

They came seemingly from nowhere, fierce and uncivilized, with their cruel god Uitzilopochtli, feeder on human hearts. In the thirteenth century the Aztecs settled on Chapultepec, the "hill of the grasshopper." Forced out by their neighbors, who detested their fearsome ways, they moved to a barren expanse of lava where they subsisted on a diet of snakes and vermin. Later they moved yet again, and as mercenary allies launched into unremitting warfare against other city-states. They threatened to conquer everything in sight, and pretty much did. By the early sixteenth century the Aztecs had brought most of present-day Mexico under their dominion. It was a rich, tribute-paying empire, at its peak when Hernán Cortés—an upstart, ruthless, cutthroat Spanish adventurer, hungry for gold, glory, gore, and conversion of heathen natives to his gentle God—landed on the coast of Mexico. With his 550 men, 16 horses, 14 cannons, and a handful of dogs, he was greeted by ambassadors of the great Montezuma II, lord of the mighty

Aztecs, who presented him with astonishing gifts. It was Good Friday in the year of grace 1519. Less than two years later it was all over. In addition to the outright murders, 3.5 million Aztecs—more than half the population—perished from smallpox, an import from the Old World.

In Aztec life church and state were one, and every detail centered around religion and its rituals, mostly of death: to keep the sun moving and the whole cosmos working, the gods needed a diet of human hearts and blood. Did their loyal servants, too? Few doubt that thousands were sacrificed, but were they also consumed? Skull racks indicate that many died; they do not prove, however, that anyone was eaten.

In *Cannibals and Kings* Professor Marvin Harris argues for the cannibalism theory; Professor Arens (in *The Man-Eating Myth*) argues against it. According to Harris:

> As well-trained, methodical butchers of the battlefield and as citizens of the land of the Inquisition, Cortés and his men were inured to displays of cruelty and bloodshed. It must have come as no great surprise to them that the Aztecs methodically sacrificed human beings, inasmuch as the Spaniards and other Europeans methodically broke people's bones on the rack, pulled people's arms and legs off in tugs-of-war between horses, and disposed of women accused of witchcraft by burning them at the stake. Still, they were not quite prepared for what they found in Mexico.
>
> Nowhere else in the world had there developed a state-sponsored religion whose art, architecture, and ritual were so thoroughly dominated by violence, decay, death, and disease. Nowhere else were walls and plazas of great temples and palaces reserved for such a concentrated display of jaws, fangs, claws, talons, bones, and gaping death heads. . . .
>
> The main source of food for the Aztec gods was prisoners of war, who were marched up the steps of the pyramids to the temples, seized by four priests, spread-eagled backward over the stone altar, and split open from one side of the chest

to the other with an obsidian knife wielded by a fifth priest [see Figure 2]. The victim's heart—usually described as still beating—was then wrenched out and burned as an offering. The body was rolled down the pyramid steps, which were built deliberately steep to accommodate this function. . . .

As [Michael] Harner* points out, there really is no mystery concerning what happened to the bodies since all the eyewitness accounts are in fundamental agreement . . . the victims were eaten. Bernardino de Sahagún's description† leaves little room for doubt:

"After having torn their hearts from them and poured the blood into a gourd vessel, which the master of the slain man himself received, they started the body rolling down the pyramid steps. It came to rest upon a small square below. There some old men, whom they called Quaquacuiltin, laid hold of it and carried it to their tribal temple, where they dismembered it and divided it up in order to eat it."

I have been pursuing the fate of the victim's body in order to establish the point that Aztec cannibalism was not a perfunctory tasting of ceremonial tidbits. All edible parts were used in a manner strictly comparable to the consumption of the flesh of domesticated animals. The Aztec priests can legitimately be described as ritual slaughterers in a state-sponsored system geared to the production and redistribution of substantial amounts of animal protein in the form of human flesh.[2]

Here is a sampling from Arens:

In a collection of popular essays on the origins of culture with the catchy title *Cannibals and Kings*, Harris concludes his selection on the pre-contact states of Mesoamerica by

---

*Michael Harner is an anthropologist.

†Fray Bernardo de Sahagún (1499–1590), who arrived in Mexico after ten years of Spanish rule, is the author of a thirteen-volume record of Aztec history titled *Historia general de las cosas de Nueva España*.

informing his readers that the term "high-civilization" is a "wildly inappropriate" characterization of the Aztec state. With this conscious misuse of a technical phrase having no relation to value-laden moral standards, he invites the audience to consider his next essay, "The Cannibal Kingdom." . . .

He supports these contentions, which could have been penned by a sixteenth-century cleric, by coopting Harner's basic premises on protein deficiency interspersed with some asides on the similar practices of the Tubinamba and Huron and judicious quotations from what he defines as the "eyewitness accounts" of the conquistadors Cortés and Díaz. Like Harner, he mistakenly assumes that large-scale human sacrifice inevitably results in an equally grand cannibalistic appetite.[3]

Where lies the truth? From the knowledge I have I tend to concur with the judgement of Ashley Montagu, one of the foremost anthropologists of our time who, in personal correspondence with me, offers this observation: "Arens is on the right track, but a little extreme. Harris, I think, is wrong."

Consider kuru.

Not so many years ago, members, especially women and children, of the Fore tribe in the New Guinea highlands were found to suffer from kuru, a rare, progressive, and fatal neurological disease named for its most obvious symptom, "trembling with fear." Cannibalistic practices were said to be the most probable mode of transmission. This etiology has in fact been described in the medical literature as a major breakthrough in microbiology, and its chief researcher, Dr. Carleton Gajdusek, received the Nobel Prize for his work. But once again nobody seems to have observed Fores engaged in eating human beings, and different hypotheses as to the disease's etiology can be advanced. The kuru controversy reads like a detective story, which we shall return to in chapter 14.

4

Summary

Claims of having observed instances of cannibalism first-hand are rampant in the travelogues of explorers, sailors, missionaries, traders, travelers, tribesmen, and others. *They may or may not be true.* Some persons may honestly misremember, many have axes to grind, and still others are seriously unhinged. The subject lends itself all too readily to distortion and fantasy by the unwary and naive, and to calculated accusation and slander by the prejudiced and mean: What, after all, could be more despicable than being "guilty" of roasting babies? Some accounts seem to be written in high Martian; others elicit a groan. In the nineteenth century beef was preserved in tins; sailors called these "bully beef" or "Fanny Adams," after an English girl who mysteriously disappeared near a tinning factory.[1] Is this connection, then, an argument for cannibalism?

Perhaps one could call all this the "over the hill" mentality, reminiscent of syphilis, which the Italians called the French disease, the French the Italian disease, and so on. A New Guinean or an African is as prone to debase someone else with the cannibal label as is a European. Thus the Chinese accused the Koreans of being cannibals and the Koreans in turn said the Chinese were. Africans charged that Europeans were cannibals and Europeans said Africans were. In fact anthropologists themselves have been mistaken for cannibals.

51

John Middleton of Yale University reported in 1970 that when he worked among the Lubgara of Uganda, the tribe had to redefine him "as one of those rare Europeans who do not eat African babies," while William Arens was seen by the Masai as a "bloodsucker." It seems that it is always someone else who indulges in our flesh and blood, or someone else who has actually observed it.*

Anthropological literature is also permeated by an unguarded tenor, while many unresolved questions of fact and interpretation remain. The need to distinguish science from authoritative pronouncements, and validated knowledge from speculation, is ever present. Even modern accounts from reputable scientists may not be convincing (and there is always an island in the South Pacific that will demonstrate almost any point—in support or refutation). Thus Margaret Mead, writing about the Mundugumor people of New Guinea, blithely described them as a "cannibal tribe," though she herself had never witnessed the act. It had been outlawed, she explained, by the Australian government three years before she got there. Again, no one ever seems to be around to verify.[2]

Mead gets worse. Often serving as a spokeswoman for American anthropology, she was once asked by a reporter for a popular magazine to account for her perennial optimism after so many years spent in the study of our species' often disheartening antics. Tellingly Mead replied, "But I have seen the children of headhunters and cannibals becoming doctors and lawyers and dealing

---

*Richard Gardner, in his book *True and False Accusations of Child Abuse*, p. 472, makes a similar point about alleged satanic rituals, to which we will return: "One must make a sharp differentiation between actually observed and proven satanic cults (which, I believe, probably exist in very small numbers and are extremely rare) and the *rumors about* their existence (which are ubiquitous). . . . Like people with 'photographic memories,' everybody seems to know someone who knows someone who knows such a person but no one has had direct personal experience with such an individual."

with complex mathematical and philosophical questions and walking around with *The Oxford Book of Verse*."

Given the strong investment in their respective theories, too many anthropologists (like other social scientists) ignore contradictory evidence, overinterpret, and confuse correlation with causation. For example, Swedes are a hundred times more likely to be schizophrenic than the presumably cannibalistic Papuans in New Guinea. It is a highly significant correlation, but almost certainly not due to Swedes' refraining from eating one another. Anthropologists have a lot to be humble about.

The cannibalism literature consequently ranges from mega-nonsense ("Man came into being through cannibalism—intelligence can be eaten") to minibattles. One of these was provoked by Arens in *The Man-Eating Myth*. Basically what Arens and his supporters argue is that the old accounts of cannibalism are not credible and that few believable modern accounts of cannibalistic societies exist. In fact, Arens essentially maintains that no anthropologist has ever seen an instance of cannibalism, and that ritual or "learned" (though not necessarily survival) cannibalism is a figment of some people's imagination. "As a consequence, the general tone of modern anthropological commentary on cannibalism emerges as little more than nineteenth-century reinterpretations in contemporary scientific jargon."[3] As Arens says of his own survey of sources dealing with cannibalism of dead bodies: "[I]t was not possible to isolate a single reliable complete first-hand account by an anthropologist of this purported conventional way of disposing of the dead. The legion of existing reports by nonspecialists were found to range from highly suspect to entirely groundless when viewed from the perspective of objective scholarship and common sense."[4]*

---

*A 1994 Smithsonian TV special, entitled "Treehouse People, Cannibal Justice," may serve as another example of this. We are told all sorts of things, including how women in this New Guinea tribe are eaten for committing adultery as well as for stealing bananas; but, lo and behold, it's that clan over the next hill again.

Thomas Riley of the University of Illinois at Urbana-Champaign counters by asserting that since Arens and his supporters reject reports of cannibalism by early explorers as well as more recent anthropological reports and archaeological evidence, their reasoning "is along the lines of those few historians who would claim the Holocaust of World War II never happened."

Conversely, Fitz John Porter Poole, an anthropologist at the University of California, San Diego, who says he has actually witnessed a form of ritual cannibalism in New Guinea, supports Arens by stating that Arens has done the field of anthropology a service in questioning the cannibalism stories.

Finally, there is Ashley Montagu again, who has maintained a cautious, scholarly position on cannibalism and has seriously undermined the entire evolutionary perspective: he points out that reports of such practices for more recent times are almost nonexistent among hunting-gathering people, who have the simplest system of adaptation. Consequently, it is not possible to posit a relationship between primitive man and cannibalism as an atavistic aggressive trait, as many have done.[5]

So it goes. There is for the interested reader more about all this in the Further Readings at the end of this book, where the good news—reasonable research—all too often alternates with the bad news—bad research, e.g., nebulous concepts; peculiar verbal gymnastics; and fanciful, if unfortunately unproven, theories of personality dynamics.

The bottom line is this: as we are about to examine the different forms of cannibalism, we once again urge you to exercise caution and to use your own judgment.

Part Two

Motivational Factors
for Cannibalism

"I know," Zerbino went on, "that if any dead body could help you to stay alive, then I'd certainly want you to use it. In fact, if I do die, and you don't eat me, then I'll come back from wherever I am and give you a good kick in the ass."

From Piers Paul Read's account
of the Andes crash, in *Alive*

Introduction

Types of cannibalism can be arranged into various categories; e.g., "in-group" and "out-group"—in other words, within or outside the tribe or other society, or chronologically, geographically, or in other ways. I have found it most useful and lucid to classify types of cannibalism according to motivations, which fall into several broad categories. While these major motivational groups can exist independently, they very often overlap. For example, magic, ritual, punishment, and presumably a good deal of sadism combine in the Melanesian custom of sacrificing criminals to the gods and eating them in order to obtain *mana* (power, talent, bravery) for warriors. Or, where the custom of eating the body of an enemy prevails, the transition from punishment to gastronomic cannibalism can be imperceptible. Put differently, there exists a fine line between devouring an enemy killed in battle and killing him purely for the sake of devouring him. Most important, no one need doubt that a socially prescribed ritual involving cannibalism conveniently legitimizes the sadist's inclinations.

5

Natural Famines

Hunger has its own logic.

Bertolt Brecht

In 1631, as has so often happened before and since, death in the form of famine reigned in India. It was the time of Shah Jahan ("Emperor of the World"), who later would build that exquisite monument, the Taj Mahal, in memory of his favorite wife, Mumtaz Mahal ("Chosen One of the Palace," who bore him fourteen children), when people were reduced to "scraping on the dunghills for food. . . . All the highways [were strewn] with dead people, our noses never free from the stink of them, especially about [the] towns. . . . Women were seen to roast their children; men traveling in the way were laid hold of to be eaten and having cut away much of his flesh, he was glad if he could get away and save his life, [and] others killed outright and devoured. A man or woman [was] no sooner dead but they were cut in pieces to be eaten."[1]

A famine (from the Latin *fames*, meaning "hunger") is a severe shortage of food, resulting in widespread starvation and death. Famines are often accompanied by violence, revolution, and cannibalism. The peasant uprisings in medieval Europe were attributable, at least in part, to famines, and it was no

59

accident that the French Revolution broke out the year following a period of acute food shortages.

Causes of famines may be natural, manmade, or a combination of the two. Foremost among the natural causes are changes in the physical environment, specifically six: droughts; excessive or fluctuating rainfall; short-term variations in temperature; floods; pests, e.g., locust plagues; and diseases/epidemics among plants, animals, or men.

The leading causes are drought and subsequent crop failure. India in particular has suffered from this fate, and for all intents and purposes droughts are endemic to that country. India relies heavily on timely monsoon rains, and while there is enough rainfall overall, it is frequently unpredictable and unevenly distributed.

Conversely, excess rainfall can cause similar havoc. Too much rain created the great European famine between 1315 and 1317: the weather was unusually frigid and wet, and crops rotted in the fields before they could be harvested.

Closely related to these causes is the relationship between the number of people and the amount of food available. Infanticide and the ritual killing of the old have always been a feature of population control, though the victims were not normally eaten. At times, however, they were.

A population control of sorts also existed in nineteenth-century Australia, where one tribe ate every tenth baby born; another, the Kaura aborigines, ate all newborn babies in time of famine. (To emphasize once more, reports like these may or may not be true. Many are cited in Volhard's book *Kannibalismus,* and it becomes a matter of judgment how much credence one gives to his sources.)

The most historically prominent famines are listed in Table 1.

Table 1
Great Famines*

436 B.C.E.	Famine at Rome, when thousands of starving people threw themselves into the Tiber
42 C.E.	Great famine in Egypt
650	Famines throughout India
879	Universal famine
941, 1022, 1033	Great famines in India; entire provinces depopulated and man driven to cannibalism
1005	Famine in England
1016	Famine throughout Europe; cannibalism widespread
1064–70	Seven years' famine in Egypt
1148–59	Eleven years' famine in India
1162	Universal famine
1200	Nationwide cannibalism during drought in Egypt
1315–17	Famine in Europe
1344–45	Great famine in India, when even the Mogul emperor was unable to obtain necessities for his household
1396–1407	The Durga Devi famine in India
1505	Famine and cannibalism in Hungary
1586	Famine in England, which gave rise to the Poor Law System
1631	Famine in India
1661	Famine in India; no rain fell for two years
1669–70	Famine in India; an estimated 3 million died
1769–70	Great famine in Bengal; a third of the population, 10 million, perished
1783	The Chalisa famine in India

---

*Sources: *Encyclopaedia Britannica* and *Encyclopedia Americana*

Table 1 (contd.)

1790–92	The Doji Bara, or skull famine, in India, so called because people died in such numbers that they could not be buried. According to tradition this is one of the severest famines ever known
1816–17	Famine in Ireland; 737,000 died
1838	Intense famine in northwest provinces of India; 800,000 perished
1846–47	Famine in Ireland due to the failure of the potato crop; 1 million died
1861	Famine in northwest India
1866	Famine in Bengal; 1 million dead
1869	Intense famine in India; 1.5 million died
1874	Famine in India
1876–78	Famine in Bombay and Madras; 5 million perished
1877–78	Famine in north China; 9.5 dead
1887–89	Famine in China
1891–92	Famine in Russia
1897	Famine in India
1899–1901	Famine in India; 1 million perished
1905	Famine in Russia
1914–18	World War I famines
1916	Famine in China
1921–22	Famine in Russia; 3 million dead
1932–33	Famine in Russia; 3 million dead
1943	Famine in India; 1.5 million dead
1943	Famine in China; 1 million dead
1960–61	Famine in the Congo
1964	Famine in India
1970–74	Famine in West Africa; 250,000 died
1979–80	Famine in East Africa
1982–83	Widespread famines in Africa

Table 1 (contd.)

1985	Famine in Africa, caused by the worst drought of this century
1993	U.S. troops enter Somalia to distribute food following a famine there

To die from hunger is very painful. Just how does one starve to death? In the cold, dispassionate language of medicine (Beeson and McDermott, *Textbook of Medicine*) undernutrition, starvation, and hunger edema feel like this:

> When a person's caloric intake is far below his daily energy expenditure, he must either bring the two into balance by reduced activity or draw upon his own tissues for energy. Initially, tissue fat is a major energy source, but protein is also required as a source of amino acids for gluconeogenesis.* . . . After several weeks of fasting, dependence on endogenous amino acids decreases, because even the central nervous system can then utilize fatty acids.
>
> Once adipose tissue has been exhausted, lassitude, loss of ambition, hypotension, collapse, and death follow if the caloric intake deficit continues. The late stages of this syndrome are also observed in anorexia nervosa, terminal carcinoma, and other wasting diseases. [One researcher] provides the most comprehensive review of the world literature on starvation, and adds important experimental observation of his own. Others have described severe malnutrition in the prisons and concentration camps of World War II and famines in many parts of the world.[2]

Here is one example of a famine, from Reay Tannahill's *Flesh and Blood*:

---

*Formation of glycogen, which is stored in the body as a sugar-supply reserve, from noncarbohydrate sources.

Cannibalism

During the great famine of A.D. 1201 in Egypt [due to a failure of the inundation of the Nile] there was a doctor living in Cairo—a man in his late thirties—who saw and heard much, and wrote it down. A whole chapter of his *Useful and instructive reflections on things that I have seen and events that I have witnessed in Egypt* (written between 1201 and 1207) is devoted to this subject.

[Excerpts follow:]

"At Misr, at Cairo, and in the surrounding areas," says Abd al-Latif, "wherever a man directed his steps, there was nowhere that his feet or his eyes did not encounter a corpse or someone in the last stages of agony, or even a great number of people in this unhappy state. Particularly in Cairo, they picked up from a hundred to five hundred dead bodies every day, to take them to the place where they were accorded burial rites. At Misr, the number of dead was incalculable; people there did not bury them but contented themselves with throwing them outside the town. In the end, there were no longer enough people to collect them and they remained where they were, among the houses and shops, and even inside the living quarters. You would see a corpse fallen to pieces—and quite near a cook-shop, or a baker's, or other places of that kind. . . .

"As for the suburbs and the villages, all the inhabitants perished except for a small number, some of whom left home to seek refuge elsewhere. . . .

"Often a traveller would pass through a sizeable village without finding a single inhabitant alive. He would see the houses open, and the bodies of those who had lived there laid out facing one another, some putrefying, some still fresh. Very often he found valuable possessions in a house, for there was no one to steal them. . . .

"It was not unusual to find people [selling] little children, roasted or boiled. The commandant of the city guard ordered that those who committed this crime should be burned alive, as should those who ate such meats.

"I myself saw a little roast child in a basket. It was brought to the commandant, and led in at the same time were a man and woman who were the child's father and mother. The commandant condemned them to be burned alive. . . .

"When the poor first began to eat human flesh, the horror and astonishment that such extraordinary meals aroused were such that these crimes formed the topic of every conversation. No one could stop talking about them. But eventually people grew accustomed, and some conceived such a taste for these detestable meats that they made them their ordinary provender, eating them for enjoyment and even laying in supplies. They thought up a variety of preparation methods. And the custom being once introduced, it spread in the provinces so that there was no part of Egypt where one did not see examples of it. Then it no longer caused surprise. The horror people had felt at first vanished entirely; one spoke of it, and heard it spoken of, as a matter of everyday indifference. . . .

"When some unfortunate who had been convicted of eating human flesh was burned alive, the corpse was always found to have been devoured by the following morning. People ate it the more willingly, for the flesh, being fully roasted, did not need to be cooked. . . . At Atfih, a grocery store was found to contain jars full of human flesh pickled in water and salt. The man was asked why he had amassed such a large quantity, and replied that he had thought that, if the dearth continued, men in future would become too skinny to eat. . . .

"Two or three children, even more, would be found in a single cooking pot. One day, they found a pot with ten hands cooking in it, prepared like sheep's trotters [feet]. Another time, they discovered a large cauldron with an adult's head and some of his limbs simmering with wheat grains. There were parallels without number.

"Near the mosque of Ahmad ibn Touloun there were people who kidnapped men. One bookseller with whom I dealt, an elderly and corpulent man, fell into their net and escaped with great difficulty and almost on his last gasp. . . .

Cannibalism

"This hideous calamity I have just described struck the whole of Egypt. There was not a single inhabited spot where eating people was not extremely common. Syene, Kush [Meroe], Fayum, Mahalleh, Alexandria, Damietta, and every other part of Egypt witnessed these scenes of horror."[3]

6

Manmade Famines

We have known everything . . .
That in Russian speech there is
No word for that mad war winter . . .
When the Hermitage shivered under bombs . . .
Houses turned to frost and pipes burst with ice . . .
The ration—100 grams . . . On the Nevskey corpses.
And we learned, too, about cannibalism.
We have known everything. . . .

Daniel Andreyev, quoted in
Harrison Salisbury, *The 900 Days*

We can divide manmade famines into two basic types: war-related and those engineered to remove "undesirables." Those that are primarily war-related affect both the enemy's soldiers and civilians. Specifically we have scorched earth policies, prison camps, and sieges. They often overlap.

From the earliest times of warfare, it has often seemed to military strategists that the easiest way to overcome an enemy was to destroy his source of food, primarily crops and livestock. Military campaigns have always left a trail of burned granaries, scorched fields, and confiscated cattle. Related to this is the damage done to transportation routes, vehicles, trains, and ships so that food cannot be moved or imported.

Cannibalism

Starvation in prison camps also goes back a long time; occasionally it was a consequence of a general food shortage, but usually it was deliberate policy. No one needed to starve to death at Andersonville, the Confederate prison camp of Union soldiers during the Civil War. In Hitler's opening campaign against the Soviet Union in 1941, approximately 3.8 million Russian prisoners were taken, and great numbers of them were deliberately left to die from hunger or cold in that cruel winter of 1941-42. Prisoners had only one right—the right to die. Of the well over 5 million Red Army soldiers captured, a bare 1 million survived the war. The major commandant of Auschwitz, SS Colonel Rudolf Höss, who was hanged for war crimes in 1947, relates the following in his autobiography:

> On the road to Auschwitz and Birkenau I once saw an entire column of Russians, several hundred strong, suddenly make a rush for some nearby stacks of potatoes on the far side of the railway line. Their guards were taken by surprise, overrun, and could do nothing. I luckily happened to come along at this moment and was able to restore the situation. The Russians had thrown themselves onto the stacks, from which they could hardly be torn away. Some of them died in the confusion, while chewing, their hands full of potatoes. Overcome by the crudest instinct of self-preservation, they came to care nothing for one another, and in their selfishness now thought only of themselves. Cases of cannibalism were not rare in Birkenau. I myself came across a Russian lying between piles of bricks, whose body had been ripped open and the liver removed. They would beat each other to death for food. . . .
>
> When the foundation for the first group of buildings [at Auschwitz] were being dug, the men often found the bodies of Russians who had been killed by their fellows, partly eaten and then stuffed into a hole in the mud. . . .
>
> They were no longer human beings. They had become animals, who sought only food.[1]

As for sieges, Julius Caesar, in his *Gallic War*, wrote that the people of Alesia in Gaul, besieged by the Roman army, ate women, old men, and others who could not fight. In 1871, when the Germans encircled Paris, a French butcher shop on the island of Saint Louis sold human flesh. This was not known until much later, after the siege had been lifted; by that time the shop had acquired a great reputation for the quality of its meat.

On June 22, 1812, Napoleon I, emperor of France, crossed the Niemen river on his way to Moscow. Like no man since Caesar he held the reigns of power over most of Europe. All that was left was Russia. Napoleon launched his attack with the Grand Armée—over 600,000 Frenchmen, Germans, Italians, Poles; 110,000 horses; thousands of supply wagons; and vast herds of cattle. Finally he reached Moscow—with only 100,000 men. The Russian territory, typhus, and Field Marshal Mikhail Illarionovitch Kutuzov's Cossacks and scorched earth policy, carried out on an enormous scale, reaped a ghastly harvest. (As in the American Civil War half a century later, many died from their wounds as well as from medical practice.)

In most European countries Napoleon would win one or two major battles, then seize the capital and dictate his peace terms. The gambit didn't work in Russia. Field Marshal Kutuzov, a big, burly man, had only one eye, but it was unusually perspicacious. When others had tried to force him to give battle, he had refused and retreated: "Time and patience; patience and time," he said. Pressured to fight at Borodino, Kutusov held his own—and immediately retreated again. At 2:00 P.M. on September 14, looking down on the glistening golden cupolas of Moscow, Napoleon saw a deserted city. That night Kutuzov set it aflame; the fire raged five days. By that act the French learned something about the Russian character. And so the arrogant little Corsican, who had once boasted that he didn't give a damn about the death of a million men ("A night in Paris will make up for it"), strutted about in the

Kremlin for five weeks, not knowing what to do next. He soon found out.

As the endless columns of hungry, exhausted, undisciplined French and allied soldiers struggled back across the same ravished path they had come, their great column stretching for fifty miles, the army of the czar followed on a parallel route. Kutuzov ordered: "Now we will attack. Now we will strike the beast at the flanks." At Borodino they found 30,000 corpses, half-eaten by wolves. At Smolensk, twenty days after leaving Moscow, Napoleon had 36,000 men left. At Vilna, Marshal Ney, commanding the Third Army Group, had a mere twenty. Snow covered the corpses of the rest.

Instead of realistically recalling the anxieties, hardships, immorality and atrocities which his war had brought both to individuals and nations, or having second thoughts about the hundreds of thousands he needlessly sacrificed in the prime of their life, the glorious emperor left his army in the lurch and hurried back to Paris. Arriving at the banks of the Niemen in his miserable sleigh, he inquired of the ferryman whether deserters had come through that way. "No," replied the Russian, "you are the first." It was December 6, and Napoleon assessed the debacle with this grotesque remark: "Perhaps I made a mistake in going to Moscow."

The following account is from *Napoleon's Russian Campaign* by Count Philippe-Paul de Ségur, who "never left the Emperor's side for more than a few feet":

> From now on there existed no fraternity of arms, no society, no human ties. An excess of hardship had made brutes of our men, and hunger, ravenous, devouring hunger, had killed everything in those unfortunate beings but the instinct of self-preservation, sole driving force of the fiercest animals, to which everything else is sacrificed. A harsh, violent, merciless nature seemed to have communicated her fury to them. Like true savages, the strong despoiled the weak: they

crowded around the dying, often not waiting to rob them until they had breathed their last. When a horse fell, you would have thought you were witnessing the fatal moment in a hunt, as the men swarmed upon the animal and tore it into scraps, over which they fought like famished hounds! . . .

On the sixth of December, the day following the departure of the emperor, the sky became still more terrible. The air was filled with infinitesimal ice crystals; birds fell to the earth frozen stiff. The atmosphere was absolutely still. It seemed as if everything in nature having movement or life, down to the very wind, had been bound and congealed in a universal death. Now not a word, not a murmur broke the dismal silence, silence of despair and unshed tears. . . .

Before long they fell to their knees, then forward on their hands. Their heads wagged stupidly from side to side for a little while, and a gasping rattle issued from their lips. Then they collapsed in the snow, on which appeared the slow-spreading stain of blackish blood—and their suffering was at an end. . . .

At Youpranoui—the same town where the partisan leader Seslawin had missed the emperor by an hour—our soldiers burned whole houses as they stood to get a few minutes' warmth. The light of these conflagrations attracted some poor wretches whom the intensity of the cold and suffering made delirious. They dashed forward in a fury [and] threw themselves into those raging furnaces, where they perished in dreadful convulsions. Their starving companions watched them die without apparent horror. There were even some who laid hold of bodies disfigured and roasted by the flames, and—incredible as it may seem—ventured to carry this loathsome food to their mouths!

And this was the army that had issued from the most civilized nation in Europe, that army once so brilliant, victorious over men up to the last moment, and whose name still inspired respect in so many conquered capitals! . . .

Issuing from the white, ice-bound desert were one

thousand foot soldiers and troopers still armed, nine cannon and twenty thousand beings clothed in rags, with bowed heads, dull eyes, ashy, cadaverous faces and long ice-stiffened beard.

Two kings, one prince, eight marshals, followed by several generals afoot and unattended, then a few hundred of the Old Guard still bearing arms, were all that remained. . . .

Such were the last days of the Grand Army: its last nights were still more frightful.[2]

Perhaps the most famous of all sieges was that of Leningrad in 1941-43. One hundred and twenty-nine years to the day after Napoleon's crossing the Niemen, at 3:00 A.M. on June 22, 1941, the pale night sky of that shortest night of the year was turned to day by the flash of thousands of guns. Adolf Hitler had invaded the Soviet Union. The basic floorplan was the same, though he had three million men along a front of 1,500 kilometers—one for every foot and a half. It was Hitler's greatest blitzkrieg of them all. He had announced to his secretaries: "In a few weeks I will be in Moscow. There is absolutely no doubt about it. I will raze this damned city to the ground. . . . The name of Moscow will vanish forever."* In November the Nazis were within sight of the Kremlin, but the swastika was not to fly over it.

Hitler had also announced: "I have no feelings about the idea of wiping out St. Petersburg [formerly Leningrad]." Hitler's troops had been in the suburbs of Russia's second largest city since early September. Now it was surrounded. Hitler forbad

---

*This engineer of Auschwitz did not like Paris or New York either. Later he gave orders to burn the former to the ground, and according to Albert Speer, his minister of armaments and munitions, Hitler had these plans for New York: "I never saw him so worked up as toward the end of the war, when in a kind of delirium he pictured for himself and for us the destruction of New York in a hurricane of fire. He described the skyscrapers being turned into gigantic burning torches, collapsing upon one another, the glow of the exploding city illuminating the dark sky."

his commanders from accepting any surrender, and so began the greatest siege at least since biblical times. Leningrad would hold—for two and a half years. One million human beings would die from starvation.

Harrison Salisbury, the veteran *New York Times* correspondent, spent twenty-five years studying diaries, memoirs, and archives, and interviewing and corresponding with survivors of the seige of Leningrad. In *The 900 Days: The Siege of Leningrad,* an epic account of human cruelty and courage, he wrote:*

"The Haymarket or Sennaya occupied the heart of Leningrad. Some years earlier it had been Peace Square, but no one called it that. The Haymarket it had been since the early days of 'Piter,' and the Haymarket it was in this winter of Leningrad's agony. But sometimes it was called the Hungry Market. . . .

"Ordinary people found they had little in common with the traders who suddenly appeared in the Haymarket. These were figures straight from the pages of Dostoyevsky or Kuprin. They were the robbers, the thieves, the murderers, members of the bands which roved the streets of the city and who seemed to hold much of it in their power once night had fallen.

"These were the cannibals and their allies—fat, oily, steely-eyed, calculating, the most terrible men and women of their day.

"For cannibalism there was in Leningrad. You will look in vain in the published official histories for reports of the trade in human flesh. But the stain of the story slips in, here and there, in casual references, in the memoirs, in allusions in fiction, in what is not said as well as in what is said about the crimes-for-food committed in the city. . . .

"But commercial anthropophagy or cannibalism-for-profit

---

*From Harrison E. Salisbury, *The 900 Days: The Siege of Leningrad* (New York: Harper and Row, Publishers, 1969). Copyright © 1969 by Harrison Salisbury. Reprinted by permission of Curtis Brown Ltd.

Cannibalism

"In the Haymarket people walked through the crowd as though in a dream. They were pale as ghosts and thin as shadows. Only here and there passed a man or woman with a face, full, rosy and somehow soft yet leathery. A shudder ran through the crowd. For these, it was said, were the cannibals. . . .

"Cannibals . . . Who were they? How many were they? It is not a subject which the survivors of Leningrad like to discuss. There were no cannibals, a professor recalls, or rather, there were cannibals, but it only happened when people went crazy. There was a case of which he had heard, for instance, the case of a mother, crazed for food. She lost her mind, went completely mad, killed her daughter and butchered the body. She ground up the flesh and made meat patties. But this was not typical. It was the kind of insane aberration which might happen anywhere at any time. In fact, the professor recalled reading of a similar case before the war. . . .

"There was hardly a dog or cat left in Leningrad by late December. They had all been eaten. But the trauma was great when a man came to butcher an animal which had lived on his affection for years. One elderly artist strangled his pet cat and ate it, according to Vsevolod Vishnevsky. Later, he tried to hang himself, but the rope failed, he fell to the floor, breaking his leg, and froze to death. The smallest Leningrad children grew up not knowing what cats and dogs were. . . .

"But no great effort was made to interfere with the grisly trade at the Haymarket. As early as November, according to some accounts, meat patties made from ground-up human flesh went on sale, although many Leningraders refused to believe the meat was human. They insisted it was horse meat—or dog, or cat. . . .

" 'In the worst period of the siege,' a survivor noted, 'Leningrad was in the power of the cannibals. God alone knows what terrible scenes went on behind the walls of the apartments.'

"He claimed to know of cases in which husbands ate their

wives, wives ate their husbands, and parents ate their children. In his own building a porter killed his wife and then thrust her severed head into a red-hot stove. . . .

"But if questions were not asked in the markets, there was terrible gossip in the queues where the women waited and waited for the bread shops to open. The talk was of children, how careful one must be with them, how the cannibals waited to seize them because their flesh was so much more tender. Women were said to be second choice. They were starving like the men, but, it was insisted, their bodies carried a little more fat and their flesh was more tasty. . . .

"There was more than one way in which the dead might help the living to survive. Again and again at Piskarevsky and Serafimov and the other great cemeteries the teams of sappers sent in from the front to dynamite graves noticed as they piled the corpses into mass graves that pieces were missing, usually the fat thighs or arms and shoulders. The flesh was being used as food. Grisly as was the practice of necrobutchery there was no actual law which forbade the disfigurement of corpses or which prohibited consumption of this flesh. . . .

"Among the fantastic tales which circulated in Leningrad in the winter of 1941-42 was one that there existed 'circles' or fraternities of eaters of human flesh. The circles were said to assemble for special feasts, attended only by members of their kind. These people were the dregs of the human hell which Leningrad had become. The real lower depths were those occupied by persons who insisted on eating only 'fresh' human flesh, as distinguished from cadaver cuts. Whether these tales were literally true was not so important. What was important was that Leningraders believed them to be true, and this added the culminating horror to their existence. . . ."

In another incident typical of the times, two men "entered a quiet lane and soon came to a good-sized building which had not been damaged by either German gunfire or bombing. Dmitri followed the tall man up the staircase. The man climbed easily, occasionally looking back at Dmitri. As they neared the top floor, an uneasy feeling seized Dmitri. There leaped into his mind the stories he had heard of the cannibals and how they lured victims to their doom. The tall man looked remarkably well fed. Dmitri continued up the stairs but told himself he would be on guard, ready to flee at the slightest sign of danger.

"At the top floor the man turned and said, 'Wait for me here.' He knocked at the door, and someone inside asked, 'Who is it?' 'It's me,' the man responded. 'With a live one.'

"Dmitri froze at the words. There was something sinister about them. The door opened, and he saw a hairy red hand and a muglike face. From the room came a strange, warm, heavy smell. A gust of wind in the hall caught the door, and in the swaying candlelight Dmitri had a glimpse of several great hunks of white meat, swinging from hooks on the ceiling. From one hunk he saw dangling a human hand with long fingers and blue veins.

"At that moment the two men lunged toward Dmitri. He leaped down the staircase and managed to reach the bottom ahead of his pursuers. To his good fortune, there was a light military truck passing through the lane.

" 'Cannibals!' Dmitri shouted. Two soldiers jumped from the truck and rushed into the building. A moment or two later two shots rang out. In a few minutes the soldiers reappeared, one carrying a greatcoat and the other a loaf of bread. The soldier with the greatcoat complained that it had a tear in it. The other one said, 'I found a piece of bread. Do you want it?'

"Dmitri thanked the soldier. It was his bread, the 600 grams he had planned to trade for the *valenki* [heavy felt boots]. The soldiers told him that they found human hocks from five bodies hanging in the flat. Then they got back into their truck and were off to Lake Ladoga, where they were part of the Road of Life."

As reported in the *Los Angeles Times*, new findings from

the Communist Party archives, opened in 1992, confirm Salisbury's contention—widely criticized by leaders of the Soviet era—that murderous gangs roamed wartime Leningrad's streets, killing for ration cards or human meat. Recently discovered documents show that the city police created an entire division to fight cannibals, and some 260 Leningraders were convicted of and jailed for the crime. With the official daily ration of 125 grams of bread, about the weight of a bar of soap, Leningraders supplemented this with anything they could: as historians Ales Adamovich and Daniil Granin wrote in their account of the siege, "with everything from the birdseed to the canary itself." They scraped wallpaper down and ate the paste, which was supposedly made from potatoes. They extracted the same paste from bookbinding or drank it straight from the glue jar. They boiled leather belts and briefcases to make an edible jelly, and plucked and pickled grasses and weeds. They ate petroleum jelly and lipstick, spices and medicines, fur coats and leather caps. Some made face-powder pancakes; others munched grimy crystallized sugar, dug out from under the sugar warehouses leveled by German firebombs.

Historians have recorded twenty-two different dishes made out of pigskin and have collected menus from military cafeterias where choices ranged from fern-leaf soup to puree of nettles and milk-curd pancakes. Scientists at the Vitamin Institute developed diet supplements by extracting vitamin C from pine needles, and swept attics and ventilation shafts at tobacco factories for tobacco dust, which contains vitamin B.

At one laboratory bacteria were also cultivated for study in a medium with meat-broth base. "We had a large stock [of this medium]. It saved many of our staff," said one survivor. "I used to extract a glassful when I arrived at work, then all the staff would sit around and I would give them each a tablespoonful."

But then there also exists something appropriately called the Law of Unexpected Consequences. Moscow had held, as had Leningrad. They were followed by Stalingrad, as we shall now see. Frustrated and furious, Hitler had became obsessed with that city on the Volga bearing the name of his counterpart. It was of little more than tactical significance in the scheme of the war, and all his senior military commanders objected to his plans. Hitler as usual ignored them. If this was to be the showdown, let it be.

This was the showdown between Germany and Russia. The slaughter on both sides was ferocious; it lasted 159 days and nights. From William Craig's *Enemy at the Gates: The Battle for Stalingrad,** we read:

> In five months of fighting and bombings, 99 percent of the city had been reduced to rubble. More than forty-one thousand homes, three hundred factories,113 hospitals and schools had been destroyed. A quick census revealed that out of more than five hundred thousand inhabitants of the previous summer, only 1,515 civilians remained. Most of them had either died in the first days or left the city for temporary homes in Siberia and Asia. No one knew how many had been killed, but the estimates were staggering. . . .
>
> The German Sixth Army was scattered to more than twenty camps stretching from the Arctic Circle to the southern deserts.
>
> One train carried thousands of Germans from the Volga to Uzbekistan, in Central Asia. Inside each car, stuffed with

---

Enemy at the Gates is the culmination of five years of research, during which Craig traveled extensively on three continents, interviewing hundreds of survivors of the battle. Harrison Salisbury has stated on the flyleaf of the book: "William Craig has written a classic account of the Stalingrad epic—here is the drama, the terror, the horror and the heroism of the greatest military encounter of our time." It was also the greatest military defeat in German history. Field Marshal Gerd von Rundstedt, one of Hitler's ablest commanders, concluded that, "After Stalingrad the war could no longer be won." One of his colleagues implied the cause of the disaster: "Too many Russians, and one German too many." Winston Churchill, no mean judge in such matters, sums it up: "The hinge of fate turned on the Volga."

one hundred or more prisoners, a macabre death struggle ensued as the Germans killed each other for bits of food tossed to them every two days. Those closest to the door were set upon by ravenous soldiers in the rear; only the strongest men survived the weeks-long trip. By the time the train reached the Pamir mountains, almost half its passengers were dead. . . .

Other prisoners, more intent on survival, took matters into their own hands, especially in camps where military self-discipline had broken down. At Susdal, Felice Bracci first noticed it when he saw corpses without arms or legs. And Dr. Cristoforo Capone found human heads with the brains scooped out, or torsos minus livers and kidneys. Cannibalism had begun.

The cannibals were furtive at first, stealing among the dead to hack off a limb and eat it raw. But their tastes quickly matured and they searched for the newly dead, those just turning cold, and thus more tender. Finally they roamed in packs, defying anyone to stop them. They even helped the dying to die. Hunting day and night, their lust for human flesh turned them into crazed animals and, by late February, they reached a savage peak of barbarism. . . .

The Russians shot every cannibal they caught, but faced with the task of hunting down so many man-eaters they had to enlist the aid of "anticannibalism teams," drawn from the ranks of captive officers. The Russians equipped these squads with crowbars and demanded they kill every cannibal they found. The teams prowled at night, looking for telltale flickers of flame from small fires where the predators were preparing their meals.

Dr. Vincenzo Pugliese went on patrol frequently and, one night, he turned a corner and surprised a cannibal roasting something on the end of a stick. At first it looked like an oversized sausage, but then Pugliese's trained eye noticed the accordion-like pleats on the object and with a sickening start, he realized that the man was cooking a human trachea.[4]

Cannibalism

In Aleksandr Solzhenitsyn's *The Gulag Archipelago* we read: "At the end of the Civil War [between the Red Army and the czarist forces, beginning in 1917], and as its natural consequence, an unprecedented famine developed in the Volga area. They give it only two lines in the official histories because it doesn't add a very ornamental touch to the wreaths of the victors in that war. But the famine existed nonetheless—to the point at which parents ate their own children—such a famine as even Russia had never known, even in the Time of Troubles in the early seventeenth century."

Later Stalin would deliberately starve millions more to enforce his policies.

In the Nazi ghettos, especially Warsaw, and in both concentration and extermination camps, human flesh was often all that was left for those who still clung to life. Thus, according to the ration scales imposed by the Nazis in Warsaw, Germans there were entitled to 2,310 calories per day; foreigners to 1,700; Poles to 934; and Jews to 183. The following account is given in Nora Levin's *The Holocaust*:

> Hunger raged through the Ghetto, more acutely felt than physical pain or the two bitter winters the Ghetto lived through. In May 1940, Ringelblum heard an eight-year-old boy scream madly: "I want to steal, I want to rob, I want to eat. I want to be a German!" Three months later, he wrote: "At a funeral for the small children from the Wolska Street orphanage, the children from the home placed a wreath at the graves with this inscription: 'To the Children Who Have Died from Hunger—From the Children Who Are Hungry.' " There was a day and night obsession with food; women tore at each other for a crust of bread. . . .
>
> Hunger drove some to madness, others to slow death. The corpses of the dead were hidden so that their precious ration cards could be used. . . .
>
> Against these accents of life rose a numbness to death from hunger and disease. As early as February 1941,

Ringelblum noted that the sight of people falling dead in the middle of the street no longer stirred people. Naked corpses were laid in mass graves separated by boards. Children began to lose their fear of dead bodies and were seen tickling them to see if they moved. Women who squatted in the streets with their children told Ringelblum they would rather die in the street than at home. . . .

The situation at the Baumann and Berson Children's hospital was no better. A diary entry by a nurse dated March 20, 1941, records the hopelessness of the staff:

"I am on duty from 3 to 11. I come to my ward. It is a real hell. Children sick with the measles, two or three in one bed. . . . Shaven heads covered with sores swarming with lice. . . . I have no beds, no linen, no covers, no bedclothes. I telephone the superintendent. . . . The answer is terse: where there are two children in one bed, put a third one in and that is the end of it. . . . There is no coal. The rooms are terribly cold. They huddle under the covers, shaking with fever. . . . In the corridor lies a child of five swollen with hunger. . . . The child moves its lips begging for a piece of bread. I try to feed him. . . . but his throat is locked and nothing goes down. Too late. After a few minutes he utters for the last time the words, 'a piece of bread.' "

Smuggling became an absolute necessity and smugglers of all ages, sizes, and kinds, including very small children, crawled through sewers and chinks in the walls. Jews even smuggled openly in carts when the guards could be bribed. Hunger-crazed children who were able to slip through to the Polish Aryan section were often given food; more often they were shot down by Nazi guards. Children reached the Aryan side of Warsaw by digging holes under walls or by hiding near the Ghetto gates and trying to sneak through when the guards turned the other way. Parents would sit at home all day nervously awaiting the return of their only breadwinner. So desperate was the need for food that not even the death penalty for smuggling (decreed in October 1941) could stop it, for strict obedience meant a lingering death by starvation. . . .[5]

Such starvation, the highest Nazi circles believed, would extinguish Jewish life. Before the accelerated exterminations began, it was assumed that this would do the job in the ghettos. But hunger, though a big killer, was not as efficient as the Nazis wished. The governor of occupied Poland, Hans Frank, therefore threatened that, "If the Jews do not die of hunger, the measures will be intensified." They swiftly were.

Postscript. The ghetto in April 1943 measured a thousand by three hundred yards. SS General Jürgen Stroop had 2,090 men, as well as tanks, artillery, flamethrowers, and aerial support; the remaining Jews who refused to be deported to their extermination had decided to fight. They possessed almost no weapons at all. They held out for thirty-seven days.

7

Accidents

Six miners went into the mountains
To hunt for precious gold;
It was the middle of winter,
The weather was dreadful cold,
Six miners went into the mountains,
They had no food nor shack—
Six miners went into the mountains,
But only one came back.

Traditional ballad

Cannibalism for survival has its history not only in the great famines—whether actual or manmade—but also in accidents—shipwrecks; planewrecks; or being lost in the mountains, desert, jungle, or on the ice. Presumably being lost in space will be the next addition. Such disasters, while involving small numbers of persons, often become highly publicized. The basic scenario is always the same: man against the elements, hunger and thirst, nothing to eat but human flesh, nothing to drink but blood.

Cannibalism has for millennia been common among shipwrecked survivors who would eat one another, or, at times, be eaten by the natives, for example, the notorious Fijis, on whose shores they had the misfortune to be stranded.

Cannibalism

A sampling. One shipwreck, that of the *Medusa*, was to become celebrated as well as notorious, in good part because of the French neobaroque painter Théodore Géricault (1791–1824), whose most ambitious work is *The Raft of the Medusa*, originally exhibited in Paris in 1819 (and now in the Louvre) (see Figure 8). The disaster attracted Géricault's attention because it was both a saga of the sea and a political scandal. Like many French liberals he opposed the monarchy, which was restored after the fall of Napoleon, and which protected the man responsible for the ship's demise—its royalist captain.

In the words of one art critic, Géricault

> went to extraordinary length in trying to achieve a maximum of authenticity: he interviewed survivors, had a model of the raft built, even studied corpses in the morgue. This search for uncompromising truth in *The Raft* is indeed remarkable for its powerfully realistic detail. Yet these preparations were subordinate in the end to the spirit of heroic drama that dominates the canvas. Géricault depicts the exciting moment when the men on the raft first glimpse the rescue ship. From the prostrate bodies of the dead and dying in the foreground, the composition is built up to a rousing climax in the group that supports the frantically waving Negro, so that the forward surge of the survivors parallels the movement of the raft itself.[1]

While not shown in the finished painting, cannibalism does appear in some of the preliminary studies Géricault made. What happened is this: On July 2, 1816, the criminally incompetent captain of the French government frigate *Medusa* ran her aground off the coast of West Africa.

On the morning of July 5, the captain and his senior officers appropriated the more seaworthy lifeboats and left the others to their fate. These crew members, soldiers, and would-be settlers in Senegal, hastily constructed a sizable raft. When 150 of them climbed aboard, it sank three feet, and they were waist-deep in water.

That night, "All the soldiers and sailórs gave themselves up to despair, and it was with great difficulty that we succeeded in calming them," recorded M. Savigny, the ship's surgeon. By the next morning twenty had perished, some swept into the ocean, others caught between the planks and drowned.

On the night of July 6, in the menacing dark, with rising waves, panic broke out. The casks of wine were broken open, and men drank themselves into a frenzy. Bodies were crushed, officers backed against the mast, and knives and sabers flashed in a free-for-all carnage. Sixty-five died.

On July 7 the sea calmed. Those still alive were exhausted and starving.

They threw themselves on the dead bodies with which the raft was covered, to cut them up in slices, which some even that instant devoured. Some passengers at first refused to touch the horrible food; but at last yielding to a want still more pressing than that of humanity, we saw in this frightful repast the only deplorable means of prolonging existence; and I proposed, I acknowledge it, to dry these bleeding limbs, in order to render them a little more supportable to the taste. Some, however, had still courage enough to abstain from it, and to them a larger quantity of wine was granted.

On July 8 a fire was made using gunpowder and flint; human flesh was cooked; and this time everyone ate.

On July 9 (day seven) only twenty-eight were left alive.

Out of this number, fifteen alone appeared able to exist for some days longer; all the others, covered with large wounds, had wholly lost their reason. However, they had a share in our rations, and might, before their death, consume forty bottles of wine; those forty bottles of wine were to us of inestimable value. We held a council; to put the sick on half rations was to delay their death by a few moments; to leave them without provisions was to put them to a slow death.

After a long deliberation, we resolved to throw them into the sea. This mode, however repugnant to our feelings, would procure to the survivors provisions for six days, at the rate of three quarts of wine a day. . . . Three seamen and a soldier took upon themselves this cruel execution. We averted our eyes, and shed tears of blood over the fate of these unhappy creatures.

On July 16 the fifteen survivors were saved by the brig *Argus*; five more died before it reached land.

Savigny and the engineer Cooréard reported the criminal incompetence of the royalist captain, provoking a major political scandal. The whistleblowers' fate, then as now, was not a happy one: they were harassed, fined, fired. They fought back, and wrote a book; published in 1817, it became a runaway success. One man who read it was Théodore Géricault.[2]

Also shipwrecked was the New England whaler *Essex*, crushed by a sperm whale off Henderson Island in the Pacific Ocean in 1820. The survivors reached the island, and two elected to stay. Given that the island did not support life, it was an unfortunate choice, and they starved to death. The others went on in open boats and eventually reached Chile— some of them, that is. After drawing lots they had dined on their fellow crew members. Herman Melville based his novel *Moby Dick* on the *Essex* incident; one of Captain Ahab's crew members was the cannibal Queequeg. Ballads were popular at the time, and the grim tale gave rise to one that included these lines (making up for its lack of style with stark drama) quoted in A. W. Brian Simpson, *Cannibalism and the Common Law*, p. 125:

The lots were drawn one man was to die,
For his wife and poor children most bitterly did cry,
To kill him says the captain or take away his breath,
But to starve with hunger is a deplorable death.

Then his messmates they killed him and cut off his head,
And all the ship's crew from the body did feed.

On August 2 or 3, 1899, the wooden three-mast sailing barque *Drot* set out from Mississippi with a cargo of lumber bound for Buenos Aires. It foundered in a hurricane off the Florida Straits on August 11. Of the crew of seventeen, nine and the captain were lost with the ship. There were five survivors on a raft when, according to a contemporary report based on conversations with survivors, the following took place:

> Another member showed signs of death in his face. He was going out fast. His hands and feet got cold and clammy: his companions all the while feeling for his heart; a knife was raised all the while to strike his breast at the signal word. His heartbeats became fewer. With life ebbing slowly but surely away the knife was plunged into his heart, and the blood trickled out to be drunk by the half-famished, thirsty mortals by his side. While the fearful feast was in progress, another member began to drop away; he was dying fast, his head fell back and his eyes were closed. Like birds after fresher prey the man-eaters rushed to the second victim, stabbed him, and sucked the milk-warm blood as it oozed from the great slash about his heart. The last of his blood was gone. The sight and taste of it had made the men mad. They refused the dead flesh, after tasting it sparingly, and then in the wild desire for more and warmer blood, they cast lots for a victim.[3]

Much more recently, in 1988, there occurred a case of cannibalism on the high seas following an encounter between a Vietnamese refugee boat and the U.S. amphibious transport *Dubuque*, Captain Alexander Balian commanding. According to the *Los Angeles Times*, in a series of articles, on May 22 a leaky, forty-five-foot junk with 110 refugees aboard made it out of the South Vietnamese port of Truc Giang destined for Malaysia and a refugee camp they believed was a gateway to the United States. Three days later, the boat's engine broke down. There was no mechanic on board, no sail. The junk began taking on water, and the refugees, who had paid an ounce of gold each for the voyage, began drifting at sea and thinking for the first time about death.

The journey to Malaysia was to have taken six days at the most. After the fifth day, the food and fresh water ran out. On the tenth day, a Japanese freighter was spotted. It came within a hundred yards. Half-mad with hunger and thirst, a dozen refugees jumped in the water and swam to it. The freighter sped off and those swimming toward it all drowned.

On June 9 the 8,600-ton *Dubuque* and the ocean-unworthy junk, which should never have left port, met in the South China Sea. There are different versions of what happened next.

According to Captain Balian, who did not personally visit them, the refugees were in "relatively good shape" when the *Dubuque* met them. He also insisted that he was speeding toward an urgent mission in the Persian Gulf when he encountered the junk, and further claimed in his depositions that the refugees misunderstood a *Dubuque* officer, who they say promised that another rescue ship would come in two days.

In interviews with half a dozen survivors of "Group 52" (so called for the number of eventual survivors), a reporter heard a very different account of the encounter with the American warship. One Dinh Thuong Hai recalled that the Americans gave them six cases of canned meat, two plastic bags each containing about six gallons of fresh water, and a map on which someone had written in Vietnamese, "Go east to reach the Philippines." Dinh said an American sailor was told that the junk's engine was broken, but no effort was made to fix it.

"And there was no doubt the Americans knew how desperate we were," Dinh added. In fact, all the survivors interviewed said one of the refugees had died of hunger during their two-hour encounter with the *Dubuque*. The body was thrown overboard, and all the survivors independently said the American sailors had photographed the body in the water.

"They knew we were all dying," said one survivor, who asked not to be identified. "But they just turned and sailed away."

International refugee workers familiar with the case also disagreed with Balian's version. They cited at least four other cases that year in which U.S. Navy ships did stop in the South China Sea, despite their mission orders. In every case, they picked up stranded "boat people" and put them ashore in the Philippines.

Again from the *Los Angeles Times*: "Never before have I heard of a case of the U.S. Navy leaving 'boat people' behind to die," said one independent refugee worker, who asked not to be named. "Even if the *Dubuque* were on an important secret mission in the gulf, why couldn't it have picked these people up and airlifted them to safety when they passed through the Strait of Hormuz? It just makes no sense."

After the *Dubuque* moved away, leaving the junk to drift toward death, one of the refugees, Phung Quang Minh, thirty-two, took charge of the foundering vessel. A former paratrooper in a South Vietnamese infantry unit known as the Red Berets, Phung was a professional survivor. He stated later that this voyage was his tenth attempt to escape, and that he had been caught twice and had spent four years in prison.

Phung first took over the food and water that Balian had given them, but they were soon exhausted, since Minh's rationing was based on the American promise that another rescue ship would come shortly. By now the refugees were dying at the rate of at least two a day. Hope was all but gone.

Once again we are told different versions of what happened next. Phung claimed that on the twenty-eighth day at sea the refugees decided "to use the dying to help the living." According to most accounts, two people (some say four) were killed for use as food, and three others who died were eaten.

Cannibalism

The first to die by force had been Dao Cu Cuong, thirty, who was weak with hunger and thirst, and who could hear them, "the men with the knife," talking when they said they needed him for food. Phung admitted to killing Dao. It was twelve days after the *Dubuque* had left them. Five days later a twelve-year-old boy, Pham Quy, was killed. It is unclear by whom.

According to the refugees' accounts, on the other hand, Phung's initial control of the boat was welcome and necessary. From the moment the engine failed, the boat began taking on water, and it was Phung and his supporters who organized bailing crews and who rationed food for survival.

As the refugees weakened, however, Phung and his men grew more cruel, using sticks and a knife to force starving passengers to bail water. Before long, the survivors said, Phung's organization for survival turned criminal.

"It was all so terrible, but we were powerless to stop him," one survivor said, "even when he and his men began killing the others. They were strong and we were so weak."

Some survivors claimed that they disapproved, but agreed only because they were too weak to resist.

"In the end, all of the passengers were forced to eat," Dinh said. "We were told we had to eat to stay strong, and if we didn't we would be next."

Dinh, in fact, was next on the list.

Captain Balian was courtmartialed at the Subic Bay Naval Base in the Philippines. Six navy captains, after hearing testimony for almost two weeks, convicted him of dereliction of duty, and gave him a letter of reprimand. However, they acquitted him of the more serious charge of disobeying orders.

Phung has emphasized that much of what has been said about him and reported in the press is not true. He said the killing and the cannibalism were not just his idea. It was agreed to by all of the remaining refugees, and the others turned on him later because they did not want to accept the blame for what they all had done. Phung also claimed that some refugees had sung songs, and about ten who were Christians offered a prayer for the dying.

"Because of the other people on the boat, I did this thing and I hoped God blessed me," Phung said in an interview. "I am a Christian. I killed this man in the boat to help the living. Personally, I think it's wrong, but so many people needed to eat."

Phung and nine others were arrested and imprisoned after the fifty-two starving, emaciated, and shocked survivors were rescued near the island of Luzon by Philippine fishermen on June 28. Fifty-eight had perished during the thirty-seven days at sea. Local officials investigated the stories of killing and cannibalism but determined that they had no authority to prosecute—the incident did not take place in Philippine waters, and the vessel involved was not registered in the Philippines. Vietnamese refugee camp leaders who have spoken to Phung said he not only feels no remorse, but is convinced that he was responsible for keeping the fifty-one others alive.

"I am afraid the people of the world misunderstand," Phung said. "I was only a member in a group of persons, so I didn't have the ability to force all of them to follow me. I was only a man who was thinking more clearly than the others. I had to do what I did to keep all the people living. We were at sea in huge waves. I had no other choice."

Phung states that he is particularly upset that his mother, who lives in San Jose, California, has rejected him. She sent him a newspaper article and demanded to know if the allegations about him were true. Although he tried to explain in a letter, she did not believe him and will no longer communicate with him.

There have been related disasters involving cannibalism on land. One is the case of Alexander Pearce, an Irish felon convicted of stealing six pairs of shoes in 1819. He was serving the remainder of a seven-year sentence under brutal conditions in a penal settlement on the west coast of Tasmania when he and seven companions escaped into the bush. There are varying accounts as to what happened next. According to Pearce, "I watched Greenhill for two nights as I thought he eyed me more than usual; he always kept an axe under his head when he lay down." The chronicler adds laconically, "So Pearce prudently engaged in a preemptive strike and killed and ate Greenhill." Recaptured, Pearce was not brought to trial for this event, for lack of evidence it seems, but was sent back to the same penal settlement, from which he promptly escaped again. This time he had one companion whom, after a quarrel, he also killed and ate. Giving himself up, Pearce had a piece of the body in his pocket, and referred to it as "most delicious food." At his trial seven officers found him guilty of murder, and sentenced him to be hanged and his body "anatomized." Pearce's skull still rests in peace in the museum of the University of Pennsylvania.

Then there is the Donner Party, part of the great westward migration of 1846. On their journey to the Sacramento Valley in California, this group of emigrants, after crossing the crest of the Rocky Mountains, organized as a separate party under George Donner, a sixty-two-year-old farmer from Springfield, Illinois. The group consisted of twenty-seven men, seventeen women, and forty-three children distributed among twenty-three wagons. Counting two Indian *vaqueros*, forty-two would eventually die. But without cannibalism only a handful of the Donner Party would have survived.[4]

The Donner Party's first major mistake was taking the Hasting's route, a so-called shortcut to California. It was much more dangerous than the relatively more hospitable Oregon Trail (over which, according to historians' estimates, 300,000 migrated from 1843 through the 1850s to Oregon, Utah, and California (see Figure 9).

The party lost much time, often barely moving a mile a

day. They lost more time crossing the Salt Lake desert, eighty miles of blazing sun and blinding white salt plain. The group was now playing against time, and they knew it. "The emigrants were no longer a 'company'; they were only a number of family groups each for itself, some of them ready to cooperate only when manifest good was to be gained for themselves. Hatred and inhumanity walked beside the wagons."[5]

The Donner group now traveled in three sections, the last, the Donners, about two days' journey behind the leading wagons. Approaching the Sierra Nevada summit on the night of October 31, those in the first section could see the deep snow on the pass ahead. (Eventually there would be twenty-two feet of it.) Caught by the first of unusually early storms that year, the party found an abandoned cabin and succeeded in building additional huts by what is now known as Donner Lake. Those who lagged behind, including the Donners themselves, made a camp of shanties covered with wagon canvas and buffalo robes five miles back down the trail.

By November 4 the trap that had closed behind them at Fort Bridger clicked shut in front. The storm did not end until November 11. By that time their situation was critical. Another storm lasted eight days, until December 4. By then, the oxen, the horses, and the mules had been eaten, as well as the dogs.

What strange thoughts had begun to grow in their minds? They have begun perhaps, as they looked about with maniacal cravings for food, to regard their comrades as offering certain new possibilities. Man might eat beef—good! Man might eat horse, too, as the need came, and mule. He might eat bear and dog, and even coyote and owl. He might also—and the relentless logic drove on—yes, man might also eat man.

Still another storm raged through Christmas night.

Cannibalism

Then they took the final step. The taboos of civilization had
held against five days of starvation, but now the will to live
was stronger. [William] Eddy* held off, and strangely enough,
the two Indians refused the food, and building themselves
a fire at a little distance sat stoically beside it. The others
cut the flesh from the arms and legs of Patrick Dolan's body,
roasted it by the fire and ate it—"averting their faces from
each other, and weeping." . . .

That morning (it was Sunday the twenty-seventh) they
set about the matter more systematically. They remained in
the camp during this and the next two days. Once the taboo
was broken, things were easier. The Indians, too, joined with
them. They stripped the flesh from the bodies, roasted what
they needed to eat, and dried the rest for carrying with them.
They observed only one last sad propriety; no member of
a family touched his own dead. But the strain was scarcely
the less for that. For as she sat by the fire Mrs. Foster suddenly
realized that spitted upon a stick and broiling over the coals
she saw the heart of her cherished younger brother.

There would be three relief parties. The second, reaching
both camps, discovered evidence of cannibalism in each. The
third found eleven refugees still alive around the fire in the
pit of snow. Three had died, and again the survivors had to
resort to cannibalism.

Mr. Foster went down to the cabin of Mrs. Murphy, his
mother-in-law, to see if any property remained there worth
collecting and securing; he found the body of young Murphy,
who had been dead about three months, with the breast and
skull cut open, and the brains, liver and lights† taken out;
and this accounted for the contents of the pan which stood

---

*A young man, a head of a family, and one of the heroes of the expedition.
†According to the dictionary, "lights" are "so called from being lighter
in weight than the rest of the body: the lungs of animals, as sheep, cattle,
etc., used as food."

beside [Lewis] Kiesburg* when he was found. It appears that
he had left at the other camp the dead bullock and horse,
and on visiting this camp and finding the body thawed out,
took therefrom the brains, liver and lights.

The food ran out. The heat ran out. The cold increased.
According to the *St. Paul Pioneer Press Dispatch* in 1991:

A new analysis of a human catastrophe has proved once
again that in times of disaster, women are more likely to
survive than men. An anthropologist (male) from the University of Washington in Seattle reached this conclusion after
a detailed study of the diaries and fate of the Donner Party.
[Roughly two-thirds of the women and children survived,
while two-thirds of the men died.]

The group was trapped for the winter by heavy snows
in the Sierra Nevada. As the members of the party perished
one by one, they became a part of a "natural experiment,"
as the anthropologist, Prof. Donald Grayson, put it. The
party's devastation demonstrated "natural selection in
action," he reported in the *Journal of Anthropological
Research.*

The detailed diaries told of desperate attempts to avert
starvation, first by slaughtering draft animals, then pets, then
making "soup" from hides and fur rugs and finally by eating
members of the group who died. A 13-year-old girl wrote
that her family survived a week on their pet dog. Another
diary told that "Mrs. Murphy said here yesterday that she
thought she would commence on Milt and eat him."

As he predicted, the analysis of the Donner Party's fate
showed that age, gender and social connectedness has a
striking effect on a person's chances of surviving until the
remnants of the group were found by a rescue party the next
March.

Also as expected, mortality rates were highest among

---

*Kiesburg had emigrated from Westphalia two years earlier.

the youngest and oldest members of the party. The men, too, "died like flies" at almost twice the rate of the women, mostly within the first three months.

Having a social support network is important to survival, he concluded, because it provides emotional support and a reason to struggle to continue living as well as mutual physical assistance.

We now come to a famous case of that famous American Wild West: Alferd Packer, also known as the Colorado maneater (see Figure 10). His legend is alive and prospering, with a substantial bibliography and dozens of recent newspaper articles; movies (the latest in 1979); a musical; a Packer fan club, including T-shirts; and the Alfred E. Packer grill at the University of Colorado in Boulder, where you can eat all the raw hamburgers you desire—or even participate in an annual hamburger-eating contest. In Lake City, a remote Rocky Mountain mining hamlet, restaurant owner Mick Harrison proudly asserts today that, "A hamburger is a hamburger, but a manburger is a meal."

Packer was born in 1842 in Pennsylvania, and ran away from home at the age of twelve. When the Civil War broke out, he enlisted in the Union Army, but was discharged in 1862 because of epilepsy. He next became a prospector in Colorado, and later a guide, though "guiding was never his strong point; given the chance, Alferd got lost." This slight deficiency had its implications.*

The party of prospectors consisted of Frank Miller, also known as "the butcher"; Shannon Wilson Bell, "a big redhead with bug eyes"; James Humphreys; Israel Swan ("Old Man Swan"); George Noon (nicknamed "California"); and Packer. They were by any standards a rough lot.

---

*For this account I am indebted to Professor Simpson's related meticulous research (see his *Cannibalism and the Common Law*).

Leaving camp on February 9, 1874, they followed the shorter but much more hazardous upper track to the Los Pinos Indian Agency—ill equipped, without even snowshoes—and into wholly uninhabited country. Fifty-five days later Packer arrived—alone. He related that first they had lost their way; next he had become lame; finally his employers had gone off to seek food, never to return.

Suspicions became aroused for a number of telling reasons. For one Packer looked remarkably well-fed; for another he seemed a bit too well-off financially, whiling away his days drinking (even demanding whiskey for breakfast), carousing, and "playing a form of poker called freeze-out." When pieces of dried human flesh were picked up along the old Indian trail over the Los Pinos Pass, threats of lynching were in the air.

According to one version, Packer had eaten rosebuds and moccasins; according to another it was more like "Friends fricasse. Campers à la carte." Eventually Packer made a sworn statement:

> Old man Swan died first and was eaten by the other five persons about ten days out of camp. Four or five days afterwards Humphreys died and was also eaten; he had about one hundred and thirty-three dollars. I found the pocketbook and took the money. Some time afterwards, while I was carrying wood, the butcher was killed—as the others told me, accidentally—and he was also eaten. Bill shot "California" with Swan's gun and I killed Bill. Shot him. I covered up the remains and took a large piece along. Then I travelled fourteen days into the Agency. Bell wanted to kill me with his rifle—struck a tree and broke his gun.

Packer also said "he had grown quite fond of human flesh, and . . . found the breasts of the men the sweetest meat he had ever tasted."

Packer's arrest caused a sensation, and he was described

in the press as a human monster. One headline read: "A Cannibal Who Gnaws on the Choice Cuts of His Fellow-Man." The legend of the Colorado maneater, Cannibal Alferd G. Packer, was born.

In due course Packer was tried for the murder of Israel Swan, convicted, and sentenced to death. His Honor Judge Gerry delivered a remarkable oration:

> God is not mocked, for whatsoever a man soweth, that shall he also reap. You, Alferd Packer, sowed the wind; you must now reap the whirlwind. . . . Close your eyes to the blandishments of hope, listen not to the flattering promises of life, but prepare for the dread certainty of death . . . prepare to meet the aged father and mother, of whom you have spoken and who still love you as their dear boy. For nine long years you have been a wanderer upon the face of the earth, bowed and broken in spirit: no home, no loves, no ties to bind you to the earth.

Gerry concluded, as was customary, by informing the doomed man that he would be "hung by the neck until you are dead, dead, dead, and may God have mercy upon your soul." Present at the time, if somewhat inebriated, was one Larry Dolan, Saquache barkeeper and one of Packer's old drinking buddies. He gave the local customers in his saloon in Lake City an immortal rendering of the judge's sentence:

> The judge says, he says, "Stand up, y' voracious man-eating son-of-a-bitch. Stand up." Then, pointing his finger at him, so raging mad he was, he says, "There was seven democrats in Hinsdale County, and you've ate five of them, God damn you. I sentence you to be hanged by the neck until you is dead, dead, dead, as a warning against reducing the democrat population of the state. Packer, you Republican cannibal, I would sentence you to hell but the Statutes forbid it."

Packer was moved off to the city jail, there to await his final reckoning. It is said that he secured peace and quiet in his cage, but that he also threatened to eat an imprisoned drunk whose behavior was noisy.

But lo and behold, Packer's lawyers found the proverbial loophole in the legal proceedings, and made the most of it. Their contention: the entire trial was invalid. The specific argument: their client had been charged with murder under a provision in the old laws of the Territory of Colorado (admitted to statehood in 1876) which had been repealed in 1881. In fact the 1882 legislation failed to allow for murder if the crime was committed before 1881. The *Daily Review Press* concluded irreverently: "The Murderer's Mirth—The Supreme Court says Murder is not a Crime if Committed before the 28th day of May 1881."

But Packer's tribulations were not over yet. In 1886 he was again brought to trial, this time charged with manslaughter of all five of his companions. The judge gave him forty years. Packer appealed, five times. The Supreme Court of Colorado denied the appeals, five times. Public opinion was mixed.

After he had served eighteen years, the governor of Colorado pardoned Packer, subject to a number of conditions, including abstinence from intoxicating liquors. Perhaps it was just as well; Packer had refused prison food, and threatened that he would be "eating his way out of jail."

So he lived on, "feeding candy to the children and telling them tales of the old days." The county museum includes a doll house Packer built for the warden's daughter. Packer's final appeal to the governor for a complete pardon, "I am dying and I am innocent of the crime," was ignored; but according to a contemporary press report his death was appropriately dramatic: "He seemed possessed of superhuman strength . . . he barked and snapped like a dog." The death certificate more graciously attributed the cause to "senility, trouble, and worry." It was 1907, and as a Civil War veteran Packer was buried with military honors.

But it was not the end. In 1950 the Republican party attempted to have set up in the Colorado capitol building a gold memorial plaque in honor of Packer, the consumer of Democrats. The move failed, after a debate on a motion that began, "Whereas it is fitting and proper that citizens who have made substantial and lasting contributions to the welfare of this great State should be suitably remembered by this Honorable Assembly . . ."

In 1977 the Department of Agriculture startled the official community by dedicating the cafeteria in its Washington building to Alferd Packer. The General Services Administration, however, removed the dedicatory plaque, accusing the Department of Agriculture of "bad taste."

Still later, one hundred and fifteen summers after the murders, James Starrs, a professor of law and forensic sciences at George Washington University who is addicted to such cases, discovered the five victims' long-forgotten graves. They were located near Lake City, Colorado, at the end of a driveway belonging to (yes, really) an orthopedic surgeon.

Says Starrs: "Everybody told me, 'You won't find anything but bonemeal if you turn up the graves at all.' " Holding a photograph of the five beautifully preserved skeletons, he elaborated that he and a team of thirteen volunteer scientists (wearing T-shirts reading "Gimme Five!") had found these remains 13 inches below ground, and removed them in July 1989 for analysis to the Human Identification Laboratory at the University of Arizona in Tucson. There identity was determined mainly by establishing the men's age and physical stature at the time of death. All the victims had scarred bones that indicated defleshing, and four of the five were repeatedly hacked with something like a hatchet. "If ever there was demonstrative evidence of overkill," the professor concluded, "this is it. There aren't too many other reasons for these marks. Now, as a scientist I can't tell you that Packer actually ate these men. But as a lawyer I can surmise that's exactly what he did."

There is a postmortem from the *Rocky Mountain News*: "Packer Victims Reburied. Is Packermania Put to Rest, Too?"

Now for a flashback to that famous accident in South America involving cannibalism. Two major books written about the events are Piers Paul Read's *Alive: The Story of the Andes Survivors* (made into the movie *Alive*, first shown in 1993), and Richard Cunningham's *The Place Where the World Ends* (1973).*

Uruguay is a small nation in a large world, and not since its soccer victory in the World Cup in 1950 did it achieve such renown when, in 1972, one of its planes crashed into the Andes.

On October 12, a cold, dreary day, an F-227, a small turbo-prop aircraft of the Uruguayan Air Force, took off from the Carrasco airport on the outskirts of Montevideo for Santiago, Chile. There was a crew of five; fourteen members of an amateur rugby team called "The Old Christians," composed mainly of socially prominent young men from Montevideo; twenty-five relatives and friends; and one other person. Of these forty-five, sixteen would survive.

Reports of bad weather in the Andes brought the plane down in Mendoza, a small town on the Argentinian side of the range. The next day flying conditions improved, and the plane took off again.

The Andes mountains, some of the highest on earth, are treacherous; only three months earlier a four-engine cargo aircraft had disappeared in them. Since the F-227's ceiling limit was 22,000 feet, it had to fly through a pass. At 15:24, with a ground speed of 180 knots, the pilot reported being over

---

*The name *Chile* comes from an Indian word meaning "the place where the world ends." Cunningham says the bulk of the material in the book is based on over fifteen hours of taped interviews with persons directly involved in the "Uruguayan affair." He further states that he gave Read a copy of the tapes, in return for a two-hour exclusive interview.

the Chilean town of Curicó. He was not. The pilot was cleared for descent to 10,000 feet and reported passing 15,000 feet six minutes later. Then the plane entered a cloud. It was not heard from again.

An investigation into the causes of the accident was later conducted by the air forces of both Uruguay and Chile. Both blamed the crash on the error of the pilot, who had begun his descent toward Santiago when still in the middle of the Andes. The actual spot where the aircraft had crashed was nowhere near Curicó.

The plane had hurtled toward jagged rock and clipped a mountain with the right wing, which immediately broke off, somersaulted over the fuselage, and cut off the tail. Out into the icy air fell the steward and the navigator with their pack of cards, followed by three others still strapped to their seats. A moment later the left wing broke and a propeller blade ripped into the fuselage. The belly of the aircraft hit a gentle downslope at around 200 knots ground speed in deep, feathery snow and plowed to a halt like a toboggan, without violent impact. Though it did not disintegrate, some more of the passengers were sucked out of the back of the plane, while others were crushed to death when their seats broke loose and were hurled forward, piling up like dominoes in the front of the cabin.

In all, thirteen died in the crash. Two more were to die during the first night; two in the following days; another nine in an avalanche that struck the fuselage, being used as a shelter, on the sixteenth day of the ordeal; and three more before rescue finally came.

For eight days after the aircraft disappeared the Chileans, Argentineans, and Uruguayans searched for the plane. Then they gave up. Ironically it was estimated that if the survivors' expeditionaries had taken a different route, they would have reached a hotel only five miles from the crash site. It was open only in the summer but stocked with supplies of canned food.

Accidents

Ten weeks later a Chilean peasant tending his cattle in a remote valley deep in the Andes saw, on the far side of a mountain torrent, the figures of two men.

This is how they had survived. One twenty-year-old survivor wrote: "One thing which will seem incredible to you—it seems unbelievable to me—is that today we started to cut up the dead in order to eat them. There is nothing else to do. I prayed to God from the bottom of my heart that this day would never come, but it has and we have to face it with courage and faith."

Piers Paul Read's *Alive* describes their ordeal:

Most of the bodies were covered by snow, but the buttocks of one protruded a few yards from the plane. With no exchange of words, Canessa knelt, bared the skin, and cut into the flesh with a piece of broken glass. It was frozen hard and difficult to cut, but he persisted until he had cut away twenty slivers the size of matchsticks. He then stood up, went back to the plane, and placed them on the roof. . . .

As the supplies grew short, an order went out from the cousins that there was to be no more pilfering. This edict was no more effective than most others which seek to upset an established practice. They therefore sought to make what food they had last longer by eating parts of the human body which previously they had left aside. The hands and feet, for example, had flesh beneath the skin which could be scraped off the bone. They tried, too, to eat the tongue off one corpse but could not swallow it, and one of them once ate the testicles. . . .

What they could do was to take the small intestine, squeeze out its contents onto the snow, cut it into small pieces, and eat it. The taste was strong and salty. One of them tried wrapping it around a bone and roasting it in the fire. Rotten flesh, which they tried later, tasted like cheese. . . .

The last discovery in their search for new tastes and new sources of food were the brains of the bodies which they had hitherto discarded. Canessa had told them that, while they might not be of particular nutritional value, they contained glucose which would give them energy; he had been the first to take a head, cut the skin across the forehead, pull back the scalp, and crack open the skull with the ax. The brains were then either divided up and eaten while still frozen or used to make the sauce for a stew; the liver, intestine, muscle, fat, heart, and kidneys, either cooked or uncooked, were cut into little pieces and mixed with the brains. In this way the food tasted better and was easier to eat. The only difficulty was the shortage of bowls suitable to hold it, for before this the meat had been served on plates, trays, or pieces of aluminum foil. For the stew Inciarte used a shaving bowl, while others used the top halves of skulls. Four bowls made from skulls were used in this way—and some spoons were made from bones.[6]

Explained a doctor, "They were eating two kinds of meat. One, of course, was that of their dead companions. In addition, their own cells were consuming themselves. For the most part, they were all big and muscular—you have to be in order to play rugby. They had their own storeroom of food, so to speak. And they ate, on an average, fifty pounds of their own bodies!"

The survivors were in apparent good mental and physical health, with some compulsion to talk, and a fear of being left alone. All agreed that the experience had changed their attitude toward life: "Suffering and privation had taught them how frivolous their lives had been; money had become meaningless. No one up there would have sold one cigarette for the five thousand dollars which they had amassed in the suitcase. . . . They now despised the world of fashionable clothes, night-clubs, flirtatious girls, and idle living. They determined to take their work more seriously, be more devout in their religious observances, and to dedicate more time to their families."

It would be interesting to do a followup study.

The speeches and articles describing the survivors' courage, endurance, and resourcefulness were abundant. One wonders if the official and public reaction would have been quite the same had they not come from some of the country's most prominent families.

The stance of the Catholic Church was unanimous.

A Chilean priest opined, "Of course one must treat the dead with respect—and one symbol of the survivors' respect was to choose them for food." As quoted by Read, the archbishop of Montevideo stated, "Morally I see no objection, since it was a question of survival. It is always necessary to eat whatever is at hand, in spite of the repugnance it may evoke." His auxiliary archbishop further argued, "Eating someone who has died in order to survive is incorporating their substance, and it is quite possible to compare this with graft. Flesh survives when assimilated by someone in extreme need, just as it does when an eye or heart of a dead man is grafted onto a living man." And finally a theologian of *L'Osservatore Romano* wrote that "he who has received from the community has also the duty to give to the community or its individual members when they are in extreme need of help to survive."

Many people in Santiago also wrote letters to the editor, justifying the cannibalism by pointing out that intentional starvation would have been suicide—a cardinal sin in the Catholic Church.

As for possible feelings or thoughts of guilt on the part of the survivors, one of them, speaking to a priest, remarked, "There is nothing better than giving to a fellow human being." When he then stated that he would like to confess, the priest replied, "You have confessed in this conversation."

There are two similar cases. In November 1982 an aircraft carrying four passengers crashed in Canada's Northwest Territory. The only survivor, Captain Hartwell, with both ankles and a kneecap broken, waited for twenty-three days before eating portions of the killed. In May 1979 a plane with three passengers crashed into the Rocky Mountains of Montana. The

105

two survivors ate the body of their father, who had died in the accident.

There was little else in the way of a postmortem on the Andes affair. Though some of the parents felt anger toward the Uruguayan Air Force for the incompetence of its pilots, it was not a moment in the political history of the country to take on a branch of its armed forces.

A few days after the rescue, Caesar Charlone, the Uruguayan chargé d'affaires in Santiago, issued the news that the bodies would be buried on the mountain. The official explanation was that it would be too difficult to bring them down. Charlone had seen photographs of the bodies, and he knew that no parent on earth should be forced to identify what was on that mountain.

Eventually the rescuers sprayed the plane's fuselage with gasoline and ignited it before leaving in their helicopters. They had been unable to remove the co-pilot's body, and the authorities had decided to burn the plane with him inside.

8

Magic

In New Zealand cannibals, believing that eating the slain enemy destroyed his soul and endowed the eater with strength and courage, therefore "preferred celebrated chiefs however old and dry they might be, to plump young men or damsels."

A patient was charged with stealing several bottles of red wine from a liquor store. The patient insisted that he should not have been charged with anything, as certain cosmic forces were draining his body of blood. He felt that since he was Jesus Christ and wine was blood, he was merely replenishing his blood supply. Therefore, he felt what he did was not a crime at all, but a matter of self-preservation.

David Shapiro,
Forensic Psychological Assessment

Magic cannibalism is that form of cannibalism based on the belief that by eating human flesh the consumer essentially incorporates certain desirable characteristics of the consumed. Strength, courage, sexual potency, health, and other good things can thus be acquired. A narrow interpretation holds that the mere event of cannibalism is efficacious, regardless of who, or what part, is eaten. More common is the belief that certain persons, and certain specific body parts, bring about the desired enrichment.

I have found basically three distinct categories of magic cannibalism, beginning with sorcery. The idea here is simple: eat human flesh or drink someone's blood, and you can become a sorcerer (or witch). In fact this may be the only way in which you can attain this lofty status.

The Ibo in the Niger delta celebrate their magic ceremonials with horrendous orgies during which they often sacrifice and devour their children.* In south Australia the sorcerers-to-be must consume flesh to obtain magic powers, specifically the fat of the kidneys, which is presumed to have superhuman qualities. If, however, you were a Marind-anim of New Guinea, you could not become a sorcerer unless you drank cadaver juice (water and other body fluids). The South African Xosa believe our flesh to be the most potent means to bewitch others. In Zanzibar two women who had opened graves and eaten the bodies were protected by the local populace, "because witches eat people everywhere." Conversely, when children were sacrificed in Mexico, their hearts were on occasion eaten as a form of protection against witchcraft. A different kind of magic cannibalism consisted of the consumption of a small portion of the body of a murdered man to prevent his ghost from troubling the murderer.

A special consideration is the Catholic Christian's belief in transubstantiation, that spiritual reunion of the Eucharist. Lest the reader think otherwise, the ceremony is not symbolic: the presumption is that bread and wine actually become flesh

---

*Many of the specific examples of cannibalism in this and the following three chapters are cited in Ewald Volhard's *Kannibalismus* (see also the Appendix). Their veracity, to state yet again, depends on the credibility one grants these sources.

and blood. On this subject, Reay Tannahill deserves to be quoted in full.*

In the year A.D. 1215, Pope Innocent III summoned not only the patriarchs of Jerusalem and Constantinople but twenty-nine archbishops, four hundred and twelve bishops, eight hundred abbots and priors, and the envoys of all the major rulers of Europe and the Levant—including the Holy Roman Emperor and the kings of England, France, Aragon and Hungary—to attend the Fourth Lateran Council. This assembly of all who were most distinguished in the Catholic world was to decree it as an article of faith that Christians must believe—when the priest at the altar pronounced the phrase "hoc est corpus meum" ("this is my body")—that the bread and wine were changed into the body and blood of Christ. In the words of the Definition: "The body and blood of Jesus Christ are truly contained under the appearance of bread and wine in the sacrament of the altar, the bread being transubstantiated into the body and the wine into the blood." Those who partook of the Host had formerly eaten it as a symbol of the body of Christ. Now it was to be no longer a symbol but an actuality, and anyone who doubted it was guilty of heresy.

This was the culmination of more than a thousand years of disagreement within the Church as to what Jesus had meant when he spoke to his disciples on the occasion of the Last Supper. In the words of Mark, "As they were eating, he took bread, and blessed, and broke it, and gave it to them, and said, 'Take; this is my body.' And then he took a cup, and when he had given thanks he gave it to them, and they all drank of it. And he said to them, 'This is my blood of the covenant, which is poured out for many.' " Matthew's version

---

*Tannahill, a graduate of the University of Glasgow with degrees in history and economics, has been engaged in historical research, especially social conditions and their influences. Her *Flesh and Blood*, perhaps written as a sequel of sorts to her previous *Food in History*, has been a valuable resource.

was much the same, and so was Luke's, although Luke added that Jesus had also said: "Do this in remembrance of me."

In A.D. 1215, however, the inconsistency had to be resolved. This, the beginning of the great century of papal supremacy, was not a time for either tolerance or dissent. The Church intended to wield temporal as well as spiritual power, and it could do so only if its followers submitted absolutely to the "will of God." Pope Innocent III was a mystic but a worldly one, and perhaps the doctrine of transubstantiation was something of a test case. Whatever the reason, Christianity adopted into its most sacred ritual an act of pure cannibalism, an unequivocal god-eating on the most primitive level. To the faithful, the bread became not a symbol of the flesh of Christ, but as real as if the flesh itself had been sliced and baked.[1]

Thinkers who have sought to interpret the Eucharist as a symbolic event have been rebuked ex cathedra by the pope. In the encyclical Mysterium Fidei (Mystery of Faith), issued in 1965,* Pope Paul VI warned the faithful that it would be spiritually fatal (this gets confusing, so pay attention) "to be so preoccupied with considering the nature of the sacramental sign that the impression is created that the symbolism—and no one denies its existence in the most holy Eucharist—expresses and exhausts the whole meaning of Christ's presence in this sacrament. Nor is it right to treat the mystery of transubstantiation without mentioning the marvelous change of the whole of the bread's substance into Christ's body and the whole of the wine's substance into his blood."

There you have it: a little extrasensory deception it seems.†

---

*It was not until 1865 that the Second Vatican Council repudiated the concept of collective Jewish guilt for the death of Christ.

†In 1993 Pope John Paul II dogmatically reasserted in his Veritatis Splendor (The Splendor of Truth) that, "The power to decide what is good and what is evil does not belong to man but to God alone"; that the [Catholic] church [i.e., John Paul] is the only authentic interpreter of the word of God;

Belonging to the second category of magic cannibalism is the belief that eating a (certain) person, or more frequently a specific part of him or her, will make you strong, courageous, or potent. It was apparently a common basic assumption held by the predynastic Egyptians, the Scythians of the Black Sea, the Chinese at various times, the Iroquois of America, and a great many more people, ranging from the Ashanti in Africa to the Maoris of New Zealand, from the aborigines in Australia to the mountain tribes of Natal (where the victims' bodies were powdered and administered to young warriors by the local priests).

We include some other examples. To gain courage and strength the Menado-Alfuren cook a bouillon made of their slain enemies' heads; the Ife make a stew of man, antelope, and some medicine; as late as 1895 the Chames of Cochin-China drank brandy mixed with the gall of their dead opponents; in northern Australia the eyes and cheeks are eaten; in the middle and south of the continent kidney fat is preferred; the Wabondei of East Africa choose the liver; the Ovambo of Angola cook their enemies' hearts; and so on. At times a part of an animal can serve this function, and the hearts of lions or leopards are in particular demand. According to Volhard's *Kannibalismus*, the Ashanti forced cowards to eat the hearts of the brave who died in battle, while a common belief in Australia held that the spirit of the slain enemy entered the slayer.

---

and that "the [Catholic] church [i.e., John Paul] has the right always and everywhere to proclaim moral principles, even in respect of the social order, and to make judgments about any human matter insofar as this is required by fundamental human rights to the salvation of souls." And the world's 900 million Catholics, in the last decade of the twentieth century, are expected to believe this. Thus the pope's inalienable and dictatorial right and competence to so judge are offered as self-evident truth. Compare the commandant of Auschwitz, Rudolf Höss: "I believed in Nazi dogma the way a Catholic believes in church dogma. It was truth without question." As an antidote, the reader may wish to peruse Wendell Watters's no-nonsense *Deadly Doctrine* (Buffalo, N.Y.: Prometheus Books, 1992).

Running a close second is the belief in increased sexual potency. Breasts of women were ingested for such a purpose. Among many others, the Lessa chiefs of Central Africa "always" consume certain female parts to better perform their marital obligations, as do the Isabel of the Solomon Islands and the Nissan (a tribe on the Solomon Islands, who also discard the male genitalia as useless). On the New Hebrides, on the other hand, the penis and testicles of fallen enemies are a favorite dish of the chiefs.

The third category of magic cannibalism, already hinted at in passing, is the consumption of human flesh and/or blood for medicinal purposes. It is another old idea. The pharaohs of Egypt, when afflicted with leprosy, used to take baths in human blood to wash the sickness away. The still-warm blood of gladiators slaughtered in the arena was the standard medicine for epileptics in Rome. "This sad medicine made an even sadder affliction bearable." It was also recommended for dropsy. Cannibalism was once thought to be a cure for illness in China, and children cut off a portion of their flesh and offered it to a sick parent. So-called pitballs containing the blood of decapitated criminals were considered a cure for consumption at the time.

There exists also an ancient Egyptian medical prescription to make a tincture of mummy as follows: "Select the cadaver of a red, uninjured, fresh, unspotted malefactor, twenty-four years old, and killed by hanging, broken on the wheel, or impaled, upon which the moon and the sun have shone once: cut it in pieces, sprinkle with myrrh and aloes; then marinate it for a few days, and pour on spirits." As the historian citing the recipe laconically remarks: "A case, it may be felt, of the remedy being worse than the disease—whatever the disease may have been. The papyrus does not say."

Around two millennia later, in 1450 in Savoy in the southeast of France, a recommended recipe was this: "Tie a naked, red-haired, male Catholic to a bench and subject him to the unrestrained attentions of a number of venomous animals. When he has expired from the bites and stings, hang him upside down with a bowl underneath to catch the drips. Mix these with the fat of a man who has been hanged, the entrails of children, and the corpses of the venomous animals who caused his death. Use as required."[2]

In the north of France, a witch was accused of feeding toads on consecrated bread and wine, of killing and then burning them, and finally mixing their ashes with powdered bones of dead Christians, children's blood, and a "number of other ingredients, unspecified."

Perhaps not unexpectedly medicinal cannibalism occupies a special niche among the old—for example, in Angola where greedy old men are said to have become addicted to it, believing that it prolongs life.

A somewhat special case, found sporadically all over the globe, and also going far back in history, is headhunting. In the Azilian deposits in Bavaria skulls were found which indicate careful decapitation and separate burial from the bodies. Others, tinted with ochre (a magical substitute for blood), were discovered on the Riviera frontier between Italy and France. In Jericho, in the seventh millennium B.C.E., skulls were fashioned into stylized portraits of their former owners by having their features molded in plaster, with inlaid shells to represent the eyes. The Greek historian Herodotus mentions headhunters in Asia, and on a bas-relief from Nineveh in the British Museum a battle between Assurbanipal and the King of Elam depicts the Assyrians cutting and carrying off the heads of the slain. In Aztec Mexico the skull of a human sacrifice was overlaid with turquoise and obsidian (volcanic glass) to create the image of a god.

In Borneo, Indonesia in general, the Philippines, and Formosa headhunting was widespread. The Igorot and Tagalog of Luzon continued it into the middle of the twentieth century. Throughout Oceania it was closely associated with cannibalism. In parts of Micronesia the head of the slain enemy was paraded about with dancing (and served as an excuse for the chief to raise a fee to defray public expenditure; the head was next lent to another chief for the same purpose). In India "all the tribes living south of the Brahmaputra" were headhunters, and in Kafiristan women showered wheat upon men returning with heads from successful raids. According to one source, "Young women were everywhere great instigators of headhunting, and refused to marry men who had not touched meat, probably with the idea that until they had taken life they were unlikely to beget offspring."

In the Solomon Islands the actual expeditions to obtain heads formed the climax in a series of ceremonial acts extending over a number of years, and the suppression of headhunting, on which depended an important part of social life, was said to be a significant factor in that society's decay and population decrease under the local British administration.

Complete heads were still taken by the Montenegrins on the Balkan until 1912, when nose-taking was substituted, the practice being to cut it off together with the upper lip and moustache (by which it was carried). Such partial substitution was known elsewhere, in Assam for example, where an ear often replaced the whole head. In North America the scalp was taken, an idea presented in the biblical story of Samson, and also common in Malaya and Indonesia. One implication seems to have been that the soul was thought to reside in the hair. Much more common was another motive: profit.

Nazi general Erwin Rommel, "the Desert Fox," found it disconcerting when dead German soldiers were discovered without their ears—collectors' items for some Commonwealth soldiers, it seems. In another part of the world at the time, in Japanese-occupied Burma of 1943-44, long-range Allied penetration units, mainly Gurkhas, were rather unhappy when their British officers doubted their claims to have killed large numbers of the enemy. Next time they returned to base they came laden with sacks of Japanese heads.

Some tribes would shrink heads. The Jibaros in South America, for instance, preserved them by removing the skull and packing the skin with hot sand, thereby shrinking it to the size of a small monkey's head yet keeping the features intact. In Melanesia the head was often mummified. In New Britain such a creation was worn as a mask so that the owner might acquire the soul of the deceased/killed. In New Guinea the Tugeris used a bamboo knife for the act of decapitation, perhaps because iron could adversely affect the soul within. In New Zealand heads were prepared in such a fashion that the tattoo marks as well as the actual features were recognizable; said Maori trophies were to become desirable curios in Europe, "and consequently a regular article of ships' manifests."

There existed elsewhere the notion that the soul of the dead could be caught and incorporated into a sort of generalized soul of the community, something akin to a soul-pool; this in turn was presumed to enhance the fertility of crops. Head-hunting by the Kagoro in Indonesia, and tribes in Nigeria, was specifically associated with crop fertility (as well as marriage). Burmese natives followed similar customs, and the Wa tribe observed a definite headhunting season when the fertilizing soul matter was required for the growing crop: "All wayfarers moved out at their peril."

How does headhunting fit into the scheme of things? The belief in a special sanctity or importance of the head is easy to understand: for one thing, it is the seat of the brain. Second, many also presumed it to be the location of the human soul, a sort of personalized life-essence. Soul and body at any rate were separate—"and the soul might sit in a tree near the graveside, looking on and observing what was happening to its bodily cover."

We find then that headhunting served a number of purposes, often in some combination: to obtain the brain, spirit, or soul for oneself; to add them to the community's "pool"; or, last and perhaps not least, to enjoy the brain of the dead as a delicacy. Whether the soul was ever eaten, or how it might have tasted, the chroniclers do not say.

9

Ritual, Religion, and Sacrifice

Custom will reconcile people to any atrocity.
George Bernard Shaw

Many kinds of cannibalism were hedged with ceremonial and religious regulations and customs. The literature indicates that certain tribes went to war to provide human flesh, and only the killers were permitted to eat it; in others only the nearest relatives could do so; in yet others related or befriended clans might be included in the feast. Conversely, all these may have been specifically excluded. In *endophagy*—the consumption of friends, relatives, or "in-tribe" members—we frequently find a veritable horror of eating an outsider. The opposite holds true for *exophagy*—no one would think of devouring a relative or fellow tribe member. Some societies prohibited women from eating human flesh; others denied it to certain classes; and so on. In short, you couldn't eat just anybody.

When practiced by a tribe or community, cannibalism as a rule seems largely to have ritual, religious, and sacrificial associations. There are five major ways in which these combine.

Cultic Cannibalism

There is little doubt that in the early days of most religions blood sacrifice was a covenant designed to ratify an allegiance with the higher powers—to win in battle, avoid divine revenge, assure health and welfare, and so on. The idea was simple; the variations, as we have already seen, almost endless. The Fijis, for example, felt obligated to eat all shipwrecked persons lest some insulted god take revenge.

Such ritual murder of animals or men to please the gods or spirits came to be combined with cannibalism apparently for a number of reasons. For one, the gods were conceived as being cannibalistic themselves, and man, or perhaps just sorcerer or priest, could partake in the prerogative. Conversely, it was mankind who first cannibalized one another, and in time the gods became included.

According to Volhard's *Kannibalismus*, perhaps the oldest form is cosmic cannibalism, prevalent in Egypt, where movements of heavenly bodies constituted the example to be imitated by man. As the sun nourishes itself when, on rising, she devours the stars of the night, thus must man eat his own kind, and in doing so also offer a sacrifice to the sun. Cosmic cannibalism also existed in parts of America, and specifically in Mexico, where the sun god as well as the moon god were cannibalistic.

Victory Celebration

In many tribes and societies major occasions for cannibalism were the feasts celebrated at the conclusion of battle or war. In that sense they were also death rituals. The consumed could be friend, foe, or both. The rationale might be an identification with one's own dead or the slain enemy. The rites were often held in secret, with only warriors taking part, sometimes just

Fig. 2. This foot-long Aztec ceremonial flint knife was used to cut the living heart out of a sacrificial victim. The crouched figure on the carved wooden handle, encrusted with a turquoise mosaic, represents a warrior knight. Copyright British Museum.

Fig. 1.

Fig. 2.

Fig. 3. Early explorer's depiction of Brazilian cannibalism: roasting and eating of human flesh. From *Historia Americae* by Theodor de Bry, Frankfurt am Main, 1634.

Fig. 4. A woodcut from Hans Staden's book recounting the cannibalism of the Tupinamba Indians. Staden, notes William Arens, *The Man-Eating Myth*, "is easily identified as the one in the fig leaf with hands folded in prayer."

Fig. 5. José Clemente Orozco, "The Epic of American Civilization: Ancient Human Sacrifice" (Panel 3), 1932-34. Commissioned by the Trustees of Dartmouth College, Hanover, New Hampshire.

Fig. 6. An imaginative woodcut, published in Germany in 1505, attempted to illustrate Spanish and Portuguese explorers' accounts of cannibalism among the Carib- and Tupi-speaking tribes along the coast of Brazil.

Fig. 5.

Fig. 6.

Fig. 7. This is a rare photograph from Volhard's *Kannibalismus*. All it says is: "Young Putumayo Indians eating enemies they killed, and whose teeth are carried as signs of victory."

Fig. 8. Théodore Géricault, *"The Raft of the Medusa."* Louvre, Paris. Art Resource, N.Y.

Fig. 8.

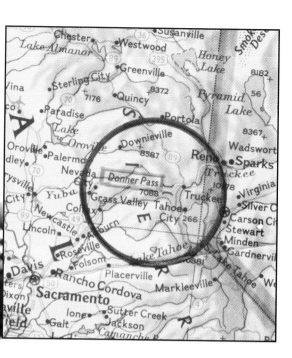

Fig. 9. Detail of a map of California showing the Donner Pass.

Fig. 10. Alferd Packer. The Denver Public Library, Western History Department.

Fig. 11. Portrait of Elizabeth Báthory. Hungarian National Museum, Historical Gallery.

Fig. 12. Gustave Doré, "Little Red Riding Hood."

Fig. 13. Joe Martin, "Mr. Boffo." Reprinted by permission: Tribune Media Services.

Fig. 14. Chikatilo being caged during his trial. AP/Wide World Photos.

Fig. 15. Jeffrey Dahmer in court. AP/Wide World Photos.

those who had done the actual killing. The eating of prisoners of war was common.

Initiation Rites

Some of man's most widespread rituals are the rites prescribed for initiation, usually of young men. Mostly puberty-related, indicating a rebirth as an adult member of the tribe, they could also involve a person's entry into a secret society.

Missionaries in Africa claimed they found a secret organization, the Leopard Society, with gruesome initiation rites. Membership required for each new leopard man to provide one blood sacrifice, traditionally a girl of fourteen or older, and either from his or his wife's family. Once she was chosen the girl's family was ritually "begged" for her body; the answer, too, was ritualistic: refusal meant their own sacrifice. On the night before the killing the initiate and four companions ran through the forest, roaring like leopards. On the night of the sacrifice members of the organization gathered, wearing leopard masks and knives—pronged, claw-like, with double-edged blades. The executioner, who also wore a leopard skin, made a U-shaped incision in the victim's chest, lifted the skin, and ceremoniously examined the organs. Next the body was split into four sections, a portion carved for each member, and the face cut away from the head. The victim's father and mother were presented with a small piece of their daughter, signifying they waived the right to start a blood feud. Members argued that this bloody ritual created powerful medicine to strengthen them. Leopard societies are believed by some to still exist in certain remote parts of Sierra Leone.

Initiates may be symbolically "killed," "eaten," and live for some time as if "dead" before being reborn. They may be tattooed in white, the color of death (not mourning). Following are two examples.

The Ovaherero in Abyssinia castrated their enemies and had their own newly circumcised youngsters eat these trophies of combat.

On reaching manhood, Kwakiutl Indian youths sought the patronage of various gods; those who selected the god Baxbakualanuxsiwae could become full-fledged *Hamatsas,* i.e., "licensed cannibals." First, however, they had to spend three months in the forest, with a required return to the village at the half point. On this occasion they stood outside, made a whistling cry (the trademark of their god), and called a female relative for human flesh. Traditionally they were ignored, charged into the assembled tribe, bit randomly into flesh, and ran back into the forest. After their final return they could then periodically exercise the privilege of eating the dead.

Harvest Ritual

The annual death and rebirth of the soil has understandably preoccupied man's thoughts since the beginning of time. As harvest was dependent upon fertilization, it had to be assured by whatever means possible. The notion that plants needed human sacrifice to prosper was likely to have been widespread.

In Egyptian legend Osiris weaned the Egyptians from cannibalism and introduced them to agriculture. When he was murdered by his brother Set, his wife, Isis, found the body and carried it home, where Set hacked it into pieces, which he scattered all over the countryside. But Isis gathered them together again, reassembled her husband, and brought him back to life.[1]

The Betschuan celebrated a feast, the "cooking of the wheat." On the occasion a young man was sacrificed; his brain, skull, and coagulated blood were burned; and the ashes spread over the field. The remainder of the corpse was eaten. The harvest ritual in Samoa was cause for extended cannibalistic feasts, the king and his consorts eating humans wrapped in coconut leaves and fruit. In order to assure a rich rice harvest, the Angamis and Semas (Assam) killed a person and threw parts of the body into the furrows. Children were sacrificed elsewhere to serve the same purpose. In Burma they were led from house to house, where one finger was cut off at a time; the owners of the house next covered themselves with the blood; then the victims were tied to a pole in the middle of the village and killed with spears. The flesh was peeled from the bones and exhibited in a basket as an offering to the god; finally, after some dancing and weeping, the basket was thrown into the jungle.

The Khonds, an ancient Dravidian tribe from Bengal in southern India, sacrificed and ate one of their own to ensure a ripe harvest. This victim, always a young man, was first treated with great reverence, then strangled; sometimes he was dismembered alive. His flesh was then distributed to the various tribal leaders.

The Kajan in Borneo tell of a woman who offended against the planting laws and had to bleed to death. "Out of her pulsating blood came rice, and after her death out of her rump bananas, out of her hair sugar cane, from the upper arms Kladi, and from the other parts of the body plants like cucumbers and yams; out of her genitals came forth tobacco; this is why the women give their lovers cigars to smoke."

According to Indonesian myth the coconut came forth from a human head.

This practice of human sacrifice in the fields to assure fertility survived into the nineteenth century when the American Pawnees killed a Sioux girl, sprinkled her blood on seeds, and ate her heart.

Funeral Rituals

Finally we find what might be called funeral cannibalism. It is not a mourning rite of the living, but a right and need of the dead that must be shared by the survivors. Blood may be poured on the grave; in one instance the victim was cut into halves, one being buried with the deceased, the other eaten by the bereaved. Whatever the ritual, it is the dead for whom the victims are sacrificed, the departed who symbolically receive flesh and blood as nourishment. The living merely share.

This final identification is still reflected in different customs elsewhere: the pulling of one's hair, tearing of clothes, or even ritual self-immolation. It was, after all, not that long ago when Indian widows shared their husbands' fate on the funeral pyre.

10

Punishment, Indifference, and Unification

The Battas of Sumatra once devoured both adulterers and, for some inexplicable reason, only those thieves who performed their crimes at night. Men discovered in the harem of the Muato-jamvos were hacked into pieces and distributed, raw and warm, to the tribe.

Cannibals in the Congo kept and fattened slaves to butcher as we do cattle and sheep. The Congo was famous for markets where human flesh hung openly for sale; where some tribes hawked living victims, leading them into the crowd so that buyers could mark with colored clay the portion they wanted.

The Cocomas of Peru eat their dead relatives and swallow the ground-up bones in fermented drinks, believing it far better to be inside a warm friend than under the cold ground.

Ewald Volhard, *Kannibalismus*

In the following three types of cannibalism hunger is not the primary consideration, and magic, ritual, and the other motivations are also irrelevant or at least immaterial. These three types have to do with punishment, indifference, and unification.

Cannibalism as a sort of societal *punishment* (also referred to as legal, penal, or vindictive cannibalism) generally affects individuals who once belonged to the community, but because of a real or imagined crime have been expelled and are now treated essentially like foreigners, enemies, or animals. Thus it is revenge enacted by more or less total annihilation of the person (the bones, too, could be ground up and consumed).

Criminals were eaten in North Nigeria by the Angas, the Warjawas, and the Sura (who also devoured women convicted of adultery). The Bangala in addition ate slaves for "obstreperous behavior"; the Jaga ate cowards, the Bapende and Kauanda the corpses of the executed. The king of Katanga ordered chests of criminals cut open so that he and his executioners could eat the hearts warm. (The proceedings were accompanied by the song, "We want to eat him.") In the king's view the heart, not the hands, had stolen.

Criminals were also eaten in New Guinea, New Caledonia, and the New Hebrides. The Battak (Bataks, Battas) in Sumatra cut up war captives alive, eating them piece by piece in order to make their destruction more degrading. The victims also included those who could not pay their debts.

Similar to the criminal's fate is that of the enemy: the victor obtains ultimate vengeance by devouring the vanquished. In the Solomon Islands eating one's enemy was the most humiliating form of punishment. The expression, "I have eaten your father, I have eaten your mother" was a sign of ultimate contempt. On Tonga the worst curses were, "Cook your grandfather!" or "Dig up your father in the moonlight and devour him." A great Samoan threat is to roast someone. Similar customs prevailed in certain South American cannibal tribes. For example, the Tubinamba (our old acquaintances) "naturally slaughter and eat a sick slave," given that it is preferable to consume him before he spoils. The Miranhas did likewise. The

Bakundu ate everyone who had offended against their strict dietary laws: chicken, for example, was forbidden.

A unique case was the following, related by Raymond McNally in his *Dracula Was a Woman*:

> The tall, hefty, red-bearded John "Liver-Eating" Johnson, an American trapper and Civil War veteran, liked to hunt alone. In 1847 he married a Flathead Indian woman. After seeing her well provided for, he left on a trapping expedition. He did not know that she was pregnant. When he returned in the spring he found the clean-picked bones of his wife and the skull of his newborn infant. A feather lying nearby told him that the killers had been Crow Indians. He declared a private war that would lead to the deaths of some three hundred Crow braves. Whenever he killed a Crow Indian he would slash the dead Indian's chest open with his Bowie knife, take out the still warm liver and eat it raw. "Liver-Eating" Johnson was apparently not averse to eating other parts of the human body. In 1861 the Blackfeet captured him with the intention of selling him to the Crows. He escaped, and amputating the left leg of one of his Blackfoot captors, he took the leg along for food. Ultimately he made his peace with the Crows. In December 1899 he entered Veterans Hospital in Los Angeles, California, and the seasoned Liver-Eater died of old age in 1900.

So-called *profane* or *indifferent* cannibalism refers to those instances when no meaningful difference exists between animal and man, between meat and flesh. Both are simply nourishment. Often those tribes practicing this form exhibit human flesh in their markets. Thus it was with the Ibo. The Nigerian Mambilas ate their dead raw, occasionally, however, boiling the intestines. They also sold their dead to neighboring tribes for food. Others, such as the Gbale in Liberia, the Tikar, and the Tupi and Guarani in South America, in different ways fattened their meals-to-be, sometimes also castrating them to speed up the process. Southern Nigeria once supported a traffic in human flesh where the meat had market prices for various "cuts." Young boys who had been kidnaped and fattened on bananas in pens were killed and baked for selling. In New Pomerania and New Mecklenburg prisoners had their legs broken and were tied to trees at times of an abundance of flesh, thereby preserving them for future use.

Profane cannibalism can be summed up in the reply given to the question about feeling any compassion for the victims. Said a surprised member of the Ekois: "But that's not a man, it's a slave, beef."

Finally, there exists *love cannibalism*, also known as *unification*: one eats a person out of some kind of "affection" or a desire to unite with him or her. It is not a very common form, but an intriguing one.

Among various tribes along the Amazon River, as well as in New Guinea, old men of the tribe are often killed at their own request (or so it is said), and eaten by their children, or relatives, or friends, who think it better to keep their parents or kin in the warmth of their bellies than in the lonely cold of the earth. Is it not, after all, a sign of dutiful piety to dispose of one's beloved's remains by devouring him, rather than having the maggots do so? Who would want to argue this point with a Papuan?

Similarly, in the Dieri and other Australian tribes the relatives of the deceased eat portions of the body in strict order of preference, and when questioned reply, "We eat him because we knew him and were very fond of him."

According to Herodotus, the Massagetae, a Scythian tribe, also ate their dead relatives out of piety. When a person became very old, all the relatives gathered to kill and eat her or him. To be disposed of in this fashion was considered a great fortune, and pity was shown to those who died from a disease and had to be buried instead. The Issidones in southern Russia had the same custom; they also scraped the skulls clean and gilded them, to be used as drinking cups.

Before 1250 B.C.E. Tibetans ate their parents from the pious desire to furnish their own bowels as a tomb. The Cashibas from eastern Peru eat their aged parents out of respect. The Bagesu from Uganda held feasts at which they consumed their dead as a means of honoring them. The Padeans in India killed and ate a sick man to prevent his flesh from being wasted by disease. A regular practice among the Hill Anga tribesmen of Nigeria was eating the old and infirm males to ensure that they left the world in full command of their faculties (they were not killed by their relatives, however, but by neighbors, who were paid for this service). The Bihors of Hindustan also ate their relatives, and it was said that this was requested by the about-to-be-devoured in preference to being left in the forests for the jackals.

The Caspiers did not eat their seventy-year-olds, but made the necessary preparations to have animals do so. They were left to die of starvation in the desert. Particularly fortunate were those, in the view of the survivors at least, who were pulled down from their last resting place in the trees by birds; less fortunate were those who were taken by wild animals or dogs; and downright unfortunate those who were not pulled down at all.

The Kaschibo of the upper Amazon slaughter their over-aged males and eat them also. "As soon as the old man is informed that his last day has come, he is happy because now he will see his friends again. He has three days to prepare himself; then his own children clobber him with a club. A great feast follows, and the *masato* (an alcoholic brew) flows in streams. No piece of the sacrifice is to be lost, everything has to be eaten, even the bones are pulverized, poured in the *masato* and drunk; some of it is put aside for the children. Females are never eaten because they are considered inferior beings as well as poisonous."

Cannibalism

We end with the custom whereby two or more persons take a certain amount of flesh or blood from one another to establish a kind of covenant or "blood relationship" between them. This "unitive" brand of cannibalism shades into the magical, and was practiced by African tribes and even some European clans.

II

The Gourmets

"*Do not enter the Kitchen, sir* . . . tonight or on any other
evening of your life: never enter Shirro's Kitchen!"
Stanley Elin,
The Kitchen in the Restaurant Robinson

The Latin proverb *De gustibus non est disputandum,* literally
translated, means "one cannot dispute tastes." More freely
it means: "Thank God I am not like other people." Cannibalism
is a gruesome subject, but in this chapter we will look at it
in a lighter vein, tongue in cheek so to speak. Fortunately not
everyone finishes up in someone else's stomach, but a notable
number of those who do seem to be considered gastronomic
delicacies (and sometimes dietary ones), and prepared accord-
ingly. In short there seem to be those who like human flesh
for its own sake. And there is no accounting for taste, as those
who believe they are blessed with it never cease to emphasize.
The relevant literature is full of examples, and we have already
come across many. Surprisingly I have found almost no actual
description of exactly *how* we taste. One I have found is this:
the Fijis compare us to pork, and favorably at that—given a
choice, they prefer the "long pig," *puakabalaua,* to the short one.

To caution yet again: not all reports and tales that follow
are necessarily the truth, let alone the whole truth; the subject

lends itself to fancy and gratuitous elaboration. The ferocious Caribs, for example, became heir to numerous legends, constantly improved upon; thus they were said to have split captured men into two, eaten their guts and limbs, and salted and dried the rest "like our hams." As the saying goes, we interrupt this fantasy to bring you a message of reality: as it happened the Caribbean people knew nothing about the process of salting until they learned it from the Europeans. With all this in mind let us see what can be done with our earthly parts, and peruse some original (or is it aboriginal?) recipes.

Humans were considered delicacies by men other than the Fijis, for example, by the Baja, Sande, Pambia, Manjema, Wadai, Haussaland, and Gerse, all of whom preferred humans to anything else; by tribes on the Solomon and other islands, such as New Caledonia, Fate, Erromango, and New Zealand; and by numerous others. When cows were given to the Basuto in order to make them give up cannibalism, they tasted them and declined the beef.

Specific preferences deal with sex, age, and race. A New Zealand chief, living in London for some years in the early nineteenth century, confessed that what he missed most about home was "the feast of human flesh . . . he was weary of eating English beef . . . the flesh of women and children was . . . the most delicious."[1] The Bele in Liberia, however, ate only men, given their belief that the flesh of women was bitter. Certain Maoris preferred a man of fifty, and a black over a white one. They also never ate the flesh raw, "and preserved the fat of the rump for the purpose of dressing their sweet potatoes." The Fijis, by all accounts among the experts in the field, also disliked the taste of white men; preferred women to men in general; and considered the arm above the elbow and the thighs the tastiest joints. Their fondness for human flesh was such that the greatest praise they could bestow on any delicacy was to describe it "as tender as a dead man."

The Gourmets

The Tartars were especially fond of females, and succulent young girls became officers' fare, "while the common soldiers had to make do with tough and stringy matrons." Breast meat, the greatest delicacy, was preserved for the princes' tables. The Baja king ate only women and girls. The chief of the Aoba had young girls slaughtered every few days, but dined only on their breasts. The Tangale, a confirmed headhunting tribe, specialized in the preparation and consumption of enemy women's heads. On the Gazelle peninsula a chief preferred the flesh of unborn children, and therefore hunted pregnant women. In eleventh-century China eating people became commonplace, and in human-meat restaurants, dishes made from the flesh of old men, women, and children all had special names, "and presumably special tastes." In sum, then, it seems that the consensus went something like this: women and children are better than men; blacks are better than whites (though at least one source stresses a preference for Chinese— perhaps because their diet was largely vegetarian); and in general the young are tastier than the old.

As for body parts, many have already been mentioned in other contexts. Nigerian tribes praised the palms, fingers, and toes, and incidentally felt that monkey meat was almost as good as man. A liking for brain and bone marrow is, as we have seen, age-old, as is the drinking of blood. Ibo cannibals favored the knuckles. The Jincang Dyaks ate only the head. The Nigerian Bafum-Bansaw tortured their prisoners before killing them by using bellows to pump boiling palm oil into their bowels and stomachs to make the meat juicier; at other times they pumped the oil into a carcass and left it to marinate. Indonesian cannibals were partial to the soles. Roasted over hot ashes the penis was regarded as a great dish by some.

A few other local preferences include: heart and liver— south and east Africa, Mexico, Fiji; kidneys—Dar For; kidney fat—Australia; navel—Bechuana; genitals—Herero; brain—New Guinea and many headhunters; eyes—Polynesia and New Zealand; cheeks—Torre; hands—New Caledonia; feet—Warega.

One description of a major dietary implication is the following from the 1972 Andes crash:

> On the other hand they all took to the marrow. When the last shred of meat had been scraped off a bone it would be cracked open with the ax and the marrow extracted with a piece of wire or a knife and shared. They also ate the blood clots which they found around the hearts of almost all the bodies. Their texture and taste were different from that of the flesh and fat, and by now they were sick to death of this staple diet. It was not just that their senses clamored for different tastes; their bodies too cried out for those minerals of which they had for so long been deprived—above all, for salt.[2]*

Additional culinary details in preparing "the long pig": In 1610, in the new colony of Virginia, a hungry settler murdered his wife, then salted/powdered her, and was eating a portion when he was discovered. He is said to have remarked that,

---

*Salt is perhaps the most important dietary consideration, and some observations seem in order. "Ye are the salt of the Earth" the Bible states, and every Nazi SS couple about to be married was presented with a cellar of salt as a symbol of "purity." You and I are 70 percent fluid, just like the oceans for the last three billion years. We also have spent our first months in a sac of saline solution, and from the cells in our brains and bones salt penetrates every aspect of our existence. Oddly enough, it is a mixture of sodium (a metal so unstable it bursts into flame when exposed to water) and chlorine, a lethal gas. Swallowed, the blend forms hydrochloric acid in our stomachs. Without salt the body suffers convulsions, paralysis, and death. Raw meat furnished the salt our prehistoric ancestors needed, and the Massai tribesmen today obtain it from the blood of their cattle. Salt starvation decimated Napoleon's troops on their retreat from Moscow— resistance to disease was lowered, epidemics spread, and wounds did not heal. Hebrews, Greeks, and Romans salted their sacrifices. The Catholic Church salts its holy water today. And liquid sodium cools our nuclear reactors.

The Gourmets

"Now whether she was better roasted, boyled, or carbonado'd, I know not." We have already met the notorious Grossmann, who transformed out-of-work peasant girls into sausages in Germany in the 1920s. The Maori of New Zealand, who keep appearing in the relevant literature, also cut the bodies of their victims into pieces, and then cooked them in holes made in the ground in which hot stones were dropped. Some Australian tribes smoke-dried the corpses of tribesmen, consuming those portions rendered liquid by the heat.

Smoking the flesh is common, and the Badinga cut off arms, legs, and heads before placing them into the smoke. The result was described as especially delicious. The Tuari of Brazil burn their dead and preserve the ashes, mixing them with daily meals. The Hamatsas also appreciated smoked meat, but believed that eating hands or feet would cause their immediate death. The Banalas broke a slave's arms and bones and lowered him into a river for three days, apparently allowing the skin to come off more easily and tenderizing the morsels. The Manjema put flesh into water for three days so it would rot and gain a strong smell. The Bassange laid a slain enemy into water over night, and on the next day cut off the head and thighs and placed these in an anthill; if the ants ate from it, "it was good." Eating cadavers in various stages of advanced decomposition is said to have been fairly widespread, and if true seems to have been a matter of taste without any other significance. Buried carcasses were unearthed after two weeks and then eaten by the Tanna. Tribes in New Guinea followed in style. The Tarianas and Tucanos in the Amazon jungle buried their dead in special houses, at the same time preparing a large batch of caxiri (an alcoholic mixture), which was left to ferment; a month later the corpse was dug up, much decomposed, and burned. The remains were powdered and mixed with the caxiri.

The following house specialty was created by Vlad, the original Dracula, whom we shall meet again soon. Boyars who had offended him were beheaded, and the heads fed to crabs;

these crabs were in turn served at a feast attended by the victims' relatives and friends. But then again, perhaps this menu is as apocryphal as Adlai Stevenson's story (related in Peter Ustinov's delightful biography, *Dear Me*): "The work of the Catholic missions in New Guinea is beginning to pay dividends. Statistics have shown that on Fridays the staple meat is fishermen."

12

The Sadists and the Mad

Missionaries have reported cannibal feasts in the Fiji Islands where 600 victims were eaten. In terms of savagery the Fijis elevated cannibalism to an almost unprecedented level—dismembering their victim alive, piece by piece, cooking and eating each limb before his eyes; stretching the tongue to its furthest extension with a fishhook and then slicing it off and taunting the victim while chewing it. Like the New Guinean Doboduras, the Fijis also permitted their children to kill captives, generally other children, by shooting arrows into them.
Ewald Volhard, Kannibalismus

What do you think about a person who kills people and has sex with their dead bodies and eats some of them—do you think he's nuts?
Chief psychologist for the
Milwaukee County Mental Health Complex

The Sadists

No one can doubt that sadism, the getting of pleasure from inflicting physical or psychological pain on another or others, constitutes a major aspect of cannibalism. Our previous chapters, especially chapter 10, abound with examples. Conversely, it may be totally absent in, say, survival cannibalism. Still there are relatively pure manifestations of sadistic cannibals.

The Iroquois, known for their incessant warfare and merciless treatment of prisoners, would pull out the prisoners' fingernails, hack off their limbs, decapitate and then eat them. At times they roasted them alive.

Chinese history reflects a preoccupation with the perfection of pleasure, be it in food, eroticism, or torture. Thus emperors employed highly respected torture masters who considered their work an art form that they constantly strove to refine. Their acme was the administration of a "Thousand Deaths." The procedure could last months. Anatomically highly sophisticated criteria were applied to stab, cut, squeeze, and burn the dying, while feeding him with his own flesh.

One additional example should suffice. The "Vampire Lady of the Carpathians" must surely rank among the most horrendous human beings who ever walked the earth. Elizabeth Báthory, born in 1560, grew up in the era of Queen Elizabeth and Ivan the Terrible. She was a highly intelligent and "cultured" woman. At a time when even the Lord Palatine of the country was barely literate, she could write fluently Hungarian, German, and Latin (see Figure 11).

Báthory tortured and butchered 650 "virgin maidens, showering and bathing in their blood . . . at four each morning—the magical hour before the dawn—and really bathe in it." She also drank their blood, all in an attempt to retain her beauty and postpone her old age. She reduced some hapless victims to cannibalism to punish them for their youth and charm. There was not a single male among the murdered. Sadistic and merciless, Báthory seems to be the only reliably recorded "vampire" in the history of Europe, making Bram Stoker's Dracula no match for this real-life horror.

At her trial—where Báthory was not allowed to be

present—her accomplices testified to unspeakable crimes. She herself raged with indignation, and power politics of the day spared her life, though not all retribution. Her offenses mattered least, though her inclusion of members of the nobility among her victims did not help. Religious consideration were more of a problem, given she was Protestant and the Hapsburg king Catholic; but above all the latter owed much money to the Báthorys—and Elizabeth had tried a little too hard to collect.

Dorottya Szentes, one of Countess Elizabeth's wiliest torturers, revealed in her trial deposition that when her Ladyship was not feeling well and could not beat anyone, "she would draw one of the serving maids suddenly to herself and bite a chunk of flesh from her cheeks and sink her teeth into her breast and shoulders. She would stick needles into a girl's fingers and say: 'If it hurts you, you famous whore, pull them out'; but if the girl dared to draw the needles out her Ladyship ordered her to be beaten and her fingers slashed up [with razors]."[1]

and:

Once the girl was hoisted up, Dorka [another torturer] would start burning and stabbing her with a red-hot iron. Recoiling from the burning iron, the girl would tear herself on the hundreds of spikes and eventually become impaled. And Countess Elizabeth, screaming obscenities and abuse in a sexual frenzy, would sit on a stool under the cage and expose her face and wrinkled neck and arms to the shower of blood and drink it.

and:

On occasion she wreaked terrible "revenge" on young lads, whom she saw looking lustful at "her" girls, by secretly feeding them with the women's flesh.[2]

The Mad

There are equally without question the mad who eat others. One case in the clinical literature describes a woman who, during an attack of temporal lobe epilepsy, put her baby in the frying pan. During the Russian Revolution a certain baron Roman von Sternberg-Ungem believed himself to be the reincarnation of Genghis Khan and proceeded to engage in drinking human blood. The Bolsheviks eventually caught up with him, and in 1920 he was tried and executed.

Not all such stories are true. The claim that in Canada's forested northland some Cree and Ojibwa Indians suffer from a bizarre mental disorder, technically known as windigo psychosis, an acute anxiety state marked first by melancholy and then a distaste for ordinary food followed by an obsessive desire for human flesh ending in homicidal cannibalism, is almost certainly fiction. A thorough literature review indicates that not a single case of this so-called psychosis has ever been directly observed by a clinician, anthropologist, or other objective observer, and it is therefore extremely unlikely that it in fact exists.

Following World War II, cannibalism was reported in the 1947 famine in the Ukraine. Nikita Khrushchev described in his memoirs how one of his subordinates related it: "The woman had the corpse of her own child on the table, and was cutting it up. She was chattering away as she worked. 'We've already eaten Manechka (little Maria). Now we'll salt down Vanechka (little Ivan). This will keep us for some time.' Can you imagine? This woman had gone crazy with hunger and butchered her own children."

But aside from these obvious cases, what are we to make of some others? Are the killers sadistic, mad, or both? Consider the following—and what would your judgment/sentence be? The setting: Berlin in the 1920s (yes, again).

We read in Otto Friedrich's *Before the Deluge*:

Of all these mass murders, the case that reverberated most throughout the 1920s was that of Georg Haarmann, a mild, soft-spoken man, who, prophetically, was an unofficial police agent, an informer on petty thieves. Like Grossmann, Haarmann liked to hang around in railroad stations, searching for his victims among the peasant youths coming to Hannover to look for work. Unlike Grossmann, he was only looking for boys. He would offer them sandwiches, beer, and help. Then, after taking one of his new friends home and putting him to bed, he would sexually attack the youth and finally tear out the victim's throat with his teeth. He never could remember the actual scene, Haarmann later told his lawyer. He would feel a kind of rage beginning to overwhelm him, he said, and then everything went blank until he woke up in the morning with another dead boy in his room.

Some children found a skull on the banks of the Leine River, and then, a few days later, a second skull was washed ashore. When the police dredged the river, they found enough bones to represent between twenty-four and twenty-six victims, but nobody associated the bones with Haarmann until the mother of a missing boy recognized her son's jacket on another boy, who proved to be the son of Haarmann's landlady. Haarmann, it turned out, did a brisk business in used clothes. He also made use of the corpses. "He . . . would cleanly dismember the body," said Vicki Baum, the novelist, who was living in Hannover at the time, "and reduce it to nicely boiled, potted meat. Said meat, labeled pork or veal and attractively packaged, reached the Black Market, where it brought good prices. When . . . Haarmann made a full confession, there was much silent shock, frightened inspection of hidden larders, some discreet vomiting, and a general throwing-away of expensive potted-meat jars."*

---

*At about this time, Klaus Mann, the son of the novelist, was sitting in the Carlton Tea Room in Munich. Across the street, in the Luitpold Cafe, bands of uniformed Storm Troopers were gorging themselves on pastry, but their leader was not among them. Apparently in search of peace and

Cannibalism

Haarmann's arrest and trial caused a national uproar. The mother of one of his victim's tried to attack him, and Haarmann lived in dread of being lynched, but he seemed to have no feelings about either his crimes or his prospective execution. A local professor of psychiatry, Theodor Lessing, argued vehemently that Haarmann was insane and not responsible for his killings, but the court barred any psychiatric evidence and sentenced Haarmann to death. . . .

Haarmann was duly executed, and as the date drew near, the schoolchildren of Berlin took to singing a song about him. "I remember," says one of them, now a teacher in New York, "there was a hit song in those days that went, 'Just wait a while, be patient, and happiness will come to you too,' or something like that, but then everybody started singing a different version that went:

> *Warte, warte nur ein Weilchen,*
> *Bald kommt Haarmann auch zu Dir,*
> *Mit dem kleinen Hackelbeilchen*
> *Macht er Pökelfleisch aus dir.*

---

quiet, Adolf Hitler, too, was sitting in the Carlton Tea Room. He ate three strawberry tarts, one after another.

As the young writer watched the Führer picking at the remains of the strawberry tarts, he began to think that Hitler reminded him of someone, and it bothered him that he could not remember the other face, someone whose picture he had seen in the newspapers.

"There was nothing but dim, rosy light," Mann recalled later, "soft music and heaps of cookies; and in the midst of this sugary idyll, a mustachioed little man with veiled eyes and a stubborn forehead, chatting with some colorless henchmen. I caught fragments of their conversation. They discussed the cast of a musical farce scheduled for the same evening at the Kammerspiele. . . . While I called the waitress to pay for my cup of coffee, I suddenly remembered whom Herr Hitler resembled. It was that sex-murderer in Hannover, whose case had made such huge headlines. . . . His name was Haarmann. . . . The likeness between him and Hitler was striking. The sightless eyes, the moustache, the brutal and nervous mouth, even the unspeakable vulgarity of the fleshy nose; it was, indeed, precisely the same physiognomy."[3]

"Which means, 'Wait, wait just a little while, and soon Haarmann will come to you. With his little hatchet, he'll make smoked meat out of you.' "[4]

It was perhaps inevitable that this case should have been disinterred. It underwent up-to-date treatment in a German movie, *Zärtlichkeit der Wölfe* (*Tenderness of the Wolves*, 1973). The police contacted Haarmann (played by an actor looking like Kojak's younger brother), trying to enlist him as an informer. Haarmann, as the good neighborhood butcher, is also making sausages of his corpses and appearing as a public benefactor at a time when there were still serious meat shortages. The orchestra meanwhile played "Plaisir d'amour" and "Johnny Is the Boy for Me." Everyone seemed to be happy with this film, especially the critics, who welcomed it as an expressionist revival and stroke of genius.

Other Forms

Finally, a number of forms of cannibalism do not fit too well in the basic motivational categories. One of the most bizarre forms of in-group cannibalism was the custom of the Lhopa in Sikkim who—if they could not capture a stranger—ate the bride's mother at a wedding. Some tribal parents consume their children, the rationale apparently being that they are entitled to take back what they had produced. Mothers of the Chavantes in Uruguay ate (and perhaps still eat) their dead children in order to recover the strength lost during childbirth. There may be a few instances of self-cannibalism. Chinese cannibalism is said to be closely related to loyalty to superiors and filial piety toward the parent. There may well be other forms of cannibalism that will be documented in time.

Intermission

The reader who has followed our tale/discussion this far deserves, I think, a little rest. It has been a lot of information. And there is more to come. Hopefully she or he has also continued to think about our three basic questions, beginning with the first, which will also be the last in this book. Here then is an entertaining reminder.

One relevant headline is "WHAT DO YOU EXPECT FROM LAWYERS?" topping a story from the *Arizona Republic,* slightly edited by me. It comes in three acts.

Act I
March 10, 1993

The Maricopa County Bar Association had issued a statement apologizing for "misjudgment" in fashioning a student essay contest touching on the subject of cannibalism, but said it would not cancel it despite complaints.

This year's contestants were asked to imagine themselves trapped with two friends in a cave where they would be unable to survive for more than thirty days without food. They were to imagine further that they decided one of them would have to be killed for food so that the other two could survive. The choice to be was determined by lot. A half hour after one of them was sacrificed, rescuers arrived. Contestants were to further determine whether the two survivors were guilty of murder. In addition, they were to determine whether the method of determining which child would be sacrificed was fair or rational. The contest offered a chance to win a fifty-dollar U.S. Savings Bond and an engraved plaque. One wonders what the engraving might say.

In a written statement on the controversial contest, spokesman Phil Riske said, "Could the county bar have selected a different question this year for its annual sixth-through ninth-grade essay contest? Yes. Should we have selected this particular question, which is part of the high school teaching manual on the law, for sixth grade pupils and junior high school students? No. We regret the misjudgment."

The statement said that 14 percent of the more than four hundred Maricopa County elementary and junior high schools that were eligible had declined to participate in this year's competition. However, because the majority had not indicated they would discourage students from participating, the bar had "no right to usurp them," Riske's statement said.

Act II
two days later

The City of Tucson Bar Association is pleased to see that the Maricopa County Bar Association is still providing a service to the public: This service being ammunition to shoot down our already tarnished image.

The Maricopa County Bar Association's contest supports the public's perception that we are all "scum sucking bottom dwellers," without a clue as to public sensitivity.

This contest, although trying to help the public's awareness of the law, ranks with the Washington attorney's performance of recreating the "Washington Map Handle Rape Case" on the "Donahue" show. Sometimes, Mr. Editor, justice and decency do go hand in hand.

Think about it. Are we trying to teach our future generations cannibalism, or "Jeffrey D.ism" and when it is acceptable? Whatever happened to the old, clean, factual problems like *Pennoyer v. Neff*? [Whoever that may be.]

It seems that although perhaps the basis of the contest was sound, the propriety of the topic was not.

Therefore, this association differs, and cannot support the Maricopa County Bar Association's means to this end.

Act III
two days after that

Under a slow roast for a week now [note the piquant language], the Maricopa County Bar Association is still being grilled for asking youngsters as young as 11 to consider, hypothetically, the grisly prospect of cannibalizing a friend in an act of survival. What were the lawyers thinking about?

As it has done for 10 years or so, the county bar association invites children in the sixth through ninth grades to enter its writing contest. The idea is to have students exercise their problem-solving skills by addressing, in 500 words or less, a problem posed by the association. . . .

These are provocative questions, recalling real-life instances of people lost at sea or otherwise stranded. The lawyers easily may have been inspired by Hollywood's January release on the subject, *Alive,* a film portrayal of the real-life experience of a Uruguayan rugby team whose plane crashed and whose survival techniques during 70 days in the Andes included cannibalism.

Yet the ethical questions are hardly appropriate for 11-year-olds, or so thought scores of parents who protested the contest. More than 45 schools are boycotting the contest as well, and even some bar association members were distraught. The outrage, however, was insufficient to cancel the contest, which is expected to draw several hundred contestants, though the bar association now concedes that the question was inappropriate for sixth grade pupils and junior high students.

Cannibalism

The *Arizona Republic* concludes earnestly, if somewhat dogmatically: "If next year the association has difficulty framing an essay question that doesn't inspire nightmares or isn't based on a Hollywood screenplay, it might turn inward for appropriate material. . . . Not just school children, but members of the bar and bench as well, might learn a thing or two."

Part Three

Cannibalism in Culture and Society

Dr. Dietz [who had examined Jeffrey Dahmer and found him sane] broke into laughter—something he often does when he's discussing the less savory aspects of his inquiries. "It was a straightforward discussion of such details as which way he held the knife when dismembering the body, and how he protected himself from getting acid burns when he was disposing of the acid in which he disintegrated the soft tissues of his victims, and the right temperature settings for properly preserving a skull."

I took a deep breath and asked him whether he'd felt any horror or revulsion, since what he had just communicated was more the feeling of one specialist comparing notes with another.

He admitted to having had a sense of the bizarre. "But no more than I would have driving past a Mormon temple," he said.

The New Yorker, May 16, 1994

13

Werewolves, Witches, and Vampires

Allegations of witchcraft and sorcery—running around the countryside in a wolf skin killing children, or sending a pack of wolves to decimate the flocks of a good Christian—were charges rather easily sustained. Fundamental nonsense was taken for irrefutable evidence. The idle word of a neighbor, the gibberish of a village idiot, a shaving cut that showed up the morning after someone claimed to have driven off a wolf with a sharp stick—for these reasons and less thousands died at the stake.[1]

Barry Lopez, *Of Wolves and Men*

Proposition 174, a California school voucher initiative in the early 90s, ran quickly into trouble when a group of Northern California witches announced they intended to open a school. When told that such private institutions would have few requirements other than taking attendance, one sen. Art Torres (D-Los Angeles) replied cryptically: "Satan worshipers are very punctual. Witches' covens are very punctual."

Los Angeles Times

149

Werewolves

A werewolf is said to be a human being who can at will change his or her shape into that of a wolf, retaining his own intelligence and cunning while gaining the beast's ferocity. A voluntary werewolf typically obtains his power of transformation from the devil in a Faustian exchange; an involuntary werewolf comes into his power as a result of a family curse or a spell cast by a sorcerer or witch—out of hate, for pay, or at the devil's behest. (He might also become one by being born in a certain tribe, say the Semitic Seiar.)[2]

The antidotes against werewolves varied also. If caught they could be bound and exorcised with potions, a common one consisting of half an ounce of sulfur, an equal amount of asafetida (devil's dung), and a quarter ounce of castor in clear spring water. Silver bullets were recommended as an alternate method.

Historically speaking, scapegoating the wolf has been one of man's favorite sports, it seems, down to our times. The Roman writer Pliny gave an account of werewolves in his *Historia Naturalis,* though he passed on the phenomenon with skepticism. However, by Roman times doctors had begun to recognize a form of mental disorder, lycanthropy, in which the patient imagines himself to be a wolf, "with the latter's savagery and lust for raw flesh."

In 1594 a case was reported in which a lycanthrope told his captors, in confidence, that he was really a wolf but that his skin was smooth on the surface because all the hairs were on the inside. To cure him of his delusions, the man's extremities were amputated, following which he died, still uncured.

More recently groups of German U-boats during the Battle of the Atlantic were known as "wolfpacks." When that war ended it was widely assumed that the eradication of Nazism would be a long and difficult process. The Nazis were thought to have prepared for a protracted guerrilla campaign by submerging in society a number of so-called werewolves, none of whom ever materialized; the plot had been a chimera. Similarly, American soldiers returning from World War II to the upper Midwest began to refer to all wolves as Nazis and hunted them down with great intensity. Even the Navajo tribe in the Southwest accused werewolves of raiding graveyards and mutilating bodies.

Barry Lopez, in his splendid book *Of Wolves and Men*, observes that "throughout history man has externalized his bestial nature, finding a scapegoat upon which he could heap his sins and whose sacrificial death would be his atonement. He has put his sins of greed, lust, and deception upon the wolf and put the wolf to death—in literature, in folklore, and in real life. . . . The wolf and the look-alike werewolf became everyone's symbol of evil."

The werewolf stories from northern Europe typically were more robust, adventurous, and inventive than the classical Greek and Roman stories. Olaus Magnus writes in his *History of the Goths* that at Christmas werewolves gathered together for drinking bouts and forcefully entered houses for the purpose of raiding the wine cellar. . . .

Debauchery and sacrilege, which became common in werewolf stories later, are not the themes of early Teutonic werewolf tales. Violence is, however. In the Icelandic saga of the Volsungs, King Volsung's daughter Signy marries a king named Siggeir. Siggeir, whose mother is a werewolf, turns around and kills Volsung and puts his ten sons into stocks to feed his mother. . . .

The Roman Church, which dominated medieval life in Europe, exploited the sinister image of wolves in order to create a sense of real devils prowling in a real world. During the years of the Inquisition, the Church sought to smother social and political unrest and to maintain secular control by flushing out "werewolves" in the community and putting them to death. . . .

Cannibalism

Among all the heretics and political enemies of the state who were marched through the courts and condemned as werewolves were an unending number of the wildly insane, the epileptic, the simple-minded, the pathologically disturbed, and the neurotically guilt-ridden. They were condemned as society's enemies, but their connection with wolves was tenuous in the extreme and that with werewolves highly imagined. . . .

At a time when no one knew anything about genetics, the idea that a child suffering from Down's syndrome—small ears, a broad forehead, a flat nose, prominent teeth—was the offspring of a wench and a werewolf was perfectly plausible.[3]

In 1275 a deranged woman named Angela de la Barthe confessed to the Inquisition at Toulouse that she had given birth to a creature that was half wolf, half snake, and that she had kept it alive by feeding it human babies she stole. In 1598 an entire family of werewolves was recorded in Western France. Two sisters, their brother, and a son were known as "the werewolves of St. Claude." One of the girls named Peronette suffered from lycanthropic hysteria and ran about on all fours. The entire family was burned to death. Later, wives of the emerging middle class referred to prostitutes as wolves because they thought of them as wenches consuming the souls of their innocent sons. Interestingly, in ancient Rome prostitutes had been called *lupae*, "she-wolves."

Nor was it just wolves. Legends of werebeasts are almost universal. Primitive beliefs in shapeshifting (the human ability to change into an animal form) combined with beliefs in sorcery to produce a fearsome local werebeast that goes about at night usually, but not always, slaying human beings. There were werehyenas and werelions in Africa, wereleopards in Assam, werefoxes in Japan, werebears in Norway, and werejaguars in South America (possibly due to an Olmec portrayal of a jaguar copulating with a reclining woman).

Lopez concludes with this grim observation:

By standing around a burning stake, jeering at and cursing an accused werewolf, a person demonstrated an allegiance to his human nature and increased his own sense of well-being. The tragedy, and I think that is the proper word, is that the projection of such self-hatred was never satisfied. No amount of carnage, no pile of wolves in the village square, no number of human beings burned as werewolves, was enough to end it. It is, I suppose, not that different from the slaughter of Jews at the hands of the Nazis, except that when it happens to animals it is easier to forget. In the case of the werewolf, however, it must be recalled that we are talking about human beings.[4]

Witches

At the end of the eighth century Charlemagne had already decreed that death was the appropriate punishment for sorcerers (of either sex) who ate human flesh, or fed it to others, as well as for anyone "believing" in cannibalism. By the end of the eleventh century, cannibalism and child murder were customary accusations, with the crimes of blasphemy and satanism added for good measure. This later brought witchcraft under the jurisdiction of the Inquisition. One legal definition of a witch in England was "a person who hath conference with the Devil to consult with him or to do some act."*

Historian Jeffrey Russell notes in his *Witchcraft in the Middle Ages*: "The wild man, both brutal and erotic, was a perfect projection of the repressed libidinous impulses of medieval man. His counterpart, the wild woman, the murderess, child-eater, bloodsucker and occasionally sex nymph, was the prototype of the witch."

---

*The word "devil" stems from the root *div*, which also gives us the word "divine." It merely means "little god." Not surprising, then, is the rather well-known fact that when a new religion is established, the god or gods of the old often become the devil or devils of the new.

Cannibalism

By the thirteenth century, Europeans were becoming disillusioned with medieval society and the Catholic Church that controlled it. To fortify its waning power, the church turned to witches as scapegoats for the ills of the world. It launched a vicious and pervasive campaign claiming that witchcraft was the greatest threat to civilized society and all those who lived within it. Witches were subsequently hunted, tortured, and viciously exterminated by the church and its henchmen for the next three hundred years across Europe and colonial North America.

Malleus Maleficarum, "Hammer of Witches" (derived from a title sometimes bestowed upon inquisitors, "hammer of heretics"), appeared in Europe in 1487. It consisted of 250,000 words of abomination and hypocrisy, one of the most odious documents in human history. It was published and republished, with language barriers, national boundaries, and even religious differences proving no obstacle. Beneath a glut of words and endless repetition, it catalogued all conceivable reasons for hunting down witches and punishing them to the greater glory of the gentle Lord of its authors. It also became the authoritative source used to condemn hundreds of alleged werewolves to be burned at the stake. We offer a few excerpts:

> What else is a woman but a foe to friendship, an inescapable punishment, a necessary evil, a natural temptation, a desirable calamity, a domestic danger, a delectable detriment, an evil of nature, painted with fair colors! . . .

> And blessed be the highest who has so far preserved the male sex from so great a crime: for since He was willing to be born and suffer for us, therefore He has granted to men this privilege. . . .

> All witchcraft comes from carnal lust, which is in women insatiable. . . . Wherefore for the sake of fulfilling their lust they consort even with devils.

The *Malleus* also advised the inquisitors to be wary about torture, given that some individuals were "so soft-hearted and weak-minded that at the least torture they will confess anything, whether it be true or not. Others are so stubborn that however much they are tortured, the truth is not to be had from them." It was church sophistry at its best; after all, witches could not be condemned and burned without having first confessed.

A similar fate befell animals, especially cats. In order to strengthen its conspiracy, the Church was also able to draw upon the witch's longstanding and traditional association with the cat. This connection with witchcraft, pagan ritual, and black magic, "probably stems from the cat's hard, cold, and often unblinking stare. Few people can look a lion or tiger straight in the eye without experiencing a certain uneasiness. At the same time, their gaze can almost be hypnotic, so it is hardly surprising that they were regarded with superstition and mistrust."[5] In colonial America alone over two thousand cat sorcery trials were recorded.

We may conclude, then, that medieval Europe under the dictatorship of the Catholic Church came to resemble a vast insane asylum.

In fifteenth-century Berne, Switzerland, one witch admitted that she and her cronies secretly took just-buried babies from their graves and cooked them in (what else?) a cauldron, "until the whole flesh comes away from the bones to make a soup which may easily be drunk."[6] In sixteenth-century Spain it was apparently more customary to bake them in a pie. In 1610 two witches were condemned at Liège for having changed themselves into werewolves and murdered a great number of children; they tore them into pieces and then guzzled them.[7]

Now a version from our own shores, from Richard Gardner's *Sex Abuse Hysteria: Salem Witchcraft Trials Revisited:*

Many have noted the similarity between the hysteria associated with the Salem witchcraft trials in 1692 and that which we are witnessing at the present time. I believe that this comparison is warranted. In fact, the similarities between the two phenomena are almost uncanny.

. . . The events began in the winter of 1691–1692 in Salem Village (now part of Danvers, Massachusetts). Betty Parris, age nine, and her cousin, Abigail Williams, age eleven, spent significant time with the family's West Indian slave, Tituba. There is good reason to believe that Tituba spent long hours with the children telling them stories about voodoo spells and witches. During the cold winter days, the Parris home became the gathering place for other girls who, we have good reason to believe, found Tituba's tales a welcome break in the boredom of the Massachusetts winter. The strict demands of their Calvinist parents provided little opportunity for enjoyable activities to pass the time. Even Christmas was not considered justification for joyous worship, let alone revelry.

It was during this period that the children developed highly emotional episodic fits associated with screaming; choking; bizarre body contortions; grimacing; inexplicable physical pains; periodic deafness, blindness, and speechlessness; epileptic-like seizures; unintelligible utterances; and trance-like states. Their father, quite concerned over these strange outbursts, summoned the village physician, Dr. William Griggs. The doctor was unable to find any physical cause for this somewhat mysterious illness and suggested that the girls had fallen under Satan's influence. This was a common explanation for diseases of unknown etiology at the time.[8]

So it started. The affliction of hysterical outbursts spread quickly, with additional "spells" during which the children saw vivid and frightening apparitions pursuing and threatening them. Then the accusations began. Tituba was the first to be jailed; by April fifty more had been accused in the nearby town of Andover alone.

The formal trial began in June. Three and a half months later twenty-seven persons had been found guilty of witchcraft. Four died in prison, nineteen were hanged, and one was executed by being pressed to death with heavy stones (he took four days to die). Tituba and some others confessed and were not even tried. Four years later twelve of the jurors signed a statement of contrition, "claiming that they had operated under the influence of the devil."

As late as the eighteenth century, in England, Scotland, and even the American colonies, the ruling powers were cheerfully burning witches after the usual preliminaries of revolting cruelty. Why not? Sir William Blackstone had laid down the law: "To deny the possibility, nay, actual existence, of witchcraft is at once to flatly contradict the revealed word of God."

Vampires

A fresh, lifelike, exhumed corpse; an evil soul; a bite with canine fangs; the sucking of blood; and a drained victim—these are the basic ingredients of vampirism.* At one time anyone hated in life by man or church, and for whatever reason, was a good candidate for being accused of having become a vampire, if not a werewolf or witch. The vampire's victims frequently took up the habit in turn, presumably to make up for their lost life elixir. To put a stop to such ravages, the most common method was to drive a stake through the vampire's body, though it could also be burned or, as in Bulgaria (where this was said to have become a full-time profession for some), bottled. (For some reason vampires were also presumed to have an

---

*There are more innocent, if also blood-sucking, "vampires," namely certain bats in South America. Actually, most of what we have read about bats is fable, story, or legend. They are really very inoffensive creatures.

inordinate horror of garlic.) In *Human Anatomy* by Elaine Marieb and John Mallatt we read:

> Although many aspects of vampire legends derive from the "behavior" of bloating corpses that shift in their graves (the "undead"), other aspects of these legends may be based on living people with skin conditions. One such condition is *porphyria* (purple), a rare, inherited disease.
>
> Sunlight creates all kinds of nasty damage to some porphyria victims (a reason, perhaps, why vampires were said to hide in dark basements and coffins during the daylight hours). When exposed to sunlight, the skin becomes lesioned and scarred, and the fingers, toes, and nose are often mutilated. The teeth grow prominent as the gums degenerate (the basis of large vampire fangs?). Rampant growth of hair causes the sufferer's face to become wolf-like and the hands to resemble paws. One treatment for porphyria is the injection of normal heme molecules extracted from healthy red blood cells. Since heme injections were not available in the Middle Ages, the next best thing would have been to drink blood, as vampires were said to do. The claim that garlic keeps vampires away may stem from the fact that garlic severely aggravates porphyria symptoms.[9]

The vampire "epidemics" that infested central Europe in the seventeenth and eighteenth centuries can probably be attributed to cannibalism, especially the well-documented psychosis that began in Belgrade in 1730 and continued for five years. Count Dracula, the notorious Transylvanian father of vampirism, had been in reality Prince Vlad V of Walachia (1431–76), not a vampire but most likely a sadist with cannibalistic habits. If he didn't drink blood, he certainly spilled it. He was affectionately known as Vlad the Impaler (with, incidentally, a noticeable underbite).

Vlad/Dracula's most memorable military exploit had come in June 1462, with a daring nighttime raid on the camp of the superior forces of invading Turks. Leaving havoc in his wake, Vlad proceeded to demoralize the survivors by "preparing a special sight" for Sultan Mohammed II along the Turkish line of march, according to a 1978 treatise published by the Romanian Academy in Bucharest. The sight consisted of twenty thousand Turkish soldiers impaled on tall poles in a field two miles wide and a half mile deep. The Turks are said to have retreated in disarray back across the Danube.

On another occasion, when Turkish envoys, in keeping with Muslim custom, refused to remove their turbans in his presence, he had them nailed to their heads. He also had hundreds of noblemen and their families impaled on suspicion of disloyalty, and is said to have eliminated poverty in his land by eliminating the impoverished. Eventually, however, the Turks caught and beheaded Vlad.[10]

Whatever else Vlad/Dracula was, modern Romanians insist with some indignation that he was not a vampire. The correct image of the prince, historian Nicolae Stoicescu argues in a book published in the late 1970s, is that of a "valiant defender of his country's independence . . . a harsh but just ruler who protected the forebears of the present Romanian nation." The former Communist government also honored him with a stamp, and, paraphrasing U.S. Senator Barry Goldwater's famous epigram, Stoicescu argued that, "Excess in defense of freedom . . . is a virtue, not a sin."

Bram Stoker's 1897 novel *Dracula* described in considerable detail such additional themes of timeless attraction as rape and pedophilia, incest and adultery, and oral and group sex. It became a heady mix, and Hollywood, as one might expect, wouldn't miss the opportunity. The film *Dracula*, starring Bela Lugosi, achieved great acclaim in 1931. The Hungarian-born Lugosi was so successful in the role that he was typecast as the prototypical diabolical madman in one Hollywood film after another, maintaining his image offscreen by holding interviews with the press while reclining in a coffin. Lugosi became a drug addict and died at seventy-three in 1956, appropriately laid to rest in the same cape he had worn as Dracula.

Real or not, vampire stories intrigue the public. Dracula scholar Leonard Wolf counts at least two hundred films and scores of books on the subject, ranging from the serious (*Nosferatu*) to the spurious (*Billy the Kid versus Dracula*). We also have a Dracula Press in New York (an affiliate of the Count Dracula Fan Club), which publishes three to five vampire books a year.

Stephen Kaplan, sixty-five, of the Elmhurst, New York-based Vampire Research Center, the self-described "father of vampirology," claims to possess dossiers on 850 living blood guzzlers. His confidential vampire census poses such questions as: "Do you have retractable fangs?" and "How much blood do you consume in a day?" and, perhaps more salient: "Have you ever been institutionalized?"

Kaplan also asserts that Los Angeles ranks as the vampire capital of the world. According to him, jurors in a recent Santa Cruz trial scoffed at a prosecutor's arguments that an accused murderer who reportedly sipped her victim's blood fancied herself a vampire. They convicted her only of assault with a deadly weapon. The prosecutor offered no apologies for the unorthodox strategy: "I thought, hey, if it was going to fly anywhere, it would fly in Santa Cruz." Ah, California.

In yet another Bay Area case, says Kaplan, a judge dismissed a man's claim that his ex-wife's habit of drinking blood in front of the children was good reason to deny her custody. The judge's ruling: Being a vampire doesn't necessarily make you a bad parent.

Francis Ford Coppola's "wildly romantic masterpiece," *Bram Stoker's Dracula,* won three Oscars in 1993. Nor will we have seen the last movie or read the last book on the subject—it seems one cannot kill a good myth, let alone a lucrative one.

Playboy interviewee Anne Rice, who came upon the literary

scene in 1976 with the extraordinarily innovative novel *Inter-view with the Vampire,* said that critics were not sure what to make of her richly imagined, deadly serious portrait of Lestat de Lioncourt, an eighteenth-century vampire who poured out his tale of centuries on the run, of the eternal struggle between good and evil and of the meanings of death and immortality. Readers, however, had no trouble seeing this vampire as an ultimate outsider—a symbolic figure for teens, gays, and lonely urban apartment dwellers. It became an instant cult classic and the basis for a series of novels collectively titled *The Vampire Chronicles*—including *The Vampire Lestat, The Queen of the Damned,* and, more recently, *Tale of the Body Thief*—which have sold nearly five million copies.

Playboy goes on:

> As the characters whirl around the world in an apocalyptic frenzy of mass killings, the intimate encounters among vampires—and between vampires and humans—become more sensual. The giving of the dark gift of immortality is as erotically riveting as any scene in Rice's pornography. The brutality of the embrace, the penetration of vampire teeth, the sucking of hot blood, the passionate moment of trans-formation—this is sexy stuff, indeed. . . .
>
> *The Tale of the Body Thief,* the fourth and latest volume of *The Vampire Chronicles* (and her lucky 13th novel), takes place in contemporary settings such as Miami, Georgetown, and aboard the *Queen Elizabeth II.* In this story, Lestat is given the opportunity to give up his immortality and return to human form. Naturally, he chooses to remain a vampire. We wouldn't want it any other way. How else could we continue to read about his adventures in volume five, which Rice promises to provide shortly?

When *Playboy* asked Rice how she came up with the idea of doing *Interview with the Vampire,* she said:

Cannibalism

It was haphazard. I was sitting at the typewriter and I thought, What would it be like to interview a vampire? And I started writing . . . had been writing the book and I said there was this little girl vampire and she's four years old, and Stan [Rice's husband] said, "Oh, no, no, no, no, not a four-year-old vampire. You can't have a vampire that young." I said, "All right, all right, a six-year-old vampire!" . . . I really see vampires as transcending gender. If you make them absolutely straight or absolutely gay, you limit the material. They can be either one. They have a polymorphous sexuality. They see everything as beautiful. . . .

I have some readers who go to the dentist and they get these little fangs made that fit on their teeth. They get them fitted by the dentist and made the same color as their teeth. In fact, I heard that I have a whole gang of fans in Los Angeles who do that. They put on their teeth and go out at night and sit in cafes, show their fangs. They've come to my door, the people with the fangs. They come to the coven party. They call me on the telephone. Let me emphasize again: All of these people know this is fiction. We're talking about people in their thirties and forties. This is fun to them. This is almost a hobby to be part of the fan club, to dress up like a vampire and to love vampire movies. They're vampire groupies. It represents the romance in their lives. They're wonderful people. I have never met a single one who's been a sinister Satan-worshipping person or anything like that.

And finally from a recent newspaper report:

Castle Bran, Romania—Cold autumn mist wreathed the gloomy towers of the 14th-century stronghold and the gray limestone crag beneath its walls. Among the branches of gnarled beech trees clinging to the bare rock, a small wren flitted enchantingly, beckoning two lone visitors up steep, mossy steps toward the iron-studded door of Dracula's Castle. "So," the guide said with an ominous hiss. "Now you are in Transylvania." . . .

"It's very hard to tell them it isn't true," he added. "Especially the Americans. They've come so far, and you should see their faces when I say it's just fiction. It's like taking a toy away from a child." . . . Until recently, off-duty hotel staffers obligingly reposed in a coffin that guests were invited to open in a dank, candle-lit basement. The practice was suspended, however, when an elderly Spanish tourist complained to the government of heart palpitations.

14

Special Cases: Medical, Legal, and Psychological

It is known that the HIV can cause brain changes similar to those in Kuru.[1]

Good skipper, use him truly
For he is ill and sad
—Hush! Hush! he cried, then cruelly
He killed the little lad.
                    "Ballad of the *Mignonette*"

Almost any night, in any major American city, adult incest and ritual-abuse survivor meetings are held in church basements and community rooms. Churches and other institutions also offer counseling for dissociative disorders and satanic-ritual-abuse victims.
                    Time, November 29, 1993

Kuru

L et us now take a look at a special case in medicine. Does it involve cannibalism? According to the American Medical Association, kuru is a progressive and fatal infection of the brain that affects some natives of the highlands of New Guinea. Kuru is caused by a virus spread by cannibalism. The condition is now rare. The disease is caused by a "slow" virus (which causes no signs of disease until many months or years after entry into the body) and the incubation period may be as long as 30 years. Symptoms include progressive difficulty in controlling movements and, eventually, dementia. Kuru has aroused special interest recently because of certain similarities between the causative virus and HIV (human immunodeficiency virus), which causes AIDS.[2]

And this from Cecil's authoritative *Textbook of Medicine*:

CJD (Creutzfeldt-Jakob disease) is closely related to kuru and scrapie. Scrapie is a spongiform encephalopathy of sheep experimentally transmissible to other animal species. Kuru is a disease previously endemic among the Fore people inhabiting an area in the eastern highlands of Papua New Guinea. Cerebellar dysfunction, dementia, and progression to death within two years were typical. Women and children were affected much more frequently than men. Circumstantial evidence indicates that the kuru agent was transmitted to them through the ritual handling of affected tissues, especially brain, from deceased relatives. This cultural practice was discontinued and the incidence of kuru has decreased dramatically since 1959. Brain tissues from patients dying of kuru were inoculated into the brains of chimpanzees which, after prolonged incubation period, developed a similar disease.[3]

The alert reader will have noticed a slight if crucial difference in the two accounts: while the AMA encyclopedia asserts that kuru is spread by cannibalism, Cecil's classic textbook refers to "circumstantial evidence of transmission . . . through ritual handling of affected tissues." These different explanations are, in fact, part of a heated debate. It goes something like this.

Dr. Daniel Carleton Gajdusek of the National Institutes of Health became interested in the mystery of kuru and claimed that infection occurred during funeral rites involving cannibalism. In 1976 he received the Nobel Prize for his research. He also published a widely cited photograph in *Science* magazine to prove his point. It purports to show a woman who died from kuru, with another photograph just below purportedly depicting some Fore tribesmen sitting around a campfire eating meat. The caption tells how the Fore tribe of Papua New Guinea prepare and eat human flesh. Most people who saw the pictures and read the caption assumed they were viewing a photograph of cannibalism in action.[4]

Though maintaining this was just a pig feast, Gajdusek strongly disagreed with anyone questioning the Fore's cannibalism as such. "The whole of Australia from the prime minister on down knows these people are cannibals," he asserted. "The old people tell of cooking and eating their relatives—they give a complete list of who ate whom and when."

Gajdusek, apparently not very accustomed to damage control, then became alarmed about the whole matter and refused to show any cannibalistic photographs he claims to have taken. "The people who are involved in it or know of it [the cannibalism] have not deigned to get into the argument. . . . It's beneath my dignity to answer [it]."[5]

One of these detractors was Lyle Steadman, who had worked with the Hewa people in New Guinea. He questioned both of Gajdusek's claims. Concerning the first argument, Steadman does not deny that New Guinea natives often say that other members of other tribes are cannibals, or that they themselves once were cannibals, or that some members still are cannibals. But he likens it to the witch hunts in Europe. "People were killed for being witches, and at the trials a lot of women said they were witches and that they ate human babies."

Concerning the second argument, Steadman bluntly stated

that, "Cannibalism is irrelevant to the transmission of kuru."
While New Guinea natives engage in mortuary rites that could
easily allow women and children to come into contact with
the kuru slow viruses, "skull handling and the handling of
corpses is prevalent, and the virus is most likely transmitted
through mucous membranes by touching them to the eyes, nose
or mouth. It is extremely unlikely that one could get kuru by
eating the virus."

Now our old acquaintance William Arens enters the fracas.

As we close in on the kuru area of the highlands, academic
standards seem to function as an almost-forgotten ideal,
rather than as standard operating procedure. Anthropologists
with well-deserved reputations based upon previous research
and publication become the victims of their own sensation-
alism or poor scholarship. The convergence in this instance
of both medical and anthropological hypotheses on the
existence of cannibalism prepares the way for astounding
leaps of fantasy and the demand for the reader to follow
along. Berndt's (1962) *Excess and Restraint*, on the kuru-
stricken Fore, is a case in point. . . .

For example, the reader is asked to accept an event
involving a husband copulating with a female corpse while
his wife simultaneously butchers the body for the roasting
fire. Unfortunately for him, he is still occupied when his wife's
knife draws near, so that she cuts off his penis. Understandably disturbed, but displaying extraordinary equanimity,
he asks, "Now you have cut off my penis! What shall I do?"
In response, his wife "popped it into the mouth, and ate it. . . ."

This is harsh punishment for adultery, but could Fore
behavior, not to mention physiology, be so far removed from
what we and the rest of the world accept as conforming to
common standards? A double dose cannibalism with sadism
and necrophilia all at once makes it difficult to determine
which of the reader's sensibilities has suffered the most.[6]

Arens concludes with this charming understatement: "During the course of the investigation of this topic, a series of personal communications with Gajdusek (1978), which he was kind enough to respond to, although helpful, did not completely resolve this matter. However, while this book was in press, Gajdusek began to treat the cannibal notion more cautiously, since he is now quoted as saying that 'there has been so far no convincing evidence that the infection can be acquired by eating or drinking affected material or by any means other than direct invasion of the bloodstream.'"[7]

Yet again the pendulum swung, and according to a later *Science* magazine article in June 1986, Gajdusek claimed that, "The whole of Australia knows that these people are cannibals; it's 100 percent documented." And, also predictably by now, it was beneath his dignity to get involved. Gajdusek's reasons for never publishing those supposedly actual cannibalistic pictures he still claimed to possess was that they were "too offensive." He then made a disparaging comment about "desk anthropologists sitting around in chairs. If they just would get off their asses and go to New Guinea, they would find hundreds of cases."[8] Sterling language for a Nobel laureate, with subtlety not exactly the order of the day.

Where does this leave us? At a great moment in medicine or caught up in an academic imbroglio? Once again the reader will need to decide the controversy as she or he sees it on the basis of the evidence presented—or defer any conclusions pending further findings.

The Last Voyage of the *Mignonette*

In 1884 two respectable seamen, survivors of the yacht *Mignonette*, were sentenced to death for killing their young shipmate, one Richard Parker, in order to eat him. The macabre incident lives on in the leading case of *Regina* v. *Dudley and*

Stephens, familiar to students of Anglo-American law. Five judges comprising a Court of the Queen's Bench division held that one must not kill one's shipmates for nourishment, however hungry one might be.

On the centenary of the *Mignonette's* foundering, Professor Brian Simpson unfolded the history of this famous case in a fascinating and scholarly book, *Cannibalism and the Common Law, The Story of the Tragic Last Voyage of the* Mignonette *and the Strange Legal Proceedings to Which It Gave Rise.* A professor of law at the University of Chicago and the University of Kent, Canterbury, and author of *Introduction to the History of the Land Law* and *A History of the Common Law of Contract* among many other publications, Simpson is an avid maritime buff who signed on as a sailor on a square-rigger as preparation for writing his book on the *Mignonette.*

I am greatly indebted to his account for the following narrative.

As the reader is aware by now, there are two basic kinds of cannibalism, and with a crucial difference: (1) eating a corpse; (2) killing a human being in order to eat him or her. In short, the significant issue here is not cannibalism per se, but the decision to kill. Simpson addresses the problem in considerable detail in his discussion of the *Mignonette* trial over a century ago. From his perspective the *Mignonette* case was and is a central authority on what is called the "defense of necessity," its aspects raising in dramatic form the problem of reconciling the instinct for survival with a moral code that respects the sanctity of human life. If circumstances make it "necessary" for one person to kill another in order to survive, does the law permit such an act? Should it?

Simpson's legal synopsis states:

> Survival cannibalism may involve the actual killing of one or more of the survivors, with or without their consent, or the acceleration of imminent death by bleeding the dying

person to secure blood to drink. In the nature of things, it can never have been easy to establish what precisely did occur in the grim conditions of shipwreck or famine at sea, particularly because the remains, such as they were, could usually be thrown overboard before rescuers had an opportunity to inspect them. However, there are a large number of cases in which it seems quite clear that deliberate killing took place, and some others that look fairly suspicious; obviously these recorded cases represent merely the tip of the iceberg.

But before we return to the legal questions involved, we need to review the events and meet Tom Dudley, the captain, who attributed the yacht's loss to "stress of weather," still a standard category today for "pilot error" in air crashes; Edwin Stephens, ship's mate, navigator, and co-defendant; Ned Brooks, able seaman, who turned prosecution witness; and Richard Parker, ordinary seaman, orphaned and illiterate, who was the unfortunate victim.

The British yacht *Mignonette* was built in 1867 in Essex, and launched in August of that year. Primarily designed as a cruiser and fishing vessel rather than a racing boat, she had a very large spread of canvas; with the topmast set up, her rig rose some sixty feet above her deck. Very strongly constructed, with timbers typical for a forty-tonner, her cost was around £850. This same year one Richard Thomas Parker was born nearby—an ominous coincidence.

The *Mignonette's* only ocean voyage began on Monday, May 5, 1884, with the final destination being Sydney, Australia, a distance of around fifteen thousand miles. Dudley and Stephens hoped to accomplish this within four months or less. As misfortune would have it, the ship was in reality unseaworthy and in need of extensive repairs. Thus for all practical purposes she was doomed from the moment she put to sea. By July 5 the *Mignonette* was caught in a gale in the South

Atlantic; Dudley, in his own words, "made up my mind to heave to for the night and have a comfortable tea." As Simpson recounts:

> When he was about to give the order to luff up and bring the *Mignonette* around, it was too late. In his own words again, "I heard the Mate who was at the tiller cry out 'Look out.' I at once looked under the boom and saw a very high sea just about to brake over us. I caught hold and had the weight of same. On looking round me I saw all the lee bulwarks was washed away and heard the Mate cry out, 'Her side is knocked in; the boat she is sinking'—not very pleasant words at such a time. I hastened to windward to my horror to prove his words only too true—get the boat out was the thing in hand." (p. 47)

Dudley realized at once that the *Mignonette* was sinking and ordered the dinghy lowered. Within five minutes the yacht had disappeared under the waves. The nearest land, South America, was two thousand miles away. Simpson continues:

> Chilled at night and burned by the sun in the daytime, the survivors' principal problem was not hunger but thirst, and by July 13, they had all begun to drink their own urine, a standard technique for prolonging life in such conditions. It did little to alleviate thirst—from a physiological point of view, the earlier this is done, the more useful it is in delaying dehydration; but understandably the men would only begin to overcome their revulsion when conditions had became very bad. . . . (p. 58)
>
> It was probably during the night of Sunday, July 20, that Richard Parker drank a considerable quantity of salt-water and became violently ill. He suffered from diarrhea (which would dehydrate him still further) and lay groaning

and gasping for breath, becoming delirious and then coma-
tose.* (p. 59)

Dudley held a conversation with Stephens that Brooks
claimed he did not overhear. According to his own account,
Dudley said, "What is to be done? I believe the boy is dying.
You have a wife and five children, and I have a wife and
three children. Human flesh has been eaten before." Stephens
replied, "See what daylight brings forth." The point of killing
Parker before he died naturally was to secure his blood.

At about 8:00 A.M. Dudley pulled himself up by the dinghy's
improvised shrouds and looked around yet again for a sail;
nothing was to be seen. He told Stephens to be ready to
hold Richard Parker's legs if he struggled and then killed
him by thrusting his penknife into the boy's jugular vein,
catching the blood in the chronometer. (p. 66)

For the following four or five days the three survivors
lived off the remains of Richard. In Brook's words, "We ate
a good deal—I should think quite half—of the body before
we were picked up, and I can say that we partook of it with
quite as much relish as ordinary food."

With parts of a decomposing body in the small dinghy
conditions must have been extraordinarily repulsive.

But on the morning of the Tuesday, July 29, a sail was

---

*Simpson makes this interesting observation: "It is now known that
small quantities of seawater, particularly if combined with another fluid,
can be drunk safely over quite long periods, as long as the practice is begun
before the body has been allowed to become grossly dehydrated. This was
dramatically demonstrated by Dr. Alain Bombard, who succeeded in crossing
the Atlantic alone in an unprovisioned dinghy, living on seawater, fluid
obtained from fish, and plankton. His account, *Naufrage volontaire*, was
published in 1956, as the first assault on what he demonstrated to be a
myth. The crew of the *Kon Tiki* also found it possible to use seawater.
But in 1884 drinking any seawater was believed to be a sure recipe for
madness and death, and to this day it is generally supposed to be extremely
dangerous to consume any."

sighted. Dudley's account runs thus: "on the 24th day as we was having our breakfast we will call it Brooks who was steering shouted a sail—true a sail it was—we then all prayed the stranger will be directed across our path." Brooks, who first saw the sail at about 6:30 in the morning, did not grasp its reality immediately; he was talking to himself and praying, but he then cried out, "Oh, my God, here's a ship coming straight towards us." [It was the German sailing ship *Moctezuma*.] (p. 69)

Nevertheless, the three survivors seem to have been generally well satisfied with what had been done. Dudley was quite convinced that it had saved all their lives: "I feel quite sure had we not that awful food to exist upon not a soul would have lived until we were rescued." . . . All three were quite astonished at being arrested, Tom Dudley in particular. There is no reason to doubt that his astonishment was entirely genuine. (ibid.)

It was to be quite a trial. Simpson stresses these four possible points of mitigation. They became a matter of life or death for the defendants.

The first and most radical thesis is that in desperate conditions, such as those confronting Dudley and Stephens, men are reduced by circumstances to a state in which it is incongruous to think of laws applying at all. The second possible basis for a defense of necessity is that in desperate conditions the actions of men are not truly voluntary, hence individuals who act under the pressures of extreme circumstances are not responsible for what they never choose to do. A third theoretical basis for such a defense is more positive in form. In desperate conditions that present a choice between two grim alternatives, it is right to take any action, including killing, that will benefit the majority. The fourth basis for his term differs from the others in treating desperate circumstances as merely an excuse for wrongdoing, not a justification, and acceptable (if at all) only because of a recognition of the frailty of human nature.

If you are confused, so was the jury, which either couldn't or wouldn't make up their minds. "But whether upon the whole matter the prisoners were guilty of murder the Jury are ignorant and refer to the court." Lord Coleridge, caught between the demands of "traditional ritualism" (Simpson's term) and common humanity, compromised and passed sentence in these words:

> You have been convicted of the crime of wilful murder, though you have been recommended by the jury most earnestly to the mercy of the Crown; a recommendation in which, as I understand, my learned brother who tried you concurs, and in which we all unanimously concur. It is my duty however, as the organ of the Court, to pronounce on you the sentence of the law, and that sentence is that to the crime of which you have been convicted, you be taken to the prison where you came, and that, on a day appointed for the purpose of your execution you be there hanged by the neck until you be dead. (p. 239)

So the judges solemnly pronounced the action of Dudley and Stephens to have been premeditated murder. But the Queen, on the advice of her home secretary, pardoned them on condition that they served six months imprisonment (not at hard labor). To some it seemed an eminently wise arrangement. Separately confined in thirteen-by-seven-foot cells, but not wholly isolated as they would have been in more rigorous prisons, they began to serve their sentences for the murder of Richard Parker, and as a legal event, the case of the *Mignonette* was now concluded.

But at the same time Madame Tussaud's exhibition was reorganized to include what was described as an excellent waxwork portrait model of Captain Dudley.

Postscript. Dudley was to die at age forty-six of the bubonic plague in Sydney, Australia, the city to which he had set out on the last voyage of his yacht *Mignonette* fifteen years earlier.

Alleged Satanic Ritualistic Abuse (ASRA)

There is also the issue of alleged so-called satanic ritualistic abuse involving sex, murder, and cannibalism. Two examples. The first was reported by the *Los Angeles Times* in 1985:

> Statements from children have convinced investigators that a child molestation ring in the Bakersfield, [California,] area engaged in ritualistic murders of infants, including cremations, cannibalism, and the drinking of human blood, the Kern County Sheriff's Department said Thursday. The children say that as many as 77 adults were involved in the rings, with as many as 27 infants slain.
>
> Conceding that the physical evidence in the case is "very light . . . very minimal," Sheriff's Cmdr. Frank Drake said the department's investigation thus far is based largely on the statements of children who were allegedly forced to witness the rituals—and engage in the cannibalism—but allowed to live.
>
> "We believe those children," he said. "We really do. . . . We have the statements of several kids who independently gave us the same stories. They named the same kids. They described the same type of acts."
>
> "We do not have any bodies. We do not have any reports of missing children. Primarily we have the statements of those kids. . . . If we can put together a prosecutable case, we will."
>
> The detective bureau commander declined to number or identify the suspects in the case other than to say that they include "parents, friends, relations and neighbors" of the young victims. Drake said several of the suspects currently are in custody in connection with other allegations, which he declined to describe.

The investigation had started in July 1984, when detectives began looking into reports of what originally was thought to be a routine child molestation case. However, at least two members of the local legal community expressed doubts about the children's stories and concern over lack of physical evidence to back them up. One concern was that the children who first denied that they had been molested then changed their stories under repeated questioning and implicated "parents, social workers, and others."

In a letter asking for a state investigation, Carleen Radanovich, foreman of the Kern County grand jury, cited "the obvious mishandling of the children involved" and raised questions about "the methodology employed by law enforcement personnel." She also requested that three agencies be investigated in connection with the cases—the sheriff's department, the county welfare department, and the county district attorney's office. The California state attorney general's office, responding to this grand jury request, "agreed to review how the Kern County sheriff's department and other local agencies have handled child molestation cases that purportedly included the cannibalistic murders of infants."

The second example is from *Ms.* magazine, which published in its January 1993 issue an article purporting to be "a first-person account of cult ritual abuse." The pseudonymous author claims not only to have been repeatedly abused during her childhood by her family's multigenerational satanic cult, but to have witnessed the ritual slaughter of her infant sister, who was then cannibalized by the otherwise ordinary middle-class people in the cult. She claims her uncle explained it this way: "Babies deserve to die. Satan wants their blood, especially girl babies, because they taste so good."

Given the implications of all this let us examine the evidence a bit. In a later case against a man similarly accused, Kenneth Lanning, the FBI's leading authority on child abuse, testified that after ten years of trying to determine the veracity of such claims (including investigating several hundred of them), he has found no evidence whatever of ritualistic sex abuse, murder, and cannibalism.

Hysteria about satanic ritual sex abuse has reached such

proportions, he said, that "hundreds of people are alleging that thousands of offenders are abusing and even murdering tens of thousands of people as part of organized Satanic cults, and there is little or no corroborative evidence." Further, "There are those who are deliberately distorting and hyping this issue for personal notoriety and profit. Satanic and occult crime and ritual abuse of children has become a growth industry. Speaking fees, books, video and audio tapes, prevention material, television and radio appearances all bring egoistic and financial rewards."[9]

For Lanning, the explanations for the lack of evidence are unconvincing.

> In none of the multidimensional child sex ring cases of which I am aware have bodies of the murder victims been found— in spite of major excavations where the abused victims claim the bodies were located. The alleged explanations for this include: the offenders moved the bodies after the children left, the bodies were burned in portable high-temperature ovens, the bodies were put in double-decker graves under legitimately buried bodies, a mortician member of the cult disposed of the bodies in a crematorium, the offenders ate the bodies, the offenders used corpses and aborted fetuses, or the power of Satan caused the bodies to disappear.
>
> Not only are no bodies found, but also, more importantly, there is no physical evidence that a murder took place. Many of those not in law enforcement do not understand that, while it is possible to get rid of a body, it is even more difficult to get rid of the physical evidence that a murder took place, especially a human sacrifice involving sex, blood, and mutilation. Such activity would leave behind trace evidence that could be found using modern crime scene processing techniques in spite of extraordinary efforts to clean it up.[10]

Lanning concludes,

Until hard evidence is obtained and corroborated, the public should not be frightened into believing that babies are being bred and eaten, that 50,000 missing children are being murdered in human sacrifices, or that satanists are taking over America's day care centers or institutions. No one can prove with absolute certainty that such activity has *not* occurred. The burden of proof, however, as it would be in a criminal prosecution, is on those who claim that it has occurred. The explanation that the satanists are too organized and law enforcement is too incompetent only goes so far in explaining the lack of evidence. For at least eight years American law enforcement has been aggressively investigating the deals with large-scale baby breeding, human sacrifice, and organized satanic conspiracies.[11]

Noted Newport Beach, California, forensic psychiatrist, Park Dietz (whom we met in connection with Omeima Nelson) has also testified that he knew of no case in the country where allegations of ritual abuse turned out to be true. A forensic psychiatrist at Columbia University, Richard Gardner, concurs:

Although I have come across many parents who are convinced with 100-percent certainty that their children were subjected to such satanic ritual sex abuse, I have never personally seen any concrete evidence of their existence over the ten-year period in which I have been involved in these cases. . . .

In one case in which I was involved, a skull was found and was sent to a pathologist, in Washington, D.C., who reported that it was the skull of an opossum. This was not surprising because the skull was found in a place where boy scouts meet. Typically, the sexual orgies that allegedly take place in association with satanic rituals include people dancing naked, people wearing a wide variety of masks and costumes, the sacrifice of babies and animals, cannibalistic orgies in which people eat the remains of the slaughtered infants, drinking blood, eating feces, and drinking urine. Typically, as well, not one drop of blood is left at the site, not one piece of skin, not one shred of concrete evidence that such an orgy has actually taken place. In fact, what is typical of these cases is that there are absolutely no *adult* witnesses to any of these events, only children whose descriptions of them vary from rendition to rendition and from child to child. I am still looking forward to the day when I will actually interview an adult who will describe in detail actual observations of such rituals. . . .

Some of these people, I suspect, are just plain psychopaths and know that they are exploiting their prey. Others, I suspect, actually believe in the existence of what they are looking for.[12]

Why does all this happen? Gardner argues as follows:
1) We are a child-oriented society.

We are very much a child-oriented society. People from most other countries generally consider Americans to be extremely indulgent of their children. Many years ago, after a visit to the United States, the Duke of Windsor was asked about his impressions of Americans. His response (as closely as I can recall): "The one thing that impressed me most about American parents was the way they obey their children."[13]

2) Human beings are extremely suggestibile.

Anyone can be made to believe anything. [Joseph] Goebbels, Adolf Hitler's propaganda minister, operated on the principle that if one tells people a lie long enough—any lie—the vast majority will come to believe it. But we do not have to go that far back to see the same phenomenon operative in our leaders in recent years. Richard Nixon—ever with a straight face—denied to the end significant involvement in the Watergate imbroglio. Of course, he knew quite well the depth of his involvement and the extent of his duplicity. He also knew quite well that as long has he kept denying involvement, there would always be a significant percentage of the public who would believe him—compelling evidence of guilt notwithstanding.[14]

3) The rising tide of fundamentalism and condemnation of sexuality, with its obtuse if not predelusional allegations. Overzealous, false accusers often vicariously satisfy their own pedophilic impulses when they "dedicate themselves to stamping out sex abuse." Gardner refers to their "hidden agenda in the psychopathological realm . . . psychopathy masked as religiosity."

4) The incompetence of many "validators." According to Gardner, "There is an element of psychopathy apparent in a person who would see a three-year-old child for a few minutes and then write a note stating that a particular individual (the father, the stepfather, a nursery school teacher, etc.) sexually abused that child. It takes a defect in the mechanisms of conscience to do such an abominable thing."[15]* Gardner notes, "Competent examiners recognize the risks of the yes/no question and generally avoid it. They realize that little information is obtained from such a question. (This is something that attorneys and judges have yet to discover.)[16]

Related to this discussion are the considerable clinical, ethical, and legal controversies regarding so-called repressed memories. Elizabeth Loftus, a professor of psychology and law at the University of Washington, gives an overview in an article, "The Reality of Repressed Memories," in the May 1993 *American Psychologist*:

> Is it true that repressed material, like radioactive waste, "lies there in leaky canisters, never losing potency, eternally dangerous" and constantly threatens to erupt into consciousness? Psychotherapists have assumed for years that repressed

---

*One well-known example is the lengthy and expensive McMartin preschool trial in California, which ended in 1984 with no convictions. Accusations of child abuse had all been started by one schizophrenic mother.

memories are powerful influences because they are not accessible to consciousness. Is there evidence for this assumption? Is it necessarily true that all people who display symptoms of severe mental distress have had some early childhood trauma (probably abuse) that is responsible for the distress? With cutting-edge research now showing that mental distress involves neuronal and hormonal systems of a much wider scope than previously realized, should not other potential causes be at least considered? . . .

How common are repressed memories of childhood abuse? There is no absolute answer available. There are few satisfying ways to discover the answer, because we are in the odd position of asking people about a memory for forgetting a memory.

Concerning so-called "recovered memory therapy," Loftus says:

The therapist can be sued if the memories are shown to be false; several have already been filed. But perhaps the most serious danger is that true accusations of childhood sexual abuse will be trivialized or discredited. As the psychologist Carol Tavris [author of *The Mismeasure of Women*] puts it, "The reality of victimization of children is diluted by a chorus of insecure adults clamoring that they are victims, too."

Perhaps even more outspoken is Berkeley social psychologist Richard Ofshe, who shared a Pulitzer Prize in 1979 for his work in exposing the Synanon cult in California.

Ofshe points out that nobody has proved the concept of "robust" repression of memory, which is far different from traumatic amnesia (forgetting a single, horrendous event) or normal memory's denial and whitewashing. Robust repression requires that one repeatedly forget a recurring event— whether it's that your father kept raping you or aliens abducted you from the time you were three. "That's like forgetting you went to high school."

And while the American Psychological Association has created a task force to investigate the validity of recovered memories, *Newsweek* concludes pessimistically that, "There is little that any organization can do to stem the popular belief—fed by recovery groups, victimization books and talk shows—that many people have abusive memories in need of recovery."

15

Our Preoccupation with Cannibalism

The significant question is not why people eat human flesh, but why one group invariably assumes that others do.[1] . . .

What is unique is that our type of society gives succor to specialized interpreters of this exotic image whose function condemns them to a never-ending search for the primitive in order to give meaning to the concept of civilization.[2] . . .

By the paradox which is religion, in the sense that it often demands a suspension of everyday reasoning and standards, the very same notion of eating human flesh and blood is transformed into the most sacred of all acts. In this way, religious systems demonstrate their ideological superiority over other moral precepts and the human mind.[3]

William Arens, *The Man-Eating Myth*

Cannibalism, as I think the reader will by now agree, enjoys a rich life within the human imagination. In addition to everything we have already read, there is the whole realm of pure fiction. Our preoccupation is really startling. Our gods and spirits, stories and fairy tales, and millennia of documentation attest to it.

Beliefs that flesh equals strength, and blood equals life, are paleolithic. Consider blood. "The blood is the life," the Old Testament tells us; and says Mephisto in Goethe's *Faust*: "Blood is a very special fluid." Many drank their enemy's blood— as did the Gauls, Carthaginians, and Sioux. Hitler's bizarre, paranoid, and murderous delusions about blood and race, "that great system of Teutonic nonsense," resulted in Auschwitz and a war that almost did us all in. Just imagine that greatest mass murderer of them all in the possession of the atomic bomb (which he could have had, with the support of Jewish atomic physicists, beginning with Einstein and Lise Meitner*).

Consider the arts. As a theme in literature, and in pictorial art, cannibalism has a long and distinguished history, stretching back to antiquity. One form is involved in the tale of the cyclops Polyphemus, who, according to Homer, consumed two of Odysseus' sailors each evening for supper. We have met Kronos, who ate his children. A relatively modern example, a long-running Broadway musical, is the melodrama *Sweeney Todd, the Demon Barber of Fleet Street*, originally a fifteenth-century story of a "demon" barber in Paris. Mrs. Lovett, the chef extraordinaire, makes meat pies from human corpses. There is also a fifteenth-century illustration showing three beatific youngsters "dining on roast heretic in the Mouth of Hell."

---

*Said Einstein: "I do not consider myself the father of the release of atomic energy. My part in it was quite indirect. I did not, in fact, foresee that it would be released in my time. I believed only that it was theoretically possible. It became practical through the accidental discovery of chain reaction, and this was not something I could have predicted. It was discovered by Hahn in Berlin, and he himself misinterpreted what he discovered. It was Lise Meitner who provided the correct interpretation, and escaped from Germany to place the information in the hands of Niels Bohr." From my *Hitler's Secret*, p. 285.

Our Preoccupation with Cannibalism

Voltaire's Candide, just having survived a shipwreck and the Lisbon earthquake, escapes from the Inquisition with the aid of his true love, Cunégonde, and an old lady, who silences their complaints by relating how she came near to being eaten by starving Turks. By mercy of a half-blind fate, they began by merely cutting off one buttock of each available woman; the siege ended before any further samplings. "Now," concluded the old lady, "Stop bemoaning your misery and rejoice that you can sit on two buttocks."

A remarkable tale is Edgar Allan Poe's "Narrative of A. Gordon Pym of Nantucket," first published in magazine form in 1837. The events include a detailed rendering of the plight of starving castaways. Eventually one of the four survivors announces that he had held out as long as human nature could be sustained, and that it was unnecessary for all of them to perish "when, by the death of one, it was possible, and even probable, that the rest might be finally preserved." Splinters of wood are used for lots, and the man who proposed the scheme draws the fatal one. He is knifed to death; head, hands, intestines and feet are cut off and thrown overboard, and the rest eaten.

One of the most extraordinary and entertaining stories is Mark Twain's "Cannibalism in the Cars" (1866). Twain's essential genius was twofold. For one there is his dark side, in part a reflection of his personal misfortunes, including the death of his beloved daughter Susy ("The difference between Papa and Momma is, that Momma loves morals and Papa loves cats"), and bankruptcy. But there is also his mastery of the whimsical, the caricatural, the practical joke, and infectious humor. It closely relates to his earthiness, his interest in American folklore, his identification with the land, its people, and their language. Following are some excerpts from this story:*

*From *The Complete Short Stories of Mark Twain,* edited and with an introduction by Charles Neider (Garden City, N.Y.: Doubleday & Company, Inc., 1957). Reprinted with the permission of Charles Neider.

Cannibalism

On the 19th of December, 1853, I started from St. Louis on the evening train bound for Chicago. There were only twenty-five passengers, all told. There were no ladies and no children. We were in excellent spirits, and pleasant acquaintanceships were soon formed. The journey bade fair to be a happy one. . . .

At two o'clock in the morning I was aroused of an uneasy slumber by the ceasing of all motion about me. The appalling truth flashed upon me instantly—we were captives in a snow-drift! "All hands to the rescue!" Every man sprang to obey. Out into the wild night, the pitchy darkness, the billowy snow, the driving storm, every soul leaped. . . .

The fourth day came and went—and the fifth! Five days of dreadful imprisonment! A savage hunger looked out at every eye. There was in it a sign of awful import—the fore-shadowing of a something that was vaguely shaping itself in every heart—a something which no tongue dared yet to frame into words.

The sixth day passed—the seventh dawned upon us as gaunt and haggard and hopeless a company of men as ever stood in the shadow of death. It must out now! That thing which had been growing up in every heart was ready to leap from every lip at last! Nature had been taxed to the utmost—she must yield. RICHARD H. GASTON of Minnesota, tall, cadaverous, and pale, rose up. All knew what was coming. All prepared—every emotion, every semblance of excitement was smothered—only a calm, thoughtful seriousness appeared in the eyes that were lately so wild.

"Gentlemen: It cannot be delayed longer! The time is at hand! We must determine which of us shall die to furnish food for the rest!"

MR. JOHN J. WILLIAMS of Illinois rose and said: "Gentlemen—I nominate the Rev. James Sawyer of Tennessee."

MR. WM. R. ADAMS of Indiana said: "I nominate Mr. Daniel Slote of New York."

MR. CHARLES J. LANGDON: "I nominate Mr. Samuel A. Bowen of St. Louis."

Our Preoccupation with Cannibalism

MR. SLOTE: "Gentlemen—I desire to decline in favor of Mr. John A. Van Nostrand, Jun., of New Jersey." . . .

MR. VAN NOSTRAND: "Gentlemen—I am a stranger among you; I have not sought the distinction that has been conferred upon me, and I feel a delicacy—"

MR. MORGAN of Alabama (interrupting): "I move the previous question."

The motion was carried, and further debate shut off, of course. . . .

MR. HALLIDAY of Virginia: "I move to further amend the report by substituting Mr. Harvey Davis of Oregon for Mr. Messick. It may be urged by gentlemen that the hardships and privations of a frontier life have rendered Mr. Davis tough; but, gentlemen, is this a time to cavil at toughness? Is this a time to be fastidious concerning trifles? Is this a time to dispute about matters of paltry significance? No, gentlemen, bulk is what we desire—substance, weight, bulk—these are the supreme requisites now—not talent, not genius, not education. I insist upon my motion."

MR. MORGAN (excitedly): "Mr. Chairman—I do most strenuously object to this amendment. The gentleman from Oregon is old, and furthermore is bulky only in bone—not in flesh. I ask the gentleman from Virginia if it is soup we want instead of solid sustenance? If he would delude us with shadows? If he would mock our suffering with an Oregonian specter? I ask him if he can look upon the anxious faces around him, if he can gaze into our sad eyes, if he can listen to the beating of our expectant hearts, and still thrust this famine-stricken fraud upon us? I ask him if he can think of our desolate state, of our past sorrows, of our dark future, and still unpityingly foist upon us this wreck, this ruin, this tottering swindle, this gnarled and blighted and sapless vagabond from Oregon's inhospitable shores? Never!" [Applause.] . . .

We improvised tables by propping up the backs of car-seats, and sat down with hearts full of gratitude to the finest supper that had blessed our vision for seven torturing days.

Cannibalism

How changed we were from what we had been a few short hours before! Hopeless, sad-eyed misery, hunger, feverish anxiety, desperation, then; thankfulness, serenity, joy too deep for utterance now. That I know was the cheeriest hour of my eventful life. The winds howled, and blew the snow wildly about our prison-house, but they were powerless to distress us any more. I liked Harris. He might have been better done, perhaps, but I am free to say that no man ever agreed with me better than Harris, or afforded me so large a degree of satisfaction. Messick was very well, though rather high-flavored, but for genuine nutritiousness and delicacy of fiber, give me Harris. Messick had his good points—I will not attempt to deny it, nor do I wish to do it—but he was no more fitted for breakfast than a mummy would be, sir— not a bit. Lean?—why, bless me!—and tough? Ah, he was very tough! You could not imagine it—you could never imagine anything like it. . . . After breakfast we elected a man by the name of Walker, from Detroit, for supper. He was very good. I wrote his wife so afterward. He was worthy of all praise. I shall always remember Walker. He was a little rare, but very good. And then the next morning we had Morgan of Alabama for breakfast. He was one of the finest men I ever sat down to—handsome, educated, refined, spoke several languages fluently—a perfect gentleman—he was a perfect gentleman, and singularly juicy. For supper we had that Oregon patriarch, and he *was* a fraud, there is no question about it—old, scraggy, tough, nobody can picture the reality. I finally said, gentlemen, you can do as you like, but I will wait for another selection. And Grimes of Illinois said, "Gentlemen, *I* will wait also. When you elect a man that has *something* to recommend him, I shall be glad to join you again." It soon became evident that there was general dissatisfaction with Davis of Oregon, and so, to preserve the good will that had prevailed so pleasantly since we had had Harris, an election was called, and the result of it was that Baker of Georgia was chosen. He was splendid! Well, well—after that we had Doolittle, and Hawkins, and

McElroy (there was some complaint about McElroy, because
he was uncommonly short and thin), and Penrod, and two
Smiths, and Bailey (Bailey had a wooden leg, which was
clear loss, but he was otherwise good), and an Indian boy,
and an organ-grinder, and a gentleman by the name of
Buckminster—a poor stick of a vagabond that wasn't any
good for company and no account for breakfast. We were
glad we got him elected before relief came. . . .

Yes, it came one bright, sunny morning, just after election.
John Murphy was the choice, and there never was a better,
I am willing to testify; but John Murphy came home with
us, in the train that came to succor us, and lived to marry
the widow Harris. . . . Relict of our first choice. He married
her, and is happy and respected and prosperous yet. Ah,
it was like a novel, sir—it was like a romance. This is my
stopping-place, sir; I must bid you good-by.

Of course, Twain concludes: "I felt inexpressibly relieved to
know that I had only been listening to the harmless vagaries
of a madman instead of the genuine experiences of a blood-
thirsty cannibal."

We have already met and discussed Dracula, a somewhat
special case: the convergence of horror fiction and political
literature creates a new dimension out of the rather simple
vision of a mysterious Transylvanian castle in a foggy forest.
For in his Romanian homeland Vlad/Dracula lives on as a harsh
but just ruler, ready to aid his people against the Turks,
Hungarians, Germans, and whatnot. As Gabriel Ronay
observes in his *The Truth about Dracula*: The Romanians are
not alone either in having a selective corporate memory or
in their myth-making. Ask a law-abiding German senior
citizens and he will say that Hitler might have made mistakes
but he ended unemployment and built the autobahns. Mussolini
might have been a trifle vain and precipitate, but he made
the trains run on time. The Russians, who lost more people
in Stalin's senseless purges and as a result of his readiness

to pay any price for industrialization than they had in the Second World War, are beginning to remember the dictator as the great builder of socialism.

Lest the reader think this is all in the past, we offer a reminder that vampirism is indeed alive and well, so to speak, in our day. Thus in 1971 the Comic Code was changed to read: "Vampires, ghouls and werewolves shall be permitted to be used when handled in the classic tradition such as Frankenstein, Dracula, and other high calibre literary works by Edgar Allan Poe, Saki, Conan Doyle and other respected authors whose works are read in schools throughout the country." Marvel Comics came up with a Dracula series titled "The Tomb of Dracula" and "Dracula Lives," which did well throughout the seventies, as did someone known as Vampirella.

The writer Gore Vidal, in his *A Search for the King*, tells the story of a French troubadour who set out to find his king, Richard Coeur de Lion (Richard the Lion-Hearted). His journey is enriched with werewolves lurking in a dark forest, though they are actually highwaymen dressed in wolfskins who merely call themselves werewolves, thus exploiting the popular belief in such creatures. There is also a giant who speaks Latin and eats shepherd boys.

Fullerton, California, horror writer Bentley Little didn't know what he was getting into when discussing vampire legends with his Chinese-American girlfriend one night in 1991. She told him about a subject he had been unaware of: Chinese vampires. "She told me that instead of crosses, jade repels vampires and instead of garlic, willow branches will do the same," Little recalled. "I thought it was an interesting twist on a rather overdone subject, and I sort of took it from there." Indeed, his new paperback horror novel, *The Summoning*, is set in the dusty Arizona town of Rio Verde, where the sheriff discovers a body in an arroyo outside town. This is no ordinary stiff, however: The body is dry, having been purged of all blood and bodily fluids. Although the sheriff, the state police, and even the FBI think it's the work of a serial killer—a case that could be solved by routine investigation—an old Chinese woman knows better.

Consider fairy tales. The world over they bear witness to cannibalism, or at least a preoccupation with the idea. The giant in *Jack and the Beanstalk* eats little boys for breakfast; the witch in *Hänsel and Gretel* entices them into her house to cook them; Baba-Yaga in the Russian *Wasilissa the Beautiful* threatens to eat Wasilissa; in the Spanish *Pulgarcito* yet another little boy gets lost in the woods and wanders into the cottage of an ogre who devours children. In perhaps most famous of them all, *Little Red Riding Hood,* "grandma" is in fact a wolf (see Figure 12).

There is also Saint Nicholas, a.k.a. Santa Claus, that fat, white-bearded, jolly old man in his red suit who lives at the North Pole and makes toys for well-behaved children that he delivers at Christmas. The patron saint of Russia, Greece, and other countries, Santa and his legend go back to the fourth century, when a Bishop Nicholas in Myra (today Kale, Turkey) brought three children back to life after a butcher had cut them into chunks and pickled them.

Consider these continuing attractions in movies, books, and related fictional media. First some movies.

The werewolf craze began in 1935, with *Werewolf of London,* which starred Henry Hull as a scientist-turned-wolf who roams the streets of London. Over the years, some forty-five films and television shows have featured werewolves. Jean-Luc Godard's 1968 film *Weekend* revolved round an obsessive, aggressive Parisian couple who capped their exploits with a bout of cannibalism. Then we had the low-budget and rather amateurish film *The Night of the Living Dead,* which, despite disparaging critical reviews, has become a contemporary cult film. In one gruesome scene the director turns back Freud's calendar to the precultural stage as a young girl is transformed into a ghoul and then begins to dine on her mother. Thus in a single instance the taboos on incest, lesbianism, and cannibalism are violated in either explicit or symbolic form. "The critics, who are very often more concerned with technique than content, were genuinely amazed and dismayed by the film's attraction."

In the early 1980s we had an American pop art contribution, *Eating Raoul*. Described as being about "lurid sex, murder, cannibalism and greed," the film was also hailed as "the best comedy of the fall season." The *Boston Globe* declared,

> *Eating Raoul* gives itself away in the title. The fun is in watching it give itself away as a movie.
>
> The film describes the outlandish adventures of a prosperous (and totally mismatched) Los Angeles couple named Paul and Mary Bland. True, Paul seems bland. He's not the most dynamic leading man you'll ever see. His wife is far more imposing, tall and quite striking-looking. In fact, your first reaction on seeing the Blands is to wonder how on earth they ever got together. One of the things distinguishing the film is its casual treatment of its characters and their actions. Nothing and no one is explained in *Eating Raoul*. They just are.
>
> Once you accept *Raoul*'s shaggy dog quality, you can relax and accept it for the sheer sake of its own uninhibited superficiality. You don't bother wondering why the studiously asexual Blands (they wear bland pajamas and sleep in twin beds) happen to be living in an apartment house inhabited by continually partying swingers—or why Paul and Mary should be distinguished by ambitious entrepreneurial dreams that seem so totally at odds with their present jobs (Paul's a clerk in a liquor store, Mary's a dietician in a hospital).
>
> It's their dreams of opening their own restaurant—and the need for money for same—that leads the Blands into involvement with the neighboring swingers they so heartily loathe. Paul kills a swinger who invades the Blands'

apartment and tries to get at Mary. Then, while rifling through the invader's wallet, he. . . .

But I can't get into this scenario without reflecting how extraneous it is to the film's success. *Raoul's* strength is in its sheer shamelessness. It stipulates that stock Hollywood situations, dormant as they so often seem, still throb when kidded with some originality and wit. In one lively sequence, Paul corners an entire swinger's orgy in a giant hot tub, tossing an electric heater into the water and electrocuting the lot. The film shows the delightfully grotesque things that can result when narrative action is allowed to tyrannize character development.[4]

There is the 1990 French contribution, *Delicatessen*. It is an old plot: a young man gets a job and falls in love with the boss's daughter. Papa disapproves. It is also a new plot: Papa supplies an apartment building full of cannibals from his butcher shop in the basement, and the suitor is on the menu. Not necessarily the preferred son-in-law. The young man is blissfully ignorant of all this, gets the job as the apartment manager while the renters begin to salivate, and the daughter, a vegetarian who wears thick glasses, of course falls in love with him. No, I will not give the ending away.

Then we have these three American contributions. One film from the early 1990s was *Fried Green Tomatoes*. A chance encounter in a nursing home between a dowdy housewife and a spry octogenarian leads to an unexpected friendship. The latter tells the absorbing story of two women, the fiercely independent Idgie and the gentle Ruth, who lived half a century before in the "town" of Whistle Stop. Idgie stands up to the Ku Klux Klan, Ruth's abusive husband, and the charge of murdering him, all at a time when a woman's place was considered the kitchen.

The evil word "cannibalism" is never mentioned, but we get the idea with the disappearance of Ruth's husband's body and such lines as, "It's hogtying time," "The secret is in the sauce," and "The best damn barbeque in the whole state of Alabama."

Two other movies are 1993's *Alive* (discussed in the section on the Andes crash), and 1992's chilling, Oscar-winning *The Silence of the Lambs*. The evil Anthony Hopkins battles it out with the heroic Jodie Foster. (The two purveyors of evil in *Lambs* are combined in a real life person, one Ed Gein, a Wisconsin slayer.) The film grossed a small fortune. Asked in an uplifting ad, "The character you portrayed in *The Silence of the Lambs* enjoyed, ahem, fine cuisine. What about you?" Hopkins reassures us, "I'm really not a connoisseur. I used to like junk food quite a bit, but I eat more sensibly now. As for cooking, I can make an egg, porridge, a pot of tea. Otherwise, I'm hopeless." On another occasion, however, he commented, "I think that if I had not become an actor I would certainly not be a very nice person. I think I would have devoured myself alive."

Not everyone was as enthusiastic as the powers that be in Hollywood. Following the Oscar accolades, one newspaper reader, a probation officer, wondered whether it was a moral movie or a slasher flick; another commented that, as usual, the female victims were all women caught up in a sadomasochistic sexual phantasmagoria.

In addition to movies there are books. Tama Janowitz not so long ago published *A Cannibal in Manhattan*. In her version of the story, a "rich, ditsy socialite" named Maria Fishburn joins the Peace Corps and brings home a cannibal by the name of Mgungu Yabba Mgungu. She uproots him from the sunny tropical island of New Burnt Norton, where he had led a peaceful if somewhat boring life with his three wives. In Manhattan she sets herself up as his mentor—and wife. Mgungu, we are told, recounts his subsequent adventures in this volume.

Given these interests, there appears little to distinguish

Mgungu from the people he meets up with in New York, even though Maria makes him dress up in full native regalia (including a penis gourd, a chain of dogs' teeth, and human jawbone jewelry) for a fashionable cocktail party.

New York seems to attract man-eaters, and so we also have Jimmy Breslin's *He Got Hungry and Forgot His Manners.* Into this nightmare city come two strangers from a strange land, Father D'Arcy Cosgrove, an Irish missionary who has spent years in Africa preaching the evils of sex, and Great Big, a seven-foot Yoruba with an enormous appetite— occasionally for people. By an intentional mistake, they are assigned to an impoverished Brooklyn parish, across from Howard Beach. To make the tale complete, above and beyond them—and controlling their fate—are the wealthy women patrons of New Opportunity Partnership, who work hand in glove with the major developers, who, in their own way, are said to dine on human flesh. Like the cannibal who forgets his manners when he gets hungry enough, the voracious men who build and run New York City are eating the rest of us alive. Or something like that.

Roy Lewis's *Evolution Man or How I Ate My Father* (Pantheon, 1993) was reviewed in *Publishers Weekly.*

This wacky, tongue-in-cheek account of human evolution as exemplified by one family of cave dwellers calls to mind TV's "The Flintstones," but wordplay and intellectual satire mix with outrageous anachronisms to lift it well above a cartoon depiction. Originally published in England in 1960, the novel is set in prehistoric East Africa, where Father ("Woman's place is in the cave") extends the use of fire and champions technological progress, despite the opposition of Uncle Vanya, who believes that ape-men and ape-women should remain innocent children of nature. The clan includes Mother, proud homemaker in their new cave ("At last the girls will get a bit of privacy"); Uncle Ian, who speaks with a Scottish lilt and travels to China ("Go north, young man"); and Ernest, the inquisitive ape-boy narrator who mates with coy, romantic Griselda. An accidental parricide, followed by a dash of cannibalism, climax this inspired, delirious hymn to the human animal's noble climb from hominid savagery to murderous civilization.

We also have books about food and related customs in history and around the world. One is by Jeremy MacClancy, a fellow of the Royal Anthropological Institute in Oxford, whose *Consuming Culture* received the following review:

> This lively look at the capriciousness of our food choices and the effect that culture has upon our eating habits and preferences should appeal to anyone interested in food in its wider context. MacClancy investigates food not as a nutritional substance but as a social, political, and religious element in our lives. Displaying a broad knowledge of both food and culture and revealing a gentle, tongue-in-cheek sense of humor, he discusses taboo foods, vegetarianism, cannibalism, aphrodisiacs, mealtimes, table manners, etc., and how they have evolved in different cultures. Through anecdotal accounts of various civilizations, both historical and contemporary, MacClancy clearly demonstrates the impact that culture has on food and concludes that man is not what he eats, but what society makes him eat.

Another comment on this work is this: "He has stocked his larder with wittily recorded gastronomic esoterica, manners and foolishness from the British isles to the Amazon. These include horrific recipes for unspeakable morsels."

There is also Stanley Ellin's splendid and legendary "The Kitchen in the Restaurant Robinson," a must reading for the aficionado.

Finally, Margaret Visser, in her *Ritual of Dinner*, addresses cannibalism in general and transubstantiation in particular:

In this ritual, Christ, who is for believers both God and human, enters not only into the minds but into the bodies of the congregation; the people present at the table eat God. No animal and no new death is needed, no bridges required; God enters directly. . . .

The ceremony uses every psychological device defined by scholars of ritual. . . . As a meal, the Mass spans all of the meanings of eating at once—from cannibalism to vegetarianism, from complete fusion of the group to utterly individual satisfaction, from the breaking of the most fearful of taboos to the gentlest and most comforting restoration. All this and more is contained, expressed and controlled by ritual: dramatic movement and structure, song, costume, poetry, incense, gesture, and interaction; every one of the five senses is employed in the service of mystical experience. There are also tablecloths and napkins, candles, cups, plates, jugs, and wash basins. The Eucharist celebration is a dinner, at which table manners are entirely necessary.

In music the 1980s saw a band called the Fine Young Cannibals, with a record titled *The Raw and the Cooked* selling millions worldwide. Another group, Cannibal Corpse, is a "death-metal" band whose subject matter runs mostly toward excruciatingly detailed descriptions of freshly exhumed women. "Singer Chris Barnes's voice brings to mind a dog with a tight collar; the album covers depict skeletons feasting on entrails. No wonder a Cannibal Corpse T-shirt is the trendiest heavy-metal uniform around." Titles from their oeuvre include: "Eaten Back to Life," "Addicted to Vaginal Skin," "Necropedophile," "Meat-hook Sodomy," and "Vomit the Soul." The disc container thoughtfully carries this notice: "Parental Tape Advisory—Explicit Lyrics."

There was even an opera by the Brazilian romantic Antônio Carlos Gomes (1836-1896), *Il Guarany*, first performed in Milan's La Scala in 1870. It featured dark jungle grottoes, Indians attacking, poisoned arrows piercing the sky, and cannibals sharpening their knives. It is being revived in Bonn, Germany, in 1994.

Lest we forget, there are also jokes and cartoons. The former range from definitions, such as "one who really loves his fellow man" and Jack Benny's "a guy who goes into a restaurant and orders the waiter," to something like this: Sydney Smith, a British clergyman and author (1771-1845) called on the newly appointed bishop of New Zealand to bid him farewell before he set sail for his diocese. Bearing in mind the reputation of the native inhabitants as cannibals, Smith advised the bishop always to keep "a smoked little boy on the baconrack and a cold clergyman on the sideboard. As for yourself," he continued, "all I can say is that when your new parishioners do eat you, I sincerely hope that you will disagree with them."[5]

We have this event in the life of Georges Léopold Cuvier (1769-1832), a French zoologist who laid the foundation of the sciences of comparative anatomy and paleontology. Cuvier's outstanding achievement resulted from his ability to reconstruct whole skeletons from fragmentary remains through his understanding of the way in which any particular features entailed the presence or absence of other characteristics. This logical approach brought no little discomfiture to a group of students bent upon a practical joke. They broke into Cuvier's rooms in the middle of the night, and one, dressed in a devil's outfit with horns, tail, and hoofed feet, approached his bed, intoning, "Cuvier, I have come to eat you!" Cuvier sat up, gave him a single glance, and announced tactfully, "All animals with horns and hooves are herbivorous. You won't eat me." Then he promptly went back to sleep.

There are also these recent newspaper headlines:

——"DONNER PARTY" NOT EXACTLY THE TIME FOR TV DINNERS
——MAN WHO ATE DEMOCRATS IS REMEMBERED WITH RELISH BY COLORADO GOP

——JUNK FOOD IN THE ANDES
——VIDEO *DELICATESSEN* DISHES UP SOME DELICIOUS
   FOODS
——EATING MISSIONARIES? STRICTLY BAD TASTE

What is behind all this joking approach to cannibalism? Does the subject really lend itself to that? We will list some possible answers in the next chapter.

So much for fiction. Equally startling is our preoccupation with factual current incidences of cannibalism.

Item: *Newsweek,* January 18, 1993, under the headline "Cannibals of the Red Guard": "The accounts were harrowing. Principals killed in schoolyards by students, then cooked and eaten. Government-run cafeterias displaying human bodies hanging from meat hooks and dishing them out to employees. Even serving suggestions on how to make a party of cooking up 'counterrevolutionaries.' Documents smuggled out of China last week described atrocities of the Cultural Revolution in grotesque detail."

Item: *Baltimore Sun,* October 1993 headline: "Book documents cannibalism by Japanese troops." Based on an Associated Press report, the story declares that Japanese soldiers lost in Asian jungles during World War II cannibalized American and Australian war prisoners, native tribesmen, and their own dead to survive.

Toshi-yuki Tanaka, professor of political science at Melbourne University, Australia, delved into war crimes archives and records of interrogations of captured Japanese soldiers to uncover long-forgotten atrocities. He found that Japanese forces on Borneo slaughtered about 1,800 Australians and 700 British POWs in what is known as the Sandakan Massacre. The Japanese were trying to move the men 160 miles through the jungle to build an airfield in the town of Api. But after months of malnutrition, mistreatment, and starvation, the prisoners dropped out of the march one by one and were shot by their captors. "That tragedy was never disclosed in Japan, and was forgotten in Australia because the six Australian soldiers who survived were too traumatized to discuss it publicly after the war. It was overshadowed in the public consciousness by the atrocities committed by Japanese forces on POWs forced to build the Burma-Thai railway, immortalized in many memoirs and in the film *Bridge Over the River Kwai*."

Of 12,000 Australian POWs, 8,000 died in Japanese prison camps. Of the 7,000 captured by Germans and Italians, 240.

Tanaka also found evidence in archives of what had previously been a dark rumor in Japan—that soldiers abandoned in the jungle by the generals in Tokyo and cut off from supplies by advancing Allied troops turned to cannibalism to survive. "These documents clearly show that this cannibalism was done by a whole group of Japanese soldiers, and in some cases they were not even starving," Tanaka added. Some, their supply lines cut off, were genuinely hungry. But in other cases, officers ordered troops to eat human flesh to give them a "feeling of victory." They cannibalized American soldiers in the Philippines, and Australians and tribesmen in Papua New Guinea, the archives further disclosed. In most cases, Tanaka said, the troops ate the flesh of soldiers killed in battle and recovered from the jungle. But in some cases captured Allied soldiers were killed for food.

Japanese soldiers also ate their own dead comrades.

The above is contained in Tanaka's *Unknown War Crimes* (1994). He has previously tried to publish it in Japan, but it was deemed "too sensitive."

Last, some individual cannibals of international renown.

Issei Sagawa was mentioned earlier in passing. Here are a few more details on him. In 1981 Sagawa, a literature student at the Sorbonne in Paris, murdered a Dutch woman friend. After shooting her, he cut up the body with an electric carving knife, and then ate her flesh—some of it raw, some fried—over the next few days, taking breaks to stroll through the Bois de Boulogne. Paris police arrested him after he was spotted trying to get rid of a blood-stained suitcase. Later Sagawa was to write, "Cannibalism has been my obsession since I was very young. It is a pleasure lying deep in the human spirit."

Today, instead of being punished for his crime, Sagawa has become a minor celebrity in Japan. His letters to novelist Juro Kara were compiled in *Letters from Sagawa-kun,* a book that won for Kara the Akutagawa Prize, the country's most prestigious literary award for a new writer. There were also prize-winning plays, and Sagawa has become the object of a popular film. Discussing his cannibalism, Sagawa said the criminal behavior was the product of long incubation. At age three, he dreamed of being cooked with his brother; he recalled *Sleeping Beauty* as a fairy tale about a cannibal witch.

Sagawa was arrested and jailed in France before his transfer to a mental institution, where he was pronounced brain-damaged, insane, and unfit to stand trial. In 1984, however, the French allowed him to be transferred to a Japanese hospital after being persuaded to do so by his wealthy family. Psychiatrists there concluded that he had a "personality disorder" but not the brain damage alleged by French authorities. The Japanese said that he belonged in jail, not in a hospital. But French police insisted that the case against him was closed. According to a criminal psychiatry professor, part of the foulup in Sagawa's case stemmed from its psychosexual nature. "The Japanese justice system," he explained, "does not regard a sexual disorder as a mental illness" requiring treatment and detention.

"The public has made me the godfather of cannibalism, and I am happy about that," Sagawa wrote recently. "I will always look at the world through the eyes of a cannibal." He is said to be writing four books on the subject. He also wants to visit the United States and is indignant that "a free country like America" has continued to deny him a visa.

The Dutch weren't at all happy with his freedom, let alone the bizarre celebrity treatment. Thus their embassy in Tokyo protested a proposed trip to Hamburg to appear on German television, labeling it "a sick act." Newspapers in the Netherlands meanwhile sounded the alarm to keep Sagawa out of Holland.

Joanna Pittman, a reporter for the London Sunday Times, had tracked him down in Yokohama, living under a pseudonym, and discovered that he had a new Dutch girlfriend, a model who had recently returned to the Netherlands without knowing about his background. Pittman said Sagawa still thinks about women, and his "memoirs" of the murder read "almost like a food review."

"I still adore the sight and the shape of young Western women, particularly beautiful ones," Sagawa said. "I was a premature and unhealthy baby, I am ugly and small, but I indulge in fantasies about strong healthy bodies. I'm essentially a romantic."

Then we have Jeffrey L. Dahmer in Milwaukee, Wisconsin (see Figure 15). Is there something seriously deranged about a man who prefers to have intercourse with a dead body in preference to a beautiful young woman (or, in this case, man)? A white homosexual whose victims were mostly gay black men, Dahmer was arrested in 1991. The former chocolate factory worker once told Dr. Park Elliott Dietz, the psychiatric consultant for the FBI who also interviewed Omeima Nelson (and who has worked for Cher, Olivia Newton-John, and Michael Jackson), that if he had found an attractive man who would have maintained an agreeable sexual relationship, "he'd never have had to kill anyone." But because that didn't happen, he was driven to drugs and ultimately to killing many of the young men he met—having sex with them before and after death, and sometimes dismembering and eating part of the bodies. Dahmer also confessed to having fantasies about sex with corpses in his early teens, and to being fascinated by road kills and the insides of animals. He told the police that he ate only those young men he liked: he wanted them to become part of him (our old unification motive). Dahmer also collected the skulls of his favorites. "At one point they were human beings," he said; "then they were reduced to four or five garbage bags."

Dahmer murdered seventeen people. Tracy Edwards, one of the few who got away, testified that Dahmer told him to open the refrigerator: inside was a human head. Then Dahmer asked him to lie on the floor next to him: "He told me he wanted to listen to my heart beating." Dahmer liked hearts. He kept them in the refrigerator, too.

Dahmer, who pled guilty but claimed insanity, faced mandatory life imprisonment for each murder unless the jury found that he was indeed insane at the time of at least one of the crimes; in that case he would have been committed to a state mental institution, probably for life as well. Wisconsin does not have capital punishment.

Under Wisconsin law, the defense had the burden of proving that Dahmer was insane at the time of the crimes. The key issue in the trial was whether Dahmer could control his bizarre impulses. He had acknowledged repeatedly that he knew his actions were wrong, leaving a claim that he could not control himself as the only basis for an insanity defense.

Of the seventy potential jurors questioned, twenty-five stated they could not serve on a jury, allegedly because they would be sequestered for an expected three-week trial. One woman said she bred birds that would die if she was unable to hand-feed them daily. Others said they couldn't be away from home or work for three weeks. "Judge, I just don't have the stomach for it," another woman honestly admitted. All twenty-five were excused.

In closing arguments in Dahmer's sanity trial, district attorney E. Michael McCann had described Dahmer as a calculating criminal who chose his victims carefully and later, "to get rid of the evidence," had to dismember their bodies. "He's fooled a lot of people," McCann told the jury before it began deliberations. "Please, please don't let this murderous killer fool you."

Conversely, defense attorney Gerald P. Boyle, describing Dahmer as "the most desolately lonely human being imaginable," told the packed courtroom that the victims of his client's grotesque murder spree "died because of a crazy man, not an evil man." Boyle said, "No human being on the face of the Earth could do anything worse than he did. Nobody could be more reprehensible than this man if he's sane. The devil would be a tie. But he's sick; he isn't the devil."

"Cannibalism, drilling, necrophilia, showering with corpses . . . murders, lobotomies, defleshing, masturbating two or three times a day. . . . This is a sick boy here, plenty sick," Boyle added. "And anybody who says he's just mean and evil is trying to sell you something that can't be sold. This is sickness."

There were disputes among the clinicians who dealt with the case, and the chief psychologist for the Milwaukee County Mental Health Complex asked, "What do you think about a person who kills people and has sex with their dead bodies and eats some of them—do you think he's nuts?" Another psychologist, Dr. Becker, opined that, "Jeffrey Dahmer is a tragic figure. He in a sense was an incredibly lonely person who believed that nobody would elect to stay with him. He did not enjoy the act of murder. . . . He felt so powerless."

Much of the trial consisted of a duel between prosecution and defense through the testimony of psychiatrists and other experts. In his closing argument, McCann attacked the credibility of the defense experts and argued that because Dahmer planned the killings, he should be responsible for them and imprisoned. Dietz, shocked at how "forthright and even analytic" his client was, said his own conclusions were firm: unlike a Ted Bundy or other notorious killers, Dahmer was driven not by a desire to kill and induce suffering, but rather by a desire to have sex with men. "Killing was not the objective," Dahmer claimed on the TV newsmagazine "Dateline." "I just wanted to have the person under my complete control to do with as I wanted." The killer was sexually deviant, but not insane. "I found him responsible for a number of things, but there were two points that had the greatest impact for public perception or at least a jury," Dietz said. "And they were that he used a condom, and that he had no particular desire or interest to kill them and had to get himself drunk to overcome the revulsion of the killing."

After twelve days of some of the most grisly testimony ever heard in a courtroom, the Milwaukee jury was asked to decide whether the confessed serial killer Jeffrey L. Dahmer was a depraved monster driven by lust or a pathetic victim of a mental illness that gave him an "insatiable appetite" to have sex with the dead.

They concluded that he was legally sane, and he was consequently ordered to spend the rest of his life in prison. (Dahmer was sentenced to serve 957 years.)

According to *People* magazine,

> Once a month, Lionel and Shari [Dahmer's father and step-mother] make the eleven-hour drive from Akron to see Jeff in the sunny visiting room at Columbia [state prison]. Jeff, who has gained more than thirty pounds in prison, passes the time studying art books and Audubon bird drawings and listening to tapes of Schubert, Gregorian chants, and humpback whales.

By early 1994, Dahmer had received over 12,000 letters from around the world.

We also have three recent cases from the former Soviet Union.

First, in 1980, one Nikolai Dzhumagaliev was sent to a

psychiatric hospital in Tashkent, the capital of the Central Asian republic of Uzbekistan, after being found guilty of murdering and eating seven women. While being transported from Tashkent to an airport in another city in 1989, he fled from two escorting medical personnel and remained on the loose until recaptured two years later.

Then we have a story of sex and cannibalism in the provincial town of Kazan. The ringleader in the affair, one Alexei Sukletin, a night watchman at a garden farm, recruited his lover, Madina Shakirova, twenty-five, to help him in the gruesome venture. The first victim was identified as a friend of Shakirova. The watchman had sexual intercourse with the woman, then, in the presence of his lover, smashed in her head with a hammer. The watchman and Shakirova ate part of the body, then buried the rest in the garden. Sukletin killed several other women, including an eleven-year-old girl, in the same way. Along the way Sukletin and Shakirova treated some of their unsuspecting friends to meals of human flesh. "The kind Madina sold several kilos of tender meat for kebabs at a token price. . . . One of them vomited in the prosecutor's office when it was explained to him why the meat had such an unusual aroma." Sukletin was executed. Shakirova got a fifteen-year prison term.

Last, but surely not least, we meet Andrei Romanovitsch Chikatilo, compared to whom "Dahmer resembles a choirboy." Since his conviction in fall 1992, at least three books have been rushed into print: *The Killer Department, Comrade Chikatilo,* and *Hunting the Devil.* "If anyone deserves such overkill, he does," a reviewer concluded.

The serial torturer, murderer, mutilator, and cannibal, born in 1936, was an ex-serviceman (stationed in East Berlin, he learned to speak German fluently), father of two, grandfather, party member, engineer, and schoolteacher who wrote articles about education. The confessions, in his own handwriting and dictated from an almost photographic memory, are a monstrous document of sadism, necrophilia, and cannibalism. Chikatilo admitted to having butchered at least twenty-one women, twenty-one boys, and ten girls between 1978 and 1990.

"The choreography of horror was always the same: suffering from impotence, he imitated the sex act with a knife—thirty times, fifty times he stabbed. He cut out hearts and uteri, ate genitals, bit tips of tongues. Then he danced around the murdered and hissed, 'I am a red partisan.' "[6] Chikatilo also gouged out his victims' eyes and stuffed their bodies with dirt. "His goal was a sexual act," said chief investigator Amirkhan Yandiyev. "When he tried to rape his victims, and found he couldn't complete the act, then he became sadistic." Chikatilo himself attributed his murderous rages to sexual inadequacy; the clinicians agreed. He also blamed the repressive Soviet system, stating that his older brother had been eaten by hungry peasants during the 1930s and that he himself almost died from starvation following World War II.

November 20, 1990, was a gray winter afternoon in the town of Nowotscherkassk. Chikatilo was on his way to buy beer when police arrested him. He did not protest, and placed his arms almost obligingly into the handcuffs. One officer remembered the anticlimactic finale: "He behaved like a man who had waited a long time for this moment." Perhaps so; during the year he had slaughtered nine persons—some almost in front of the police; the Rostov militia had reported that, "The murderer is now playing *va banque*."

Thus ended the greatest manhunt in the history of the Soviet Union. It had lasted twelve years and involved 127 detectives, an entire specially created section of the Moscow district attorney's office, and hundreds of informers and other persons used as baits. In addition, there were 165,000 blood tests made, 500,000 individuals checked, and five million identification cards reviewed.

The hunt also engendered a terrifying dynamic of its own. The Soviet criminal justice system reflected the country's backwardness and dictatorial methods. A lack of forensic know-how and expert forensice clinicians, antiquated equipment, and plain incompetence resulted in a continuous botching of the investigation. Moreover, during the pre-glasnost era crime was considered a capitalist phenomenon and was seldom publicized in the Soviet Union. As a result, Rostov-on-Don residents had not been warned that a maniac was killing young women and children in their city of 1.4 million about 600 miles south of Moscow. It was not until 1989 when, thanks to Gorbachev's policy of openness, the public was at last made aware of what was going on.

Chikatilo was once imprisoned for three months but released, apparently because his blood type, A, did not match the AB type found in the sperm on the victims' mutilated bodies. The Moscow Health Ministry later attributed this to the murderer being an "abnormal secretor," i.e., the ministry claimed that Chikatilo's sperm, sweat, and saliva had a different blood type than his blood. This theory of "biological exceptionalism" is not shared by the international medical community. It is much more likely that the blood testing was done sloppily. Chikatilo also escaped on another occasion, in 1985, not surprisingly: as an informer of the militia he was one of the posse tracking himself.

In April 1992, in Rostov, the trial began. Held inside a steel cage like a wild animal (see Figure 14), Chikatilo blared the Internationale, and also exposed his buttocks, screaming, "I am pregnant!" The three-judge panel had ordered paramedics to sit in the courtroom and an ambulance to wait outside because of the impact of such testimony on victims' families. Once the ambulance crew rushed into the second row of spectators to take the blood pressure of an elderly woman who had sobbed for nearly two hours, then fainted. They gave her an injection and took her to a hospital. Nearby, another woman slumped against a court officer and covered her tear-streaked face with her hands. Chikatilo kept his shaved head bent forward and his eyes on the floor as a judge read details of one of the fifty-three acts of murder, mutilation and cannibalism attributed to him.

"I understand why you cannot look into the eyes of the families of the victims, but I order you to look at the pictures," Judge Leonid Akubzhanov said as pictures of a girl's corpse were held up to Chikatilo's six-foot-square cage.

Russian psychiatrists declared Chikatilo to be abnormal but sane, thus precluding any mental institutionalization. President Boris Yeltsin rejected an appeal for clemency. Chikatilo once said, "I know I have to be destroyed. I understand I was a mistake of nature, a mad beast." According to the Interfax news agency in Moscow, a firing squad concurred in February 1994.

Conclusion

The worst insult which could be made to a Samoan was to talk of roasting him—which meant that missionaries had to guard their tongues and leave hellfire out of their sermons.

Reay Tannahill, *Flesh and Blood*

After all, if you believe in Nessie, the Loch Ness monster, or in Bigfoot, no big deal; but if you go to a psychic healer to remove a cancer, you are dead. And the intellectual climate that fosters one fosters the other.

The Skeptical Inquirer

The Diyarbakir gendarmerie commander reportedly told Leyla Zana, a Kurdish member of parliament in Turkey, "You are my enemy. I will only be satisfied when I have spilt your blood. Even if I killed you and drank your blood, I still would not be content. I am going to kill you."

From a 1993 investigation
by Amnesty International

The death figure in the ghetto still hovers around 5,000 per month. A few days ago, the first case of hunger-cannibalism was recorded. In a Jewish family the man and his three children died within a few days. From the flesh of the child who died last—a twelve-year-old

boy—the mother ate a piece. To be sure, this could not
save her either, and she herself died two days later.

Nazi propaganda division,
Warsaw, March 21, 1942

Before arriving at our conclusions and implications, let us
summarize our discussion so far. We began with a chapter
entitled "By the Dawn's Early Light," reviewing facts, prob-
abilities, and guesses about prehistorical cannibalism. This was
followed by some examples of recorded historical cannibalism
up to our time, to give the flavor of the subject, so to speak.
Next we looked at a geographical distribution. Finally we
stressed caveats concerning the frequently pronounced lack
of reliable evidence, resulting in numerous falsifications, mis-
interpretations, misconceptions, and often rather acrimonious
controversies by laymen and anthropologists alike. Horror
stories tend to wipe away rationality. Let us therefore emphasize this point one last time: we need to judge for ourselves
what is scientifically compelling and what is not. What do
the data, fairly read, mean? What conclusions do they reasonably support?

While on some issues persons of similar integrity and intelligence can reasonably differ, on others they cannot. Failing
to meet factual criteria, common sense, and customary standards of determining reality, such claims should raise one's
index of suspicion correspondingly.

We continued by describing the different kinds of cannibalism. I have found it most useful and lucid to classify them
according to *motivation,* and while these major motivational
groups can exist in pure form, they very often overlap. Let
us next briefly review them. First and foremost there is hunger,
above all a consequence of famines, natural or man-made, or
disasters on land or sea. A crucial distinction to which we
will return is that of eating an already dead person, or killing
him/her in order to do so.

Conclusion

We next looked at magic. What does the cannibal think he is eating or, in the case of blood, drinking? If he is starving, it may well be just meat or fluid; but in magic he believes he is incorporating one or more of the victim's characteristics—say courage, or strength, or health, or virility, or sorcery. Thus before beginning a caravan the Ovimbundu in southwest Africa are said to have practiced cannibalism to ensure good luck on their journey. The placebo effect, so well known in psychological research, alone probably accounts for a significant reinforcement of the already existing belief.

Then we reviewed a very broad category: ritual, religion, and sacrifice. Many kinds of cannibalism were hedged with ceremonial and religious regulations and customs. Ludovic Zamenhof, the brilliant and humane creator of the artificial language Esperanto, summarizes one crucial elementary for consideration:

> The majority of human beings need for their lives some submission to external rules, without which they would feel as if they were hanging in the air; not only some concrete ethical programme, but also some kind of customs, festivals, ceremonial arrangements in the most solemn of moments of their lives and at death; they can have all this only when they are registered as members of a definite religious community.[1]

Primitive tribes worshiped spirits of many kinds: natural powers such as sun, moon, earth, lightning; tribal founders and ancestors; basic life-cycles like birth, puberty, illness, and death. Unable to cope with often unknown forces, they assigned identity and power to spirits, and innumerable related rituals became part of everyday life. After appropriate ceremonies, the dwelling place of such a spirit was often believed to be in a carving. From here it was but one more step to offer flesh or blood, of man or animal, to feed the spirit and thereby gain his support. Men—or some exalted ones among them—next claimed the privilege or duty to partake.

Continuing with motivational factors, we mentioned punishment, total annihilation by what might simply be called one form of execution. The *corpus delicti* (the body of the crime) becomes, so to speak, the *corpus delicati*. There have always been societies that taught their members to be merciless toward real or imagined enemies, on the battlefield or elsewhere. By all indications it takes an amazingly short period of time for the average person to become inured to such brutality, especially if advocated or required in the name of some belief or ideal. Eating the enemy also means literally to derive strength from his annihilation.

One wonders about the indifferent, whose only concern is food, and who maintains that plant, animal, and man are interchangeable. He is closely related to the gourmet, for if the issue is merely nourishment, why not prepare the food according to the best in known culinary art? Unification with the magic component of food seems, psychologically speaking, relatively benevolent, at least in spirit.

We finally come to the mad and the sadist. The explanation for the mad can be simple: there is such a thing as insanity. But what about the person starving to death? Might he be "insane"? Or does he suffer from "diminished capacity"? How would we know? And what would be the moral and legal implications?

As for the sadist, clinically speaking there are many of them in this world, sexual and otherwise, and what they can do to us is not entirely left to our imagination. But they are of no particular interest except to the psychologist, who should study them, and the judge, who should take them out of circulation. Of profound interest to us all, however, is the average person when he or she behaves sadistically. The Doboduras in New Guinea "always try to wound a man so that they can slowly torture him to death, keeping him tied up in a small hut and cutting out pieces of meat only when they want to eat, eating him practically alive. So skilled are they that they can sometimes retain him for more than a week, until he is almost dead, then they chop a hole in the side of his head and scoop out the brains."

We next looked at the related subject of werewolves, witches, and vampires. At one time anyone hated in life by man or church, and for whatever reason, was a good candidate for being accused of being one of these. For most it would be a death sentence, and often a horrible one. Werewolves (and other werebeasts) were usually thought to have achieved their transformation by a pact with the devil. Witches tended to be accused as murderesses, child eaters, and evil sexual temptresses incarnate. Vampires, with their canine teeth and bloodsucking, found their patron saint—if that is the correct term—in Vlad/Dracula. They were not confined to Transylvania, making their appearance in many other countries. Thus, for example, according to an old Japanese folktale, the two-tailed demon vampire cat of Nabeshima sucked the blood of a beautiful maiden and assumed her form in order to bewitch her lover, the prince.*

In the medieval mind there also existed something called the succubus, a female demon believed to have sexual intercourse with sleeping men. But as Ronald Siegel, a neuropsychologist at the University of California at Los Angeles, perhaps disappointingly points out in his challenging book *Fire in the Brain,* in the final analysis succubi, like vampires and other

---

*To bring the reader up to date, a 1993 *Weekly World News* contained this story: "Mobile, Ala.—A howling, snarling werewolf escaped from a foreign freighter, savagely bit seven cops and turned a police cruiser over before he was captured in a darkened alley near the docks. Heavily armed police are now guarding the wolfman around the clock at an undisclosed location in Mobile County until he can be placed back aboard the ship he escaped from." When questioned how one might get in touch with the author of this article, a Mr. Shelly, to verify it, the tabloid's editor, Eddie Clontz, replied it might be difficult since Shelly was in Venezuela "covering our vampire beat."

spirits, are invading only the mind, not the bedroom. Siegel adds: "My opinion of these 'scientific reports' was best illustrated by the location I assigned them on my bookshelves. I placed the books, with such titles as *Phone Calls from the Dead* and *Journeys Out of the Body*, next to my collection of Woody Allen. . . . No one was able to explain a séance described by him in which 'a table not only rose but excused itself and went upstairs to sleep.' "

How could reasonable people believe such things? While painful to admit, the evidence here is overwhelming: easily. They always have and still do today. The omnicredulity and scientific illiteracy given the underwhelming evidence is remarkable. As Tannahill concluded, "The supernatural is still alive and well and living in Occultsville. . . . Astrology, dreams, witchcraft, and satanism are all aspects of that single area of ignorance. So, of course, is religion."

There has never been a shortage of bizarre belief systems. If you doubt this, you will now hear something interesting. These are the results of a June 1990 Gallup "Mirror of America Survey" of 1,236 adults, i.e., presumably rational human beings in the late twentieth century:

• One of every four Americans believes in ghosts.
• One of every four Americans believes he has had a telepathic experience in which he communicated with another person without using the traditional five senses.
• One in six Americans has felt he has been in touch with someone who has died.
• One in ten claims to have seen or been in the presence of a ghost.*

---

*Elvis Presley, who asserted that he had slept with over a thousand women *before* his marriage, lost interest in this activity as he became increasingly drug-addicted. His later comment, "A bed is for sleeping," didn't stop the mass hysteria following his death, including women who claimed to be making love to his ghost.

- More than half believe in the devil, and one in ten claims to have talked to him.
- One in seven says he has personally seen a UFO.
- Three in four at least occasionally read their horoscopes in a newspaper, and one in four says he believes in the tenets of astrology.*

There is an abundance of true believers who, with what can mercifully be described as comic book simplicity, assert the existence and special implications of the Bermuda triangle and channeling, black cats and the number 13, creationism and cold fusion, iridology and lunar effects on oysters, palmistry and tea leaves, Shirley MacLaine and reincarnation, the Oedipal complex and penis envy. Increasingly contemptible news media editorial choices emphasizing such nonsense are predictable; you know how it goes: "The public is making us do it." It all seems basically to have something to do with primitive explanations of human behavior and the notion that humans are free to think and do anything they want. This encourages people not to ignore their limitations but to defy them: the dominant myth is that the old can grow young, the indecisive can become leaders of men, housewives can become glamour girls, glamour girls can become actresses, the slow-witted can become intellectuals. One is reminded of Einstein's absorbing conclusion: "Two things are infinite, the universe and human stupidity. . . . and I'm not yet sure about the universe." Compare this from the winter 1994 issue of the *Skeptical Inquirer* by Robert Park, a physics professor:

> Even a Ph.D. in physics, I should warn you, is no inoculation against irrational beliefs. This past summer, an organization

---

*I am delighted to have my horoscope shared by that fellow Pisces Einstein; conversely, and unfortunately, my horoscope is also shared by the Nazi chief of the Gestapo, Reinhard Heydrich (and for all I know, Caligula, Attila the Hun, or Jack the Ripper).

calling itself the Institute of Science, Technology, and Public Policy, headed by John Hagelin, a Harvard-trained particle theorist, launched a two-month, $4 million experiment to reduce crime in Washington, D.C. Hagelin explained that a thousand trained experts would generate a powerful anti-violence field by meditating in unison. The field would not only reduce crime by spreading tranquility throughout the city but also make President Clinton more effective in running the nation.

You will not be at all surprised to learn that the expert mediators, all followers of the Maharishi Mahesh Yogi, declared the experiment to have been an enormous success— experimental proof of the creation of an anti-crime field by meditation. They seemed genuinely convinced that they had succeeded, even though the murder rate in Washington soared to a record level during the period of the experiment. The murders, they cheerfully explained, were less brutal. They requested $5 million in public funds to continue meditating.

To return to our review, we finally analyzed in some detail three special cases: one of medical, another of legal, and a third of psychological interest.

The kuru virus controversy may be a regrettable affair, but it is hardly the stuff of a Greek tragedy. While basically a matter of fact, it is piquant since it involves a Nobel Prize winner. (And there is the HIV connection, wherever that may lead.) Gajdusek does not make the most elegant arguments, and his style tends to go off the scale. (François Rabelais, that phenomenally polymathic monk and physician, had this to say to those who questioned his inventive *Gargantua and Pantagruel*: "If you don't believe me, may your ass fall off.") It is possible Gajdusek is right about the cannibalism of the Fore, possibly not. Take your pick from the evidence you have seen. You can guess mine.

The *Mignonette* case and the legal issues involved make for a very different story. The problem here is not cannibalism per se, but killing. Professor Simpson outlined four theoretical defense-of-necessity arguments: (1) laws don't apply at all, (2) there is diminished responsibility, (3) the majority is benefited, and (4) behavior can be excused but not justified.

The second point deserves some consideration. How "normal"—and therefore responsible for their actions—are those caught in the grip of starvation? Insanity and diminished capacity, difficult concepts at times, are generally recognized in extenuation or mitigation. But where do we draw the line?

Simpson addresses this point concerning our old acquaintance Alferd Packer:

> There is, however, one other possibility, which is that Alferd himself never actually knew what had happened out there in the wilderness, having been reduced by the combined effects of his long-standing epileptic condition (coupled possibly with the effects of lead poisoning) and by privation almost to automatism. His own retelling of his experiences in 1893 was punctuated by a fit, of which he was quite unaware. . . . His story was dreamlike in quality: "There I was alone in the middle of my dead companions, and I had killed one of them. It must have been then that I began to get leery." . . . Eventually he was overtaken by a frenzy to get away, and he left, carrying fire in a coffee pot; how long he stayed near Dead Man's Gulch he did not know. His condition could well have been aggravated by starvation.[2]

Stewart, the author of our story of the Donner Party, has his reservations, too (though the issue here is not killing):

> Surely the necessity, starvation itself, had forced them to all they did, and surely no just man would ever have pointed at them in scorn, or assumed his own superiority. "There but for the grace of God, go I!"—such an attitude is the only one which a decent man can assume in the case.
> Even the seemingly ghoulish actions involved in the story

may be rationally explained. To open the bodies first for the heart and liver, and to saw apart the skulls for the brain were not acts of perversion. We must remember that these people had been living for months upon the hides and lean meat of half-starved work-oxen; their diet was lacking not only in mere quantity, but also in all sorts of necessary vitamins and mineral constituents, even in common salt. Almost uncontrollable cravings must have assailed them, cravings which represented a real deficiency in diet to be supplied in some degree at least by the organs mentioned. If Keseberg said that human liver was better than lean beef, most likely a starved body more than a perverted mind was speaking.

I myself am a man somewhat squeamish in dietary habits; I am not comfortable in the presence of tripe, and pass with a certain feeling those little shops in the back-streets of French towns where one sees displayed the freshly flayed side of a horse. And yet this horror of cannibalism seems to me disproportionate. Humanity may fall into many worse degradations.

In the *Mignonette* affair, as the reader will recall, Dudley and Stephens were sentenced to be hanged, though in 1886 the Queen, in the view of some very wisely, pardoned them. Basically survival cannibalism involving killing still remains premeditated murder under the law in Great Britain and the United States.

Finally we discussed alleged satanic ritualistic abuse supposedly involving cannibalism. Children are often said to partake in the proceedings, in which babies are not only being eaten but, believe it or not, bred for this purpose.

There seems to be a significant preponderance of opinion among respected experts that in the vast majority of cases convincing evidence simply does not exist, despite extensive efforts by the FBI and many other agencies and individuals to find it. We are thus confronted, once again, with yet another instance of social hysteria—and, as usual, one involving deliberate distortions and accusations for personal notoriety and profit. Thus we have so-called cult-crime law-enforcement officials. As Robert Hicks put it in his *Police Pursuit of Satanic Crime*: "The law-enforcement model of cult crime exaggerates levels of satanic and cult involvement, is derived largely from news articles, and is rife with errors and ignorance. . . . Fundamentalist Christianity drives the cult-crime model. Cult officers invariably employ fundamentalist rhetoric, distribute fundamentalist literature . . . and sometimes team up with clergy to give satanism seminars."

In the previous chapter we also looked at some jokes, cartoons, and amusing newspaper headlines about our subject (as well as a Mark Twain story). How does such a grim topic lend itself to this approach? Isn't funny cannibalism an oxymoron? Humor is a complex phenomenon. As someone once concluded, "If humor is, as it has been interminably touted to be, tension-releasing, thought-clarifying, and otherwise medicinally wondrous, it behooves us to discover what we can of how, when, and why it happens."

One review of humorists such as Charlie Chaplin and Groucho Marx suggested that two things stand out in one's mind after reading them: first, the preponderance of testimony in favor of a genial as opposed to a derisive view of instinctive laughter, and second, the frequent recurrence of the idea that humor is closely associated with pain. In addition to a purely enjoyable and entertaining function, much of humor thus appears also to serve as a vehicle to defuse other emotions, such as aggression and defense (as it happens, the theme of my doctoral dissertation). We can speculate a little more, and it seems to me that there may well be the additional elements of awkward discomfort, stress, disbelief or inability to handle the truth, passive-aggressiveness, a making the best of a bad situation, and plain shock value.

Cannibalism

Another way of organizing our major data could be that of a table of basic considerations.

Cannibalism and Its Implications

Category	Primary Motivation	Example	Ethical Considerations	Legal Considerations
Eat the already dead	Hunger/ Thirst	Andes crash	None	Minor/ None*
Kill to eat	Hunger/ Thirst	*Mignonette*	?	Major†
Eat the already dead	Social custom	Unification cannibalism	Local belief system	None
Kill to eat	Social custom	Punishment cannibalism	Local belief system	None

*A lawyer advised me that he is unaware of any specific prohibition but that one might expect some low-level charge, e.g., defacing a corpse.

†See the four legal defense-of-necessity arguments mentioned under the *Mignonette* discussion; the law considers them immaterial. A colleague of mine, however, raised the question of whether it could be argued that there may in fact be a legal *obligation* to sacrifice someone for the benefit of the majority, given that, say, the captain of a ship or an airplane has such a duty to his passengers. Take this scenario: a surfacing U-boat in wartime is surprised and attacked by enemy planes. The captain crash-dives, even though this will lead to the certain death of the sailors left on the deck. Not only did he do the right thing, i.e., saving the vessel and majority of the crew, but he would have been courtmartialed had he not done so. Is a military emergency, then, so different from a civilian one? Further, an acquaintance, who I think should have become a lawyer, suggested an out: draw straws, and the loser has to commit suicide.

Conclusion

At the beginning of this book we asked ourselves three questions; let us return to them now after having looked at some of the stranger dining-out (or -in) habits of our species.

One question concerned eating flesh for its own sake. For example, even under normal circumstances why should we not eat the dead? You may recall the dicussion that anthropologically speaking, the fact that we ourselves should persist in a superstition, or at least sentimental prejudice against human flesh, is more puzzling than the fact that the Orokaiva in Papua, born hunters, should see fit to enjoy perfectly good meat/flesh when they get it. It could be argued that from a purely economic or materialistic viewpoint this assertion is impeccable.

Anthropologist Marvin Harris concluded:

> Neither the prohibition of cannibalism nor the decline of human sacrifice in the Old World had the slightest effect on the rate at which the Old World states and empires killed each other's citizens. As everyone knows, the scale of warfare has increased steadily from prehistoric times to the present, and record numbers of casualties due to armed conflict have been produced precisely by those states in which Christianity has been the major religion. Heaps of corpses left to rot on the battlefield are no less dead than corpses dismembered for a feast.[3]

In a sense what has to be explained is why cultures that have no scruples about killing people should ever refrain from eating them. Is it perhaps something genetically programmed in us, because cannibalism would be counterproductive to our species' survival? This raises a related question: Is there an instinctive revulsion against human flesh? Perhaps, perhaps not. Some maintain that no evidence of any such generalized instinct exists, and that in fact what is at first a novel taste quickly becomes an acquired one.

Cannibalism

Food preferences and taboos are admittedly subjective and often irrational. Romans ate nightingale tongues, ostrich brains, parrot heads, camel heels, elephant trunks, and even, it is said, eels that had been carefully fattened on a diet of slave meat. During the Middle Ages Europeans considered swans and peacocks great delicacies. In our time baked dog is popular in Asia but almost unthinkable in the Western world, though until a century ago North American Indians ate both dogs and snakes (until they themselves, not the dogs and snakes, disappeared). Insects are regarded as culinary treats in Asia and Africa (with chocolate-covered ants and even wasps having made an occasional entry into the United States). And so on. I have eaten horsemeat (like beef, a bit tough); bloodsausage (a matter of taste); salted grasshoppers (salty); and the more common rattlesnake (which tastes like tender chicken, and is expensive). On markets in Taiwan I have also seen rats for sale.* In fact there isn't much that crawls, flies, or swims which, short of being poisonous, hasn't been eaten by someone or other. Do you eat frog legs, sweetbread, snails, brains? All are available in your neighborhood store.†

Early in 1994, Russian President Boris Yeltsin invited President Bill Clinton and aides to his country dacha southeast of Moscow for a three-hour summit feast, and if some of the culinary elements of the evening were familiar, others were

---

*According to an article in the *Los Angeles Times* in 1986, more than two billion rats had been killed in China during the preceding three years, with, however, an estimated three billion still devouring fifteen million tons of grain annually, enough to feed fifty million people. In an effort to gain public support for the extermination campaign, the Chinese press urged citizens to find new uses for rats, and newspapers published recipes for rat steaks and stews, praised champion rat-killer squads, and told of craftsmen who made rat skin shoes and other goods.

†Hoping to capitalize on the food shortages that the Second World War had brought about, a book came onto the U.S. market in 1942 titled *How to Cook a Wolf*, by M. F. K. Fisher—a woman eventually to become one of the nation's most revered and eloquent food writers.

like nothing the man from Hope, Arkansas—or even the most cosmopolitan of his aides—had ever seen before.

The evening began with some sober talk of Russian politics and East-West issues; but when it came time for dinner, the menu featured a traditional Russian delicacy: moose lips. "And I don't mean a chocolate dessert," a senior presidential advisor said later in a briefing for reporters. The taste? After just the slightest pause for the diplomatically correct word, an aide added, "It was unusual."

Therefore, it has also been argued that most people regard eating human flesh with an irrational repulsion entirely out of proportion to any experience they themselves can have had with it, namely none. It is regarded as one of the unclean things, like certain sexual practices, not to be discussed or even thought of.

Conversely it can be argued that man is not a mere animal, and that to eat a maiden isn't quite the same as to cook a swan, that to consume one's mother-in-law is not quite the same as baking a dog.

In 1973 the Hollywood film *Soylent Green* and David Sale's novel *The Love Bite* both used cannibalism to provide a gruesomely logical answer to, first, the world's food problem, and, second, its related population problem.

The issue brings to mind the "neocannibalism" of modern medicine: with the great advances in life-support technology and organ transplantation, the dead today do indeed have much "protein" to offer us—in the form of their organs and other body parts. You may recall that the auxiliary archbishop in Montevideo argued similarly concerning the Andes crash survivors.

Is eating human flesh, then, one of those ideas whose time has come? Or is it one that should be strangled at birth? Once again, this is above all a value judgment, and the reader is entitled to her or his own opinion.

A second question we asked at the beginning concerned

mankind's preoccupation with the subject of cannibalism throughout history and, for some reason, especially today—and all this regardless of the veracity of the evidence. Just as with abstinence from sex, abstinence from interest in cannibalism does not seem to be very popular. Why should this be so? An unlovely consequence of our time?

I do not claim to know the answers, but three possibilities come to mind. First, there may be something atavistic about man eating man, something instinctive buried in the recesses of our brains and perhaps, therefore, making it all of primal emotional and intellectual interest. We eat other species, and at times they eat us; there also flourish numerous flesh-eating plants on earth. One literary reference always seemed to me a kind of self-cannibalism: the boat in Jules Verne's *Around the World in 80 Days,* devouring all of its burnable parts to keep going, and looking like a floating carcass when finally reaching port; and black holes are said to swallow everything, including light. As for our origins, Richard Gardner speculates about the beginning of cannibalism:

> Ultimately the free-floating smaller molecules in the primordial soup become scarce as they are utilized ("eaten up") in the formation of the larger DNA molecules. Some sort of competition, then, arises as the DNA molecules compete with one another for the ever scarcer simpler radicals. The next step, according to Dawkins [author of *The Selfish Gene* (London: Oxford University Press, 1976)], was basically the phase of cannibalism. Because of the scarcity of free-floating smaller molecules in the primordial mixture, the DNA strands began breaking off segments of their neighbors in order to be provided with "food" for the replication process. The next step—and this was an extremely important one—was the formation by DNA molecules of protective coatings, a physical wall that served as a kind of armor that protected the DNA strand from being cannibalized by its neighbors. These entities (DNA strands surrounded by protective shells)

are basically what we are talking about when we discuss viruses. The protective shell is necessary for the survival of the internal core of DNA. Dawkins refers to this entity as a "survival machine," and this is the term he uses for all subsequent living forms, the function of which is to provide a housing for DNA molecules, especially with regard to the protection.[4]

Second, our preoccupation with cannibalism may be explained by the combination of violence, weirdness, death, and taboo, the last, remember, being defined as something "banned on grounds of morality or taste." I think there is little doubt that this powerful combination accounts for a good part of the variance in our interest. For many the subject will be as alluring as it is repelling. Consider this: One Shi Hu, who ruled the Huns of northern China between 334 and 349 C.E., from time to time "used to have one of the girls of his harem beheaded, cooked and served to his guests, while the uncooked head was passed round on a platter to prove that he had not sacrificed the least beautiful." True or not, this blood, gore, sex, *bizarrerie*, and excitement translates into a potent mix for a civilization preoccupied with violence.

There are apparently few taboos left to us. Sex used to be, but no more. By making sex as remarkable and marketable as peanut butter, the media have so eroticized society that we can hear all we ever, or never, wanted to know about it on the morning news. The most lurid stories of celebrities' sexual habits barely raise an eyebrow.

Third, our interest in cannibalism may be explained by the need for a scapegoat, or what can be called the "barbarian just beyond the gate" syndrome. Arens in particular subscribes to the idea that rather than cannibalism itself, the belief that others are cannibals is the universal phenomenon. Since the notion of consuming the human body is often viewed as the most profane act imaginable, all over the world the fear of such a possibility is commonly used "to express the most basic form of malevolence." Some decades ago newspaper critic H. L. Mencken of the *Baltimore Sun* emphasized what he saw as the superficiality of Franklin Roosevelt's democratic pose. "If he became convinced tomorrow that coming out for cannibalism would get him the votes he so sorely needs," Mencken charged, "he would begin fattening a missionary in the White House backyard come Wednesday."

On December 14, 1993, U.S. Senator Ernest Hollings, as reported in the *Los Angeles Times,* compared African leaders to cannibals in just the latest in a series of remarks that have angered minority voters and made even his supporters cringe. The South Carolina Democrat, who is white, criticized African diplomats who traveled to Switzerland for international trade agreement talks. "Everybody likes to go to Geneva," Hollings said at a press conference in Washington. "I used to do it for the Law of the Sea conferences and you'd find these potentates from down in Africa, you know, rather than just eating up each other, they'd just come up and get a square meal in Geneva."

Black leaders protested, and some white Democrats were embarrassed. "The man is mentally sick. As an African-American, I condemn him for making those kinds of accusations against leaders of African nations," said William Gibson, a Greenville dentist who is chairman of the National Association for the Advancement of Colored People, the day after the press conference. Said Don Fowler, a state Democratic Party leader, somewhat more circumspectly: "Senator Hollings has a unique way of expressing himself. It would serve him better to think through some of these things."

There has existed throughout history a pervasive cultural theme of viewing outsiders (say those of "foreign origin, you know") as wicked, depraved, ferocious, and akin to animals (as if animals behaved like man), a source of danger and therefore deserving of punishment no matter how foul. Common decency and common sense have been of no account in such considerations. This rubbish of the human mind has resulted in the torture and annihilation of hundreds of millions, as we have seen.

The cannibalism theme has not infrequently played a significant part in the definition of malevolence in "those others." Culture, in turn, implied a deletion of human flesh from the food inventory, and since Christians, of course, did not devour one another, it became their duty to civilize the mindless savages. Resistance to the Church's colonization, for example, by the Indians of Middle and South America, was therefore often laid at the door of cannibalism, with nakedness, incest, and assorted wicked and sinful sex often thrown in for good measure.

It also follows, from the dominant Western cultural viewpoint, that other "inferiors," namely, women, long considered by many a source of pollution to men, were accused of the cannibal's bestial practices. We are surprised that gay men and lesbians haven't been implicated. Whatever the future of actual cannibalism (a very real problem in times of famine), its fictitious use as an accusation against "undesirables" by the racist, sexist, and chauvinist is likely to continue, no matter how absurd.

And so, having come full circle, we return to our primary question: Is cannibalism one of man's last taboos? The answer, it seems to me, is yes and no. For while there were many who practiced it frequently, and not just out of hunger, and while they apparently were quite happy doing so, most of us still shudder at the thought and would (almost, one concludes) rather starve. Most human beings appear to need a few taboos, and for the time being cannibalism seems to serve that purpose admirably.

William Arens rather wickedly concludes, "Without anthropophagists, anthropologists would find themselves in much the same position as the inquisitors of the Middle Ages who quickly exhausted the supply of mortal heretics and therefore had to conjure up supernatural ones lest their industry and wisdom become superfluous. . . . Indians without souls to be saved or bizarre customs to be interpreted would be of little value to missionaries or anthropologists."[5]

To return to our hypothetical crash scenario: If the only apparent alternative to certain death is the survival of some through killing and then cannibalizing others, what would we do? What should we do? If anyone is to be killed, who? The youngest or oldest? The healthiest (fattest) or sickest? Women and children first? Or last? Why? Or is it to be a sort of final lottery with everyone drawing straws? Who is to do the killing? How is that to be done? And the cooking? And last, but not least, who is to make all these decisions? And if we should be lucky and survive, are we and our fellow cannibals to be tried in a court of law? On what charges? With what "punishment" to fit what "crime"?

Once again we need to find the answers to these questions individually, as we see the evidence and as our moral standards compel us to. And this is making the considerable assumption that we can do so sitting in a comfortable room reading this book, rather than, say, drifting somewhere on a dark, stormy ocean in a liferaft full of starving people.

Logically it seems to me that one could make a reasonable argument in favor of doing whatever may be necessary for the benefit of the majority. But judges, though presumed to be reasonable, have seen this differently, as of course they did in the *Mignonette* case, still applicable today in at least Anglo-Saxon law. Then again, how logical or legal-minded are people under those extraordinary circumstances?

But all this, it could be argued, is merely a theoretical exercise—after all, how many Donner parties, Andes crashes, and Chickatilos are there? As for famines, yes, they go on, but seem to happen elsewhere, to others.

Yet there is one final consideration: the future. The cold

war is over, but the existence of weapons of mass destruction and people willing to use them is not: Iraq, North Korea, and South Africa are warning shots. Such is the progress of civilization that human beings now have it in their power to eradicate Florence, Athens, Paris, Rome, St. Petersburg, New York, Berlin, Cairo, London, Moscow, Tokyo, Vienna, and Stockholm, all in a single morning. And, for that matter, any place you and I might live. As Einstein warned, "The unleashed power of the atom has changed everything save our modes of thinking, and we thus drift toward unparalleled catastrophe."

A chilling flash-forward article on the sociocultural effects of a nuclear war contains but one reference to cannibalism, six words: "Citizens would even prey on corpses." The reader can imagine for himself or herself the ghastly details of this greatest and final famine of them all.[6]

A bumper sticker I've seen reads: "One Nuclear Bomb Can Ruin Your Whole Day"—and, we may add, our last supper. For everything left to eat for the famished survivors, including human flesh, will be a radioactive witches' brew that will make what you have read in this book sound like a picnic by comparison. It is food for thought.

Postscript

A fter writing this book I did a computer search on media mentions of cannibalism since 1985. My reasons were to get up-to-date information (as it turned out, there wasn't much new); to see how popular the subject is (quite); and to note how it is handled by the press (see below). A final question I asked myself was: Are the major points made in this book exemplified in media headlines? Let's see.

First the basic findings. Books in print (worldwide): sixty-three. U.S. newspaper articles were divided into national (e.g., *USA Today*) and northeast, southeast, central, and western sections. Here is the western breakdown.

Los Angeles Times	342 entries
Arizona Republic and Phoenix Gazette	196
(Portland) Oregonian	122
Sacramento Bee	100
San Jose Mercury News	277
Seattle Times	95

This total of over 1,100 entries in about the last ten years in just six major newspapers nicely supports the argument that we have something of a preoccupation with the subject of cannibalism today. We can conveniently divide article titles into three broad groups: (1) directly related to cannibalism, (2) more or less related, and (3) possibly tangentially related.

Here are some examples.

Directly related:

- NO MEAT ON THE BONES OF DONNER PARTY PLAY
- DONNER DOCUMENTARY TO START SEMINAR ON WESTERN WRITING
- THESE DAYS DONNER LAKE MEANS SUMMER FUN
- PROFESSOR DIGS UP FRESH DIRT ON MYSTERY OF THE COLORADO CANNIBAL
- ALFERD PACKER ISN'T THE ONLY REASON TO VISIT LAKE CITY
- *ALIVE*: NOT MUCH MORE THAN A GREAT CRASH SCENE
- ALIVE & WELL SURVIVORS OF ANDES PLANE CRASH GIVE FILM HIGH MARKS
- U.S. WARSHIP SAILED AWAY. CANNIBALISM AT SEA. VIET REFUGEES RELIVE HORROR
- ADMIRAL PRAISES ACCUSED SKIPPER FOR HIS "INTEGRITY"
- JURY FINDS NAVY CAPTAIN GUILTY
- *DELICATESSEN*: THE LATEST VULGAR TURN FROM FRANCE
- IN *DELICATESSEN* THE CHARACTERS ARE WHAT THEY EAT
- "LAMBS" STEW BATTLE OVER "SILENCE"—SEQUEL MAY CHANGE HOLLYWOOD DEAL MAKING
- A DELICIOUS PART FOR ANTHONY HOPKINS
- SUCCESS OF DRACULA LIES IN HIS ABILITY TO MUTATE WITH THE TIMES
- VAMPIRES OF THE 80'S ARE EROTIC BUT PONDEROUS
- 25 BEG OFF DAHMER DUTY
- MADNESS IF DAHMER WINS. SYSTEM IS INSANE

- MORE SERIAL KILLERS ON LOOSE. DAHMER NOT THE LAST, FBI SAYS
- SERIAL KILLER TRIAL LEAVES RUSSIAN SPECTATORS FAINT
- FIRST USED IN CANNIBALISM CASES, "NECESSITY" DEFENSE IS POPULAR TODAY
- ATROCITIES ALLEGED IN 60'S REPORTED IN CHINA. IT WAS A MEANS OF PROVING IDEOLOGICAL ZEAL
- "KURU" A SAVAGE MIXTURE OF HUMOR, HORROR
- DECADES AFTER SIEGE, LENINGRAD GOES HUNGRY, BUT THIS TIME GERMANS LEND HELP

More or less related:

- EATING PEOPLE IS WRONG
- VOTE FOR CANNIBALISM
- CORPORATE CANNIBALISM
- A DISTINGUISHED GUEST LIST FOR THE FIRST BUSH DINNER
- ARE VAMPIRES AS SCARY AS FREEWAY SHOOTINGS?
- SPIDERS, CANNIBALISM, AND OTHER LIGHT TOPICS
- DON'T START CUTTING ARMS UNTIL ALL ATOMIC WEAPONS ARE GONE TO NUKES
- CANNIBALISM YES; BUT THAT ISN'T THE SCARIEST PART
- HOLLYWOOD DREAM FACTORIES ARE CRANKING OUT NIGHTMARES
- TABLE MANNERS AS SELF-DEFENSE
- DELIGHTFUL DIGRESSION THROUGH KENYA (MAN-EATERS MOTEL AND OTHER STOPS)
- ENTOMOLOGISTS ZERO IN ON ITSY-BITSY CANNIBAL
- "FORGOTTEN ANCESTORS" SHAPE BEHAVIOR TODAY, SAGAN WRITES
- DON'T READ THIS AT THE DINNER TABLE
- IS OUR MILKY WAY GETTING BIGGER BY GOBBLING A GALAXY?

Cannibalism

Obscure:

(This category may tax your mind; it did mine, and I have given up. Remember, though, that we are dealing with that idiot-savant, the ubiquitous computer; the instructions were to list *any* article in which the word "cannibalism" appears. How might the word have appeared in the following? Good luck.)

- WOULD YOU BELIEVE JEWISH ESKIMOS?
- WACHTLER CASE: IS INSANITY IDEA CRAZY?
- MARILYN QUAYLE: WRITING FOR DOLLARS
- WHY THINGS ARE
- FREUD'S TROUBLE WITH WOMEN
- BILL WOULD OUTLAW BLASPHEMY
- IS PORN POLITICALLY CORRECT?
- FEMALE PILOTS WAIT FOR COMBAT SLOTS
- LOTS OF SEX, LITTLE ENJOYMENT
- CONTENDING WITH KEVORKIAN
- AFRICAN DICTATOR LETS EX-RULER, EVERYONE OUT OF PRISON
- CLINTON'S PRIVATE LIFE SHOULD REMAIN JUST THAT—PRIVATE
- FOR HOLLYWOOD'S CREATIVE GENIUSES, THE LIGHT BULBS NEVER DIM
- THE BEST ARGUMENT AGAINST ABORTION? A BABY
- SHOULD THE TAXPAYERS BE FORCED TO SUPPORT LARGE POOR FAMILIES?
- BUSH OPPOSES BASIC RIGHTS FOR WOMEN
- A CENTURY AGO THE MAIL WAS A DEADLY MISSION
- SOUTH POLE TIDBITS MAY LEAVE YOU COLD
- APOCALYPSE ANY DAY NOW. ANGRY INDIAN WRITER CALMLY PREDICTS END.

Well, how did you do?

Further Readings

A brief overview of some books on the subject indicates a continuum ranging from the absurd through the debatable to the substantiated. As we noted earlier there is little disagreement about the essentials of the Donner Party, the Leningrad siege, or the Andes crash, but there is a lot about the Tupinambas, Aztecs, kuru victims, and many others.

1. Oscar Kiss Maerth's *The Beginning Was the End* (Westport, Conn.: Praeger Publishers, 1973, translated from the German), is perhaps best summarized in its subtitle: "Man came into being through Cannibalism—intelligence can be eaten." That should speak for itself.

2. Garry Hogg's *Cannibalism and Human Sacrifice* (London, 1958) reflects his frustrations.

> No book covering the subject generally exists in the English language. Inquiries from the Royal Anthropological Institute of Great Britain and Ireland elicited this reply: "We know of no comprehensive work on cannibalism. The material on the subject is unfortunately scattered through many books and periodicals." [*Books in Print* (1993–1994) lists twenty-six titles.] Subsequent inquiries at the British Museum met

239

with the same result: on the 80 miles of shelves in that incomparable library of 8,000,000 books, there is no single work in the English language that covers the immense field of cannibalism and human sacrifice. The Germans would appear to be the only people who have made any attempt to deal comprehensively with the subject on a large scale, and the work in question has not been translated into English [Volhard, one presumes].

3. Reay Tannahill's *Flesh and Blood* (New York: Stein and Day, 1975) is an easily readable popular survey of cannibalism and some of its major implications. At times I found it somewhat uncritical. One example: "In some regions (usually islands, or isolated areas deep in the continental interior) livestock suitable for domestication were entirely lacking. Farmers could raise nothing but starchy foods, and it was, in fact, the resultant craving for meat that turned such peoples as the Caribs and Papuans into the great cannibals of the post-medieval world." Perhaps, perhaps not. Hindus and vegetarians in general do not seem to crave meat.

4. In her *Divine Hunger: Cannibalism as a Cultural System* (New York: Cambridge University Press, 1986), Peggy Reeves Sandy, who holds a doctorate in anthropology from the University of Pennsylvania, appears psychoanalytically oriented, and at times might as well be talking about the tenth day of the fifth moon. The following gives the flavor: "I suggest that ritual cannibalism expresses the ontological structures for being-in-the-world in terms of which humans understand the facts of life," and, "In rendering cannibalism comprehensible, I found it necessary to balance the divergent styles of hermeneutics and hypothetico-deductive explanations." Not surprisingly, to Sandy a meal of human flesh was not simply a matter of nutrition, but almost always had a cultural and spiritual significance.

5. The title of Maggie Kilgour's book gives away the content: *From Communion to Cannibalism: An Anatomy of Metaphors of Incorporation* (Princeton, N.J.: Princeton University Press, 1990). From the final paragraph we read: "To pretend that there are no termini at all is to remain in Lacan's Imaginary or Freud's oral stage of total symbiotic imagery: the difficulty is recognizing their existence without turning them into not only laws but even gods." Kilgour mentions Montaigne but not Montagu, Aquinas but not Arens.

6. Others are even worse, playing fast and loose with the facts, and we are treated to megadoses of meta-anthropology. Eli Sagan's *Cannibalism, Human Aggression and Cultural Form* (New York: Harper and Row, 1974) states in the foreword, "The chief theoretical resource for the study is drawn from Sigmund Freud. . . . It thus falls under the rubric of psycho-history or psychoanalytic sociology." No wonder, then, that the author claims that, "Cannibalism is the fundamental form of institutionalized aggression—it is impossible to comprehend the true nature of human culture without understanding its role in human history." This is not thinking but free association. In still more cognitive slippage we are also treated to the bizarre notion of the "Fijian Oedipal drama," and such pearls as "The satisfaction of Oedipal desires brings down the aggressive condemnation, 'You mother fucker.' " Alas, perhaps such productions confusing Oedipal and edible should be titled "Meditations on Transcendental Gastronomy."

7. Ewald Volhard's *Kannibalismus* (Stuttgart: Strecker and Schroeder, 1939) is a very different book. As noted before, it is almost five hundred pages long, including thirty pages of bibliography adding up to around 750 references. With sometimes an abundance of minutiae of details and customs of tribes and societies with unpronounceable names, the book has yet to be translated into English. Volhard was associated with

the Frobenius Institute of Natural History in Frankfurt am Main, and *Kannibalismus* is in many ways a very scholarly work. It certainly cites a wealth of information, whatever the actual worth of the books and articles. Volhard, however, describes and attempts to explain cannibalism *only* as a substantial cultural custom. He therefore disregards individual incidences, survival cannibalism, and so on, considering them physiological or psychopathological problems. As we already know, Arens in his *The Man-Eating Myth* takes issue with precisely this approach.

Volhard's essential conclusion is this: cannibalistic societies possessed remarkably high cultural levels compared to their noncannibalistic neighbors. "This fact is unquestionably proven scientifically, and to have thereby firmly destroyed the myth of the cannibalistic original condition of mankind, must be considered one of the most important insights of cultural history research in the nineteenth century." Volhard maintains that by and large these societies are not warlike, and that their character is often well-meaning, courteous, and peaceful. He cites numerous examples to make his point, such as the Tangale, who are said to have been "mellow, talkative, and most grateful for presents"; the loving family father on New Lauenburg; the higher cultural level of the Battack in Sumatra as compared to their noncannibalistic neighbors; and the Botokuden in South America, who live "in harmony, cleanliness, and order" and exhibit an extraordinary love for their children.

What are we to make of all this? Where is the bottom line? What of the husband who eats his wife "with whom he has been living happily for many years"? What of the mother who cooks her child? What of the Aztec priest, the Fiji sorcerer, the Tartar prince, the Iroquois chief, and the hundreds of others whom we have met in these pages? Are they *really* ordinary, good-natured, well-meaning folk, killers and cannibals merely because of necessity and custom? I for one wouldn't bet my life on it. While I have used many of Volhard's references,

I have equally emphasized the need for very cautious interpretation. They are often difficult if not impossible to sub-
stantiate, to put it mildly.

8. The alert reader will recall Marvin Harris, chairman of the
Department of Anthropology at Columbia University in the
1960s, and author of several books, among them *Cows, Pigs,
Wars, and Witches: The Riddles of Cultures,* and *Culture,
People, Nature: An Introduction to General Anthropology.*
   Harris is a proponent of the ecological interpretations of
cannibalism, complete with cost/benefit analyses and caloric
counts. He tries to make a strong case for his belief that the
thousands of bodies slaughtered atop the Aztec pyramids were
thereafter distributed and eaten—not in a ritualistic way, but
in an organized, state-sponsored program of production and
allocation of high-protein food in the form of human flesh.
(Sandy, mentioned above, agrees with Harris that the corpses
of the victims were rolled down the stone steps of the pyramidal
shrines and then eaten by nobles and warriors.) The following
is vintage Harris (from his *Cannibals and Kings* [New York:
Random House, 1977]):

> If an occasional finger or toe was all anyone could expect,
> the system would probably not have worked. But if the meat
> was supplied in concentrated packages to the nobility,
> soldiers, and their retainers, and if the supply was
> synchronized to compensate for deficits in the agricultural
> cycle, the payoff for Montezuma and the ruling class might
> have been sufficient to stave off political collapse. If this
> analysis is correct, then we must consider its inverse
> implications, namely, that the availability of domesticated
> animal species played an important role in the prohibition
> of cannibalism and the development of religions of love and
> mercy in the states and empires of the Old World. Christianity,
> it may yet turn out, was more the gift of the lamb in the
> manger than the child who was born in it. (p. 110)

9. Finally there is William Arens again, and his *The Man-Eating Myth* (New York: Oxford University Press, 1979). Its jacket copy reads:

> Belief in the existence of cannibalism just beyond the borders of one's own culture is a time-honored, universally accepted notion. In advanced societies, man-eaters are presumed to inhabit mysterious lands on the fringes of civilization. Among primitive peoples, cannibals are said to reside over the next mountain or farther along the river.
>
> The author of this provocative book has meticulously viewed the evidence from all fields on the world's classic man-eaters, from the 16th-century Aztecs to contemporary African and New Guinean cultures. He comes to a conclusion certain to cause shock waves in anthropological circles: despite the massive literature alluding to cannibalism, the author finds that there is *no* satisfactory first-hand account of this act as a socially proved custom in any part of the world.
>
> Arens adds that recourse to cannibalism under survival conditions or as a rare instance of antisocial behavior is not denied for any culture, but that whenever it occurs this is considered a regrettable act rather than a custom.*

Arens then goes on the attack:

> As we have constantly observed, the cannibal has a great fascination for the academic mind, as this horrible creature

---

*However, Simpson in his *Cannibalism and the Common Law* counters that, "Arens has argued that cannibalism, as a socially accepted practice, is a myth; he excludes from this thesis 'survival' cannibalism. I should myself argue that maritime survival cannibalism, preceded by the drawing of lots and killing, was a socially accepted practice among seamen until the end of the days of sail; it is therefore not an exception but a counterexample. . . . There was general understanding of what had to be done on these occasions and that survivors who had followed the custom could have the certain professional pride in a job well done."

demands further exculpation until every potential explanation has had its day. . . . Learned essays by profession-
als are unending, but the sustaining ethnography is lacking.

Next Arens cites numerous examples to make his case.
A sample:

The most recent concern is the ecological debate, complete
with caloric counts of the potential nutritional value of human
flesh. Predictably, there is little agreement as some (Garn
and Block 1970) claim there is no nutritional sense to the
practice, while others (Dornstreich and Morren 1974) argue
that there is some worthwhile sustenance entailed. The following quote conveys the objective nature of present publications. "Data from different New Guinea societies indicate
that the balance between different protein inputs varies with
such things as ecological zonation and the structure of local
ecosystems involving human populations (Dornstreich and
Morren 1974:10)." Which side of the argument this is meant
to support is unclear, but the discussion is obviously meant
to be "scientific."

At the other extreme are the structuralists. This camp
shows little interest in the concrete implications of the act
out of preference for a symbolic interpretation which will
permit integration of the idea with broader cultural patterns.
Thus the master of structuralism, Lévi-Strauss (1966),
suggests that boiling is the usual preparation of food for
domestic consumption while roasting is more typical for food
to be served to guests. As an extension of this model, he
proposes that among cannibals boiling will be most often
employed in preparing kin, with roasting the preferred
method for enemies. However, Shankman (1969) finds this
logic faulty. After examination of sixty cases of reported cannibalism, he concludes that Lévi-Strauss's boiling-roasting
efforts have been undermined by "the natives who have
discovered a veritable smorgasbord of ways of preparing
people" (1969:61). Again, agreement is scarce, even among

those who share a common theoretical perspective. Medieval scholars encountered similar problems, since an exact count of the number of angels able to dance on the head of a pin is never a simple task.[1]

If the reader is beginning to feel amazed by these wondrous associations, he is not alone. Ashley Montagu, quoted before and one of the great names in anthropology, called *The Man-Eating Myth* "a splendid book. . . . It makes excellent reading and should cause not a little fluttering in academic dovecotes. . . . There's a good deal more than cannibalism here, and it says some long overdue things about the credulity and self-fulfilling prophetic methods of some anthropologists."

Endnotes

A s stated in the Preface, this book, while intended primarily for the intelligent layperson, should also be of more than passing interest to scholars and serious students, who will find additional details and documentation here and in the Further Readings. The idea is to avoid weighing the general reader down with technical data, yet make them available to those who wish to explore further.

As emphasized in the text, the majority of claims (and that is the word) concerning cannibalism as some kind of social custom (especially in the chapters of Part Two on magic, ritual, religion, sacrifice, punishment, indifference, unification, and the gourmets), are found in Volhard's extensive *Kannibalismus* (and to a lesser extent in Arens's and Tannahill's books).

The interested scholar needs to be warned, however, that further research may not lead to an enlightening, clear-cut answer. Take the Bakundu. According to Volhard, p. 41, they were alleged to be cannibals by someone named Zintgraff, author of a work on the North-Cameroun, published, presumably in German, in Berlin in 1885. "He was told so by London Bell, the brother of Chief Bell." Volhard also places this tribe in the Cameroun in West Africa (with a map on p. 22), and further asserts (p. 389) that anyone who broke

247

their dietary laws (with chicken, for example, being forbidden food) was punished by being eaten himself.

One can but wonder how readily available Herr Zintgraff's book is, what exactly one would find in it, and if the statements are really more than mere hearsay. Which, of course, is Arens's major argument.

Chapter L. By the Dawn's Early Light

1. See Donald Johanson, Lucy: The Beginning of Humankind (New York: Simon and Schuster, 1981).
2. Richard Cunningham, The Place Where the World Ends (New York: Sheed & Ward, 1973).
3. William Arens, The Man-Eating Myth (New York: Oxford University Press, 1979), p. 13.
4. Isaac Asimov, Asimov on Science (New York: Windsor, 1989), p. 395.
5. Jane Goodall, "Life and Death at Gombe," National Geographic, May 1979.

Chapter 2. Recorded History

1. Brian Gagan, Archeology 47, no. 1 (January–February 1994): 11-16.
2. Reay Tannahill, Flesh and Blood: A History of the Cannibal Complex (New York: Stein and Day, 1975), pp. 104, 105.
3. Ernest Dodge, Islands and Empires (Minneapolis: University of Minnesota Press, 1976), p. 16.
4. Otto Friedrich, Before the Deluge: A Portrait of Berlin in the 1920s (New York: Harper and Row, 1972), p. 332.
5. Ibid., pp. 332–34.

Chapter 3. Caveats

1. Arens, The Man-Eating Myth, p. 31.

2. Marvin Harris, *Cannibals and Kings* (New York: Random House, 1977), pp. 108, 109.

3. Arens, *The Man-Eating Myth*, p. 73.

Chapter 4. Summary

1. Robert Massie, *Dreadnought* (New York: Random House, 1991), p. 379.

2. See Margaret Mead's *Sex and Temperament in Three Primitive Societies* (New York: Mentor Books, 1950).

3. Arens, *The Man-Eating Myth*, p. 183.

4. Ibid., p. 181.

5. Ibid., p. 134.

Chapter 5. Natural Famines

1. Tannahill, *Flesh and Blood*, p. 107.

2. Paul B. Beeson and Walsh McDermott, *Textbook of Medicine* (Philadelphia: W. B. Saunders, 1975), p. 1367.

3. Excerpts as quoted in Tannahill, *Flesh and Blood*, pp. 48–55. See also Abd al-Latif, *Relation de l'Égypte par Abd-Allatif, Médecin arabe de Bagdad* (Paris, 1810).

Chapter 6. Manmade Famines

1. Rudolf Höss, *Commandant of Auschwitz* (New York: Public Library, 1951), p. 113.

2. Philippe-Paul de Ségour, *Napoleon's Russian Campaign* (Alexandria, Va.: Time-Life, 1958), pp. 267–69, 271, 281.

3. Harrison Salisbury, *The 900 Days: The Siege of Leningrad* (New York: Avon Books, 1970), pp. 521, 522, 543–53.

4. William Craig, *Enemy at the Gates* (New York: Readers Digest Press, 1973), pp. 385, 386, 389–92.

5. Nora Levin, *The Holocaust* (New York: Thomas Crowell Co., 1968), pp. 205ff.

Chapter 7. Accidents

1. H. W. Janson, *History of Art* (New York: Harry N. Abrams, 1963), p. 481.

2. See Tannahill's *Flesh and Blood,* pp. 139–42. Savigny's story was published in the London *Times,* September 17, 1816, p. 2.

3. A. W. Brian Simpson, *Cannibalism and the Common Law* (Chicago: University of Chicago Press, 1984), p. 267.

4. See George Stewart's *Ordeal by Hunger* (Boston: Houghton Mifflin, 1960), from which I'll be quoting. There is, too, the very successful essay in investigative journalism, Charles Fayette McGlashan's *History of the Donner Party: A Tragedy of the Sierras,* which originally appeared in serial form in the *Truckee Republican* between January and June 1879. The book's first edition sold out in two weeks; it has since gone through eleven subsequent editions. In 1987 the author's granddaughter, Nona McGlashan, was editing 450 handwritten letters from twenty-four survivors describing events at Donner Lake during that awful winter. In 1911 interest was also revived by a remarkable book by Aliza P. Houghton (née Donner), who as a child survived the disaster.

5. Stewart, *Ordeal by Hunger.*

6. Piers Paul Read, *Alive: The Story of the Andes Survivors* (Philadelphia: J. B. Lippincott, 1974), pp. 160, 199, 200.

Chapter 8. Magic

1. Tannahill, *Flesh and Blood,* pp. 56, 60.

2. Jeffrey Russell, *Witchcraft in the Middle Ages* (Ithaca, N.Y.: Cornell University Press, 1972), pp. 251, 240.

Endnotes

Chapter 9. Ritual, Religion, and Sacrifice

1. Tannahill, *Flesh and Blood*, pp. 20, 21.

Chapter 11. The Gourmets

1. Tannahill, *Flesh and Blood*, p. 151.
2. Read, *Alive*, p. 199.

Chapter 12. The Sadists and the Mad

1. Gabriel Ronay, *The Truth about Dracula* (New York: Stein and Day, 1972), p. 238.
2. See Tannahill, *Flesh and Blood*, pp. 67–71.
3. Friedrich, *Before the Deluge*, pp. 349, 350.
4. Ibid., pp. 335, 336.

Chapter 13. Werewolves, Witches, and Vampires

1. Barry Lopez, *Of Wolves and Men* (New York: Charles Scribner's Sons, 1978).
2. Ibid., p. 236.
3. Ibid., pp. 208, 227, 234.
4. Ibid., p. 233.
5. Caroline Brett, *Wild Cats* (New York: Dorsett Press, 1992), p. 124.
6. Tannahill, *Flesh and Blood*, p. 112.
7. See H. R. Trevor-Roper, *The European Witch-Craze of the 16th and 17th Centuries* (Harmondsworth, England: Penguin Publishing Co., 1969).
8. Richard Gardner, *Sex Abuse Hysteria: Salem Witch Trials Revisited* (Cresskill, N.Y.: Creative Therapeutics, 1992), pp. 127, 128.
9. Elaine Marieb and John Mallatt, *Human Anatomy* (Redwood City, Calif.: The Benjamin Cummings Publishing Co., 1992), p. 112.
10. Tannahill, *Flesh and Blood*.

Chapter 14. Special Cases: Medical, Legal, and Psychological

1. American Medical Association, *Encyclopedia of Medicine* (New York: Random House, 1969), p. 623.

2. Ibid.

3. Cecil, *Textbook of Medicine*, 18th ed. (Philadelphia: W. B. Saunders, 1988), pp. 2205, 2206.

4. *Science* 197 (September 2, 1977): 956.

5. *Science* 232 (June 20, 1986).

6. Arens, *The Man-Eating Myth*, pp. 99, 100.

7. Ibid., p. 115.

8. *Science* 232 (June 20, 1986).

9. Kenneth Lanning, *Investigator's Guide to Allegations of "Ritual" Child Abuse* (Quantico, Va.: U.S. Department of Justice, National Center for the Analysis of Violent Crime, 1992), p. 29.

10. Ibid., pp. 18–19.

11. Ibid., p. 40. See also F. Matzner, "Does Satanism Exist?" in the *Journal of the American Academy of Child and Adolescent Psychiatry*: "There has never been a single piece of objective evidence documenting such systematic cult activity in connection with any crime or reported abuse." See also sociologist J. Victor, "The Satanic Cult Scare and Allegations of Ritual Child Abuse," *Issues in Child Abuse Accusations* 3, no. 3 (1991): 135–43, and *Santanic Panic: The Creation of a Contemporary Legend* (Chicago: Open Court, 1993).

12. Richard A. Gardner, *True and False Accusations of Child Sex Abuse* (Cresskill, N.J.: Creative Therapeutics, 1992), pp. 472–77.

13. Gardner, *Sex Abuse Hysteria*, p. 125.

14. Ibid., pp. 37, 38.

15. Ibid., p. 83.

16. Ibid., p. 58.

Chapter 15. Our Preoccupation with Cannibalism

1. Arens, *The Man-Eating Myth*, p. 53.

2. Ibid., p. 54.

3. Ibid., p. 55.

Endnotes

4. Bruce McCabe, *Boston Globe,* October 29, 1982.
5. Clifford Fadiman, *The Little Brown Book of Anecdotes.*
6. *Der Spiegel,* May 1993.

Conclusion

1. Marjorie Boulton, *Zamenhof* (London: Routledge and Kegan Paul, 1960).
2. Simpson, *Cannibalism and the Common Law.*
3. Harris, *Cannibals and Kings.*
4. Along these lines is phagocytosis. In order to prevent diseases, our white blood cells, the leukocytes, literally eat bacteria, viruses, fungi, and parasites. "Obviously phagocytes must be selective of the material that is phagotized, or normal cells and structures of the body would be ingested. . . . Motion pictures of phagocytosis by Kupffer cells have demonstrated this event involving a bacterium to last less than 0.01 seconds." Arthur Guyton, *Textbook of Medical Physiology* (Philadelphia: W. B. Saunders, 1991), p. 184.
5. Arens, *The Man-Eating Myth,* p. 184.
6. For the gory details, see Bem Allen, "After the Missiles," *American Psychologist,* August 1985.

Further Readings

1. Arens, *The Man-Eating Myth,* pp. 16, 17.

Bibliography

(Abd al-Latif). *Relation de L'Égypte par Abd-Allatif, Médecin arabe de Bagdad.* Paris, 1810. Translated from the Arabic by Silvestre de Sacy.

American Medical Association. *Encyclopedia of Medicine.* New York: Random House, 1989.

Arens, William. *The Man-Eating Myth.* New York: Oxford University Press, 1979.

Asimov, Isaac. *Asimov on Science: A Thirty-Year Retrospective.* New York: Windsor, 1989.

Beeson, Paul B., and Walsh McDermott. *Textbook of Medicine.* Philadelphia: W. B. Saunders, 1975.

Bem, Allen. "After the Missiles: Socioeconomic Effects of Nuclear War." *American Psychologist,* August 1985.

Boulton, Marjorie. *Zamenhof.* London: Routledge and Kegan Paul, 1960.

Breslin, Jimmy. *He Got Hungry and Forgot His Manners.* New York: Ticknor & Fields, 1988.

Brett, Caroline. *Wild Cats.* New York: Dorset Press, 1992.

Cecil. *Textbook of Medicine.* Edited by James R. Wyngaarden and Lloyd H. Smith. 18th ed. Philadelphia: W. B. Saunders, 1988.

Chong, Key Ray. *Cannibalism in China.* Wakefield, N.H.: Longwood Academics, 1990.

Craig, William. *Enemy at the Gates: The Battle for Stalingrad.* New York: Readers Digest Press, 1973.

Croy, Homer. *Wheels West.* 1955.

255

Cunningham, Richard. *The Place Where the World Ends*. New York: Sheed & Ward, 1973.

Dodge, Ernest. *Islands and Empires*. Minneapolis: University of Minnesota Press, 1976.

Dornstreich, M. D., and G. E. B. Morren. "Does New Guinea Cannibalism Have Nutritional Value?" *Human Ecology* 2 (1974): 1–12.

Elgar, Mark, and Bernard Crespi (eds.). *Cannibalism—Ecology and Evolution among Diverse Taxa*. New York: Oxford University Press, 1992.

Feynman, Richard. *What Do You Care What Other People Think?* New York: W. W. Norton, 1988.

Freud, Sigmund. *Totem and Taboo*. New York: W. W. Norton, 1950.

Friedrich, Otto. *Before the Deluge: A Portrait of Berlin in the 1920s*. New York: Harper and Row, 1972.

Gardner, Richard A. *Sex Abuse Hysteria: Salem Witch Trials Revisited*. Cresskill, N.J.: Creative Therapeutics, 1991.

———. *True and False Accusations of Child Sex Abuse*. Cresskill, N.J.: Creative Therapeutics, 1992.

Garn, S. M., and W. D. Block. "The Limited Nutritional Value of Cannibalism." *American Anthropologist* 72: 106.

Gerster, Patrick and Nicholas Cords. *Myth in American History*. Encino, Calif.: Glencoe Press, 1977.

Goralski, Robert. *World War II Almanac 1933–1945*. New York: Perigree, 1981.

Guyton, Arthur. *The Textbook of Medical Physiology*. Philadelphia: W. B. Saunders, 1991.

Harris, Marvin. *Cannibals and Kings*. New York: Random House, 1977.

Hicks, Robert. "Police Pursuit of Satanic Crime," *Skeptical Inquirer* 14, no. 3 (Spring 1990): 276–86.

Höss, Rudolf. *Commandant of Auschwitz*. New York: Public Library, 1951.

Hogg, Garry. *Cannibalism and Human Sacrifice*. London: 1958.

Janowitz, Tama. *A Cannibal in Manhattan*. New York: Crown, 1987.

Janson, H. W. *History of Art*. New York: Harry N. Abrams, 1963.

Johanson, Donald, and Maitland Edey. *Lucy: The Beginning of Humankind*. New York: Simon and Schuster, 1981.

Johnson, Joyce. "Witness for the Prosecution." *The New Yorker,* May 16, 1994.

Kilgour, Maggie. *From Communion to Cannibalism: An Anatomy of Metaphors of Incorporation.* Princeton, N.J.: Princeton University Press, 1990.

Lanning, Kenneth. *Investigator's Guide to Allegations of "Ritual" Child Abuse.* Quantico, Va.: U.S. Dept. of Justice, National Center for the Analysis of Violent Crime, 1992.

Levin, Nora. *The Holocaust.* New York: Thomas Crowell Co., 1968.

Lévi-Strauss, Claude. *The Raw and the Cooked.* New York: Harper and Row, 1969.

Loftus, Elizabeth. "The Reality of Repressed Memories." *American Psychologist,* May 1993.

Lopez, Barry Holstun. *Of Wolves and Men.* New York: Charles Scribner's Sons, 1978.

MacClancy, Jeremy. *Consuming Culture.* Henry Holt, 1993.

McNally, Raymond. *Dracula Was a Woman.* New York: McGraw-Hill, 1983.

Maerth, Oscar Kiss. *The Beginning Was the End.* Praeger, 1973.

Marieb, Elaine, and John Mallatt. *Human Anatomy.* Redwood City, Calif.: The Benjamin/Cummings Publishing Co., 1992.

Massie, Robert K. *Dreadnought: Britain, Germany and the Coming of the Great War.* New York: Random House, 1991.

Matzner, F. "Does Satanism Exist?" *Journal of the American Academy of Child and Adolescent Psychiatry* 20, no. 5: 848.

Mead, Margaret. *Sex and Temperament in Three Primitive Societies.* New York: Mentor, 1950.

Polo, Marco. *Travels.* Harmondsworth, England: 1958.

Read, Piers Paul. *Alive: The Story of the Andes Survivors.* Philadelphia: J. B. Lippincott, 1974.

Ronay, Gabriel. *The Truth about Dracula.* New York: Stein and Day, 1972.

Russell, Jeffrey. *Witchcraft in the Middle Ages.* Ithaca, N.Y.: Cornell University Press, 1972.

Sagan, Eli. *Cannibalism: Human Aggression and Cultural Form.* New York: Harper and Row, 1974.

Salisbury, Harrison E. *The 900 Days: The Siege of Leningrad.* New York: Avon Books, 1970.

Sandy, Peggy Reeves. *Divine Hunger: Cannibalism as a Cultural System.* New York: Cambridge University Press, 1986.

Savigny, Henri, and Alexandre Corréard. *Naufrage de la frégate La Méduse faisant partie de l'expédition du Sénégal en 1816.* Paris, 1817.

Ségur, Philippe-Paul de. *Napoleon's Russian Campaign.* Alexandria, Va.: Time-Life, 1958.

Shankman, Paul. "Le Rôti et le Bouilli: Lévi-Strauss' Theory of Cannibalism." *American Anthropologist* 71: 54–69.

Siegel, Ronald K. *Fire in the Brain.* New York: Plume, 1993.

Simpson, A. W. Brian. *Cannibalism and the Common Law.* Chicago: University of Chicago Press, 1984.

Solzhenitsyn, Aleksandr. *The Gulag Archipelago.* New York: Harper and Row, 1973.

Stewart, George R. *Donner Pass.* San Francisco: The California Historical Society.

———. *Ordeal by Hunger.* Boston: Houghton Mifflin, 1960.

Tannahill, Reay. *Flesh and Blood: A History of the Cannibal Complex.* New York: Stein and Day, 1975.

Trevor-Roper, H. R. *The European Witch-Craze of the 16th and 17th Centuries.* Harmondsworth, England: Penguin, 1969.

Twain, Mark. *The Complete Short Stories.* New York: Doubleday, 1957.

Victor, Jeffrey S. "The Satanic Cult Scare and Allegations of Ritual Child Abuse." *Issues in Child Abuse Accusations* 3, no. 3 (1991): 135–43.

———. *Satanic Panic: The Creation of a Contemporary Legend.* Chicago: Open Court, 1993.

Visser, Margaret. *The Rituals of Dinner.* New York: Grove Weidenfeld, 1991.

Volhard, Ewald. *Kannibalismus.* Stuttgart: Strecker and Schroeder, 1939.

Watters, Wendell W. *Deadly Doctrine: Health, Illness, and Christian God-Talk.* Buffalo, N.Y.: Prometheus Books, 1992.

Index

Abd al-Latif, Egyptian physician, 64–66

A Cannibal in Manhattan, 196

Accidents, 83–106

Alive, 14, 56, 101–106, 196

Alleged satanic ritualistic abuse, 52, 165, 176–83, 222–23

Anasazi, 27

Andamanese, 18

Andersonville, Civil War prison camp, 68

Andes crash, 44, 101–106, 132, 224

Anga, 124

Angami, 121

Angola, 113

Animal cannibalism, 24–25

Anthropophagy, definition of, 10

Aoba, 131

Arens, William, anthropologist, 16, 21, 46, 48–49, 52–54, 168–69, 185, 229, 231–32, 242, 244–46

Arizona Bar Association controversy, 143–46

Ashanti, 111

Asimov, Isaac, 22

Assam, 114

Assyrian, 113

Atavism, 54

Auschwitz, 68

Australia, 18

Australopithecus afarensis, 17

Aztec, 46–49, 113, 224

Baba-Yaga, in fairy tale, 193

Badinga, 133

Bafum-Bansaw, 132

Bagesu, 127

Baja, 130–31

Bakundu, 125, 247

Balian, Alexander, navy captain, 87–91

Banala, 133

Bangala, 124

Bapende, 124

Bassange, 133

Basuto, 130

Báthory, Elizabeth, Hungarian murderess/cannibal, 136–37

Batta (Batak, Battak), 123–24
Beane, Sawney, English cannibal, 28–29
Bele, 130
Betchuana, 120, 132
Biaka-Boda, Ivory Coast politician, 32
Bihor, 127
Birkenau, 68
Bokassa, Jean, African dictator, 34
Borneo, 113
Bosnia, 41
Brecht, Bertolt, 30, 59
Breslin, Jimmy, 197
Brooks, Ned, British seaman, 171–75
Burma, 121
Bushmen, 18

Caesar, Julius, 69
Candide, 187
Cannibal Corpse, band, 199
Cannibalism
  in accidents, 83–106
  among animals, 24–25
  and alleged satanic ritualistic abuse, 176–83, 222–23
  and Arizona Bar Association's controversy, 143–46
  and atavism, 54
  and caloric debates, 11, 47–49, 243, 245–46
  caveats, 43–54, 214
  in China, 18–20, 27–28, 111–12, 131, 136, 201
  Comic Code, 192

computer search, 235–38
and controversies; see Tupinamba, Aztec, Kuru, Further Readings
cosmic, 118
cultic, 118
defined, 10
dietary considerations, 132
and diminished capacity; see Mignonette
distribution, 19
early history, 17–24
in famines, man-made, 67–82
in famines, natural, 59–66
in fiction, 186–97
in films, 193–96
in funeral rituals, 122
geographical overview, 18–19, 214
and gourmets, 129–34
as harvest ritual, 20–21
headhunting, 113–16
historical overview, 17–24
HIV connection, 155–56
in humor, 200–201, 223
and indifference, 125–26, 216
in initiation rites, 119–20
in kuru, 165–69, 220
legal issues, 143–46, 224, 232; see also Mignonette
and madness, 138–41, 216
Medical; see kuru
for medicinal purposes, 112, 143–46
Mignonette, case/debate, 169–75, 220–22
in magic, 107–16

in music, 199–200
in news media, 235–38
penal, 124
prehistoric, 214
profane, 125–26
as punishment, 124–25, 216, 224
in recorded history, overview, 27–41, 214
and repressed memories, 181–83
in ritual, religion, and sacrifice, 117–22
sadism, 135–37, 216–17
in satanic ritual abuse; *see* alleged satanic ritual abuse
and sorcery, 108
transubstantiation, 108–11
types, 57
and unification, 126–28, 224
and vampires, 157–63, 217
in victory celebrations, 118
vindictive, 124
and werewolves, 149–153, 217
and witches, 153–57, 217
"Cannibalism in the Cars," 187–91
Carib, 13, 130
Carthaginians, 186
Cashiba, 127
Caspier, 127
Castle Bran, 162–63
Catholic Church
and reaction to Andes crash, 105
and transubstantiation, 18, 108–11
and vampires, 157

and werewolves, 151–52
and witches, 153–57
Cats and sorcery trials, 155
Chames, 111
Chaplin, Charlie, 223
Charlemagne, 153
Chavante, 141
Chikatilo, Andrej, Russian mass murderer/cannibal, 14, 208–11
Chimpanzees and cannibalism, 24
China, 18–20, 27–28, 111–12, 131, 136, 141, 201, 226
Chinese vampires, 192–93
Chong Key, 18
Clinton, Bill, U.S. president, 226
Cocoma, 123
Colorado maneater; *see* Packer, Alferd
Columbus, Christopher, 13
Comic Code, 192
Computer search, 235–38
Congo, 30, 123
Cook, James, British explorer, 29–30
The Cook, the Thief, His Wife and Her Lover, French/Dutch film, 35–36
Cortés, Hernán, Spanish explorer, 46–47
Craig, William, journalist, 78–79
Cree, 138
Crocker, W., anthropologist, 45
Cro-Magnan man, 23
Cultic cannibalism, 118
Cunningham, Richard, 101

Cuong, Dao Cu, Vietnamese boat refugee, 90
Cuvier, George, French zoologist, 200

Dahmer, Jeffrey, mass murderer and cannibal, 14, 148, 204–207
Dar For tribe, 131
Dart, Raymond, anatomy professor, 20
Darwin, Charles, 21
Death from starvation, 63
Defense of necessity arguments; see Mignonette
Delicatessen, French film, 195
Denke, Karl, German murderer and cannibal, 30
Derek, Indonesian cannibal, 36–38
Dieri, 126
Dietz, Park Elliott, forensic psychiatrist, 39, 148, 179, 204, 206–207
DNA molecules, 228–29
Dobodura, 135, 216
Donner, George, 92–93, 221–22
Donner Party, 44, 92–96, 221–22
Dracula, 14, 158–61, 191–92, 217
Dracula Press, 160
Drot, ship, 87
Dubois, Eugene, Dutch physician, 22
Dubuque, U.S. ship, 87–91
Dudley, Tom, British captain and cannibal, 169–75, 222
Dzhumagaliev, Nicolai, Russian cannibal, 207–208

Eating Raoul, film, 194
Egypt, 64–66, 111–12, 118, 120
Einstein, Albert, 186, 219, 233
Ekoi, 126
Ellen, Stanley, writer, 198
Endophagy, 117
Erromango, 130
Eskimo, 18
Essex, ship, 86
"Evolution Man or How I Ate My Father," 197
Exophagy, 117

Famines, 59–82
Fanny Adams, 51
Fate, 130
Feynman, Richard, physicist, 43
Fiji, 18, 30, 83, 129–31, 135
Fine Young Cannibals, band, 199
Fires on the Plain, Japanese film, 32
Fish, Albert, murderer/cannibal, 32
Fisher, M. F. K., food writer, 220
Fontbrégoua Cave, 23
Food preferences and taboos, 226–27
Fore tribesmen, 49, 167–69
Foster, Jodie, actress, 196
Formosa, 113
French Revolution, 60
Freud, Sigmund, 21–22
Fried Green Tomatoes, film, 195
Friedrich, Otto, journalist, 30–32
Fuegian, 18
Funeral rites, 122

Gabon, 34–35
Gajdusek, D. Carleton, research-
er, 49, 167–69, 220
Gallup Poll, 218–19
Gardner, Richard, forensic psy-
chiatrist, 72, 155–56, 179–81,
228–29
Gaul, 69, 186
Gazelle peninsula, 131
Gbale, 125
Gein, Ed, murderer/cannibal, 196
Géricault, Théodore, French
painter, 84–86
Gerse, 130
Godard, Jean-Luc, French film
director, 193
Gomes, Antònio, Brazilian com-
poser, 199–200
Goodall, Jane, researcher, 24–25
Gourmets, 130–34
Grossmann, Carl Wilhelm, Ger-
man mass murderer/canni-
bal, 31–32, 133
Group 52; see Vietnamese
boatpeople
Guarani, 125
Gulag Archipelago, 80
Gurkha, 115

Haarmann, Georg, German mass
murderer/cannibal, 139–41
Hänsel and Gretel, 193
Hai, Dinh Thuong, Vietnamese
boat refugee, 88–91
Hamatsa, 120, 133
Harner, Michael, anthropologist,
48–49

Harris, Marvin, anthropologist,
47–48, 225, 243
Hartwell, pilot, 105
Harvest rituals, 120–21
Haussaland, 130
Headhunting, 113–16
*He Got Hungry and Forgot His
Manners,* 197
Herero tribe, 131
Herodotus, 23–24, 113, 126
Heston, Charlton, actor, 12
Hewa, 167
Hill Anga, 127
Hindu, 18
Hitcher, film, 34
Hitler, Adolf, 68, 72, 78, 139–40,
186, 191
Höss, Rudolf, commandant of
Auschwitz, 68, 111
Hogg, G., anthropologist, 11, 239
Hollings, Ernest, U.S. senator,
230
Homer, 186
Homo erectus, 22
Homo sapiens, 22
Hopkins, Anthony, actor, 196
Hu, Shi, Chinese cannibal, 229
Humor, 200–201

Ibo, 108, 125, 131
Ichikawa, Kon, Japanese film
director, 32
Ife, 111
Igorot, 113
Il Guarany, Brazilian opera, 199–
200
India, 18, 114, 121

Indifference, 125–26
Indonesia, 36–38, 113–14
Initiation rites, 119–20
Interview with the Vampire, 161
Iroquois, 111, 136
Isabel tribe, 112
Isis, Egyptian goddess, 120
Issidone, 126
Ivory Coast, 32

Jack and the Beanstalk, 193
Jaga, 124
Jahan, Shah, 59
Janowitz, Tama, 59
Japanese army and cannibalism, 201–202
Java Man, 22
Jibaro, 115
Jincang Dyak, 131
John Paul II, Pope, 110–11
Johnson, John, "Liver eating," cannibal, 125

Kafiristan, 114
Kagoro, 115
Kajan, 121
Kaplan, Stephen, "father of vampirology," 160
Kara, Juro, Japanese author, 33, 203
Kaschibo, 127
Katanga, 124
Kauanda, 124
Kaura, 60
Kenya, 32
Khonds, 121
Khrushchev, Nikita, 138

Kilgour, Maggie, 241
"Kitchen in the Restaurant Robinson," 198
Knossos, Minoan palace, 27
Krapina, Neanderthal site, 23
Kronos, 24
Kuru, neurological disease, 49, 220
Kutuzov, Mikhail, Russian field marshal, 69–70
Kwakiutl, 120

Lanning, Kenneth, FBI child abuse expert, 177–79
La Vey, Anton, satanist, 33
Lecter, Hannibal; see *Silence of the Lambs*
Leakey, Louis, researcher, 20
Leakey, Mary, researcher, 20
Leningrad (St. Petersburg), 44, 67, 72–77
Leopard society, 119
Lessa tribe, 112
Letters from Master Sagawa, 33, 203
Levin, Nora, 80–82
Lévi-Strauss, Claude, French structuralist, 245
Lewis, Roy, 19
Lhopa, 141
Linguissa, Philippe, 34
Little, Bentley, 192
Little Red Riding Hood, 193
Loftus, Elizabeth, psychologist/author, 181–82
Lopez, Barry, 149, 151–53
Love Bite, film, 227

Love cannibalism; *see* unification cannibalism
Lubgara, 52
Lucy, hominid, 17
Lugosi, Bela, 159-60
Lycanthropy, 150, 152

MacClancey, Jeremy, 198
MacLaine, Shirley, 219
McMartin School trial, 181
Madness, 138-41
Maerth, Oscar, 239
Magic cannibalism, 107-16, 215
Malaya, 114
Malleus Maleficarum, 154-55
Mambila, 125
Man-Eating Myth; see Arens, William
Manjema, 130, 133
Maori, 111, 115, 130, 133
Maricopa County Bar Association, 143-46
Marind-Anim, 108
Marx, Groucho, 223
Masai, 18, 52
Massagetae, 126
Matto Grosso, 13
Mau Mau, 32
Mayoruna, 11
Mba, Ntem, African mass murderer/cannibal, 35
Mead, Margaret, anthropologist, 52-53
Medusa, 84-86
Meitner, Lise, nuclear physicist, 186
Melanesia, 18, 57, 115

Melville, Herman, 86-87
Menado-Alfuren, 111
Mencken, Henry, journalist, 230
Middleton, John, anthropologist, 52
Mignonette, British yacht, 169-175, 220-22, 224
Minh, Phung Quang, Vietnamese boat refugee, 189-91
Miranha, 11, 124
Moby Dick, 86-87
Montagu, Ashley, anthropologist, 49, 54, 246
Montezuma, Aztec emperor, 46-47
Moscow, 69-70
Muato-jamvo, 123
Mundugumor, 52

Nabeshima, Japanese vampire cat, 217
Napoleon I, 69-72
Napoleon's Russian Campaign, 70-72
"Narrative of A. Gordon Pym of Nantucket," 187
Natural famines, 59-66
Navajo, 151
Neanderthals, 22-23
Nelson, Omeima, murderess/cannibal, 14, 38-41, 204
Neocannibalism, 227
New Britain, 115
New Caledonia, 111, 124, 130, 132
New Guinea, 13, 18, 49, 53, 54, 115, 124, 126, 131, 134, 167
New Hebrides, 112, 124

New Mecklenburg, 126
New Pomerania, 126
New Zealand, 18, 107, 115, 130, 132-33
Nigeria, 126, 131
Night of the Living Dead, 193
Nine Hundred Days: The Siege of Leningrad, 73-76
Nissan, 112
Nosferatu, 160

Ofshe, Richard, sociologist, 182
Ojibwa, 138
Orokaiva, 11, 225
Osiris, Egyptian god, 120
Other forms of cannibalism, 141
Ovaherero, 120
Ovambo, 111
Ovimbundu, 215

Packer, Alferd, cannibal, 96-101, 221
Padean, 127
Pambia, 130
Parker, Richard, seaman, 169-75
Pawnee, 121
Pearce, Alexander, Irish murderer and cannibal, 91-92
Peking Man, 20-21
Penal cannibalism; *see* punishment cannibalism
Phagocytosis, 253
Philippines, 32, 91, 113
Pithecanthropus erectus, 22
Pittman, Joanna, English journalist, 204
Pliny, 150

Poe, Edgar Allan, 187, 192
Polo, Marco, Venetian traveler, 27
Polynesia, 18, 30, 132
Polyphemus, 186
Poole, Fitz, anthropologist, 54
Porphyria, inherited disease, 158
Presley, Elvis, 218
Pulgarcito, 193
Punishment cannibalism, 124-25, 216
Pygmy, 18

Queequeg, cannibal, 86

Ra, Leda Amun, 33
Raft of the Medusa, painting, 84-86
Ramona malpractice decision, 183
Raw and the Cooked, 199
Read, Piers Paul, 101-106
Red Guard cannibals, 201
Reeves, Peggy, 240
Regina v. *Dudley and Stephens*, 169-75
Religion, 117-22
Repressed memories, 181-83
Rice, Anne, 161-62
Rice, A. P., 11
Riley, Thomas, anthropologist, 54
Ritual, 117-22, 215
Ritual of Dinner, 198-99
Robinson, Edward G., 12
Rodriguez, Aryon, Brazilian linguist, 45
Rommel, Erwin, German field marshal, 114

Rwanda, 41

Sacrifice, 117–22
Sadism, 135–37, 216
Sagan, Eli, 241
Sagawa, Issed, Japanese murderer/cannibal, 33, 202–204
Sahagún, Bernardo de, 48
Saint Nicholas, 193
Salem witch trials, 156–57
Salisbury, Harrison, 73–76, 78
Salt, 132
Samoa, 120, 124, 213
Sande, 130
Sandy, Peggy Reeves, 240
Satanic ritualistic abuse, alleged, 52, 176–83, 222–23
Satanic Rituals Book, 33
Scythian, 111
Search for the King, A, 192
Ségur, Phillipe-Paul de, French general and author, 70–72
Sema, 121
Semang, 18
Set, Egyptian god, 120
SETI (Search for Extraterrestrial Intelligence), 24
Sex Abuse hysteria, 155–57
Shakirova, Madina, Russian cannibal, 208
Sheffner, David, forensic psychiatrist, 39
Siegel, Ronald, neuropsychologist, 217–18
Silence of the Lambs, 14, 196
Simpson, A. W. Brian, 86–87, 96, 170–75, 221, 244

Sinanthropus pekinensis, 20
Sioux, 186
Solomon Islands, 30, 112, 114, 124, 130
Solzhenitsyn, Aleksandr, 80
Sorcery, 108
Survival cannibalism, 9–10, 143–46, 220–22
Soylent Green, film, 12, 227
Staden, Hans, German sailor, 44–46
Stalin, Joseph, 80, 191
Stalingrad, 78–79
Starrs, James, 100
Steadman, Lyle, 167
Stephens, Edwin, British cannibal, 169–75, 222
Stewart, George, 92–95, 250
Stone Age man, 24
St. Petersburg; see Leningrad
Sukletin, Alexei, Russian murderer/cannibal, 208
Sumatra, 18, 124
Summoning, The, 192
Sura, 124
Survival cannibalism, 9–10, 17, 143–46, 220–22, 232; see also Accidents, *Mignonette*
Sweeney Todd, musical, 186

Tagalog, 113
Tahitian, 18
Tanaka, Toshi-juki, 201–202
Tangale, 131
Tanna tribe, 133
Tannahill, Reay, 240
Tariana, 134

Tartars, 131
Tasmania, 92
Tavris, Carol, 182
Thermonuclear war, 18, 233
"Thousand Deaths," Chinese torture, 136
Tibetans, 127
Tikar, 125
Tonga, 124
Toole, Otis, mass murderer/cannibal, 33–34
Torre, 132
Transubstantiation, 108–10, 199
Tuari, 133
Tucano, 134
Tucson City Bar Association, 144–46
Tugeri, 115
Tupi, 125
Tupinamba, 44–46, 124
Tutsi, 41
Twain, Mark, 187–91

Ukraine, 138
Unification cannibalism, 126–28, 224
Uruguay; see Andes crash
Uzbekistan, 79, 208

Vampire Chronicles, 161
Vampires, 157–63, 217
Vedda, 18
Victory celebrations, 118
Vidal, Gore, 192
Vietnamese boat people, 87–91
Viruses, 229

Visser, Margaret, 198–99
Vlad V., Walachian prince, 133–34, 158–59
Volhard, Ewald, German anthropologist, 19, 60, 108, 123, 241–43
Voltaire, François Marie, 187

Wa tribe, 115
Wabondei, 111
Wadai, 130
Warega, 132
Warjawa, 124
Warsaw ghetto, 80–82, 213–14
Wassilissa the Beautiful, 193
Weekend, French film, 193
Werebeasts, 152
Werewolf of London, film, 193
Werewolves, 149–53, 217
   of St. Claude, 152
Witches, 149, 153–57, 217
Windigo psychosis, 138
Wolf, Leonard, Dracula scholar, 160

Xosa, 108

Yeltsin, Boris, 211, 226

Zärtlichkeit der Wölfe, 141
Zamenhof, Ludovic, physician and inventor of Esperanto, 215
Zanzibar, 108
Zerbino, Andes crash victim, 56
Zulu, 18